FROM NEWMAN TO CONGAR

FROM NEWMAN TO CONGAR

*The idea of doctrinal development
from the Victorians to the Second
Vatican Council*

AIDAN NICHOLS, O.P.

T&T CLARK
EDINBURGH

T&T CLARK
59 GEORGE STREET
EDINBURGH EH2 2LQ
SCOTLAND

First Published 1990

ISBN 0 567 291812

British Library Cataloguing in Publication Data
Nichols, Aidan
From Newman to Congar: the idea of doctrinal development
from the Victorians to the Second Vatican Council.
1. Christian doctrine, history
I. Title
230.09

Typeset by Barbers Highlands Ltd, Fort William
Printed and bound in Great Britain by Billing & Sons Ltd, Worcester

Contents

1. Introduction: the Importance of the Question   1
2. John Henry Newman   17
3. Alfred Loisy   71
4. George Tyrrell   114
5. Maurice Blondel   136
6. Ambroise Gardeil   155
7. Other Neo-Scholastic Figures   177
8. Henri de Lubac and Pierre Rousselot   195
9. Karl Rahner   214
10. Edward Schillebeeckx   236
11. Yves Congar   248
12. Conclusion: Retrospect and Prospect   263

Appendix: The Idea of Doctrinal Development in Eastern Orthodox Theology   279

Index   287

I

The Importance of the Question

Why is the issue of doctrinal development worth studying?
In what respects is it a significant, or even a crucial, issue for
theology, and, indeed, for faith?

In the first place: for Catholic theology, the issue of
doctrinal development is vital to the justification of
specifically Catholic Christian doctrinal insights, *vis-à-vis* the
serious objections to these which other historic Christian
communities can lodge. For it may be said that certain
elements met with in Catholic teaching today, such as, for
example, the doctrine of Purgatory, were not found in the
early Church, or, at any rate, can be found there only with
difficulty. But if an aspect of the public faith of the Church
today was not a constitutive part of the original apostolic
preaching, at least not in any obvious sense, how can this
aspect be supported, or even tolerated?

Put negatively, in terms of apologetics, this is a matter of
defending the Catholic Church against the claim that it has
corrupted the Gospel by adding to it elements which are not
divinely revealed, being of merely human devising. The
classic case against Catholicism in just such terms was made
by John Henry Newman in his Anglican period. Writing in
1837, in pursuance of the theme of Anglican identity,
Newman wrote:

> Romanism may be considered as an unnatural and mis-
> shapen development of the Truth; not the less dangerous
> because it retains traces of its genuine features, and
> usurps its name ... However the Church of Rome may

I

profess a reverence for Antiquity, she does not really feel and pay it. There are in fact two elements in operation within her system. As far as it is Catholic and Scriptural, it appeals to the Fathers; as far as it is a corruption, it finds it necessary to supersede them. Viewed in its formal principles and authoritative statements, it professes to be the champion of past times; viewed as an active and political power, as a ruling, grasping, ambitious principle, in a word, as what is expressively called popery, it exalts the will and pleasure of the existing Church above all authority, whether of Scripture or Antiquity, interpreting the one and disposing of the other by its absolute and arbitrary decree.[1]

Nor should it be supposed that such objections to Catholic belief are no longer met with in the contemporary period. Thus in the wake of the proclamation of the dogma of the Bodily Assumption of the blessed Virgin Mary in 1950, the Lutheran Friedrich Heiler commented that, in the matter of dogmatic evolution:

Roman Catholic apologetic has not only happily adopted, overnight, one of the basic affirmations of the Modernist concept of dogma, but has outdone the Modernists themselves.[2]

Or again, R. P. C. Hanson, one of the most classically Anglican theologians of recent times, had this to say:

Their (Catholics') religion is a religion which looks to the present, and to the future for its revelation, indeed one which may confidently expect new revelations and new fundamental doctrines of Christianity to emerge in the future into public gaze ... In this insistence it has

---

[1] J. H. Newman, *Lectures on the Prophetical Office of the Church* (London 1837), p. 100.

[2] F. Heiler, 'Katholischer Neomodernismus. Zu den Versuchen einer Verteidigung des neuen Mariendogmas', in *Oekumenische Einheit* II. 3 (1951), p. 233.

entirely deserted the whole emphasis and outlook of primitive Christianity, it has reversed the current of original faith.[3]

And pointing out that the Church must consider itself bound by its original tradition, expressed in Scripture, Hanson maintains that such apparent doctrinal advances as the affirmation of the Son's consubstantiality with the Father, made at the First Council of Nicaea, are not development of that tradition, in the sense of adding fresh articles to its faith. Rather are they measures of defence expressed in the thought-forms of a period, and constructed in such a way as to meet some particular attack on an original identity.

> Genuine development of Christian doctrine … has taken place only in the enunciation of certain formulae necessary to protect the original tradition of the Church from error. These formulae are only *de fide*, necessary to salvation, in as far as points of controversy have been raised to which they could be the only answer if the witness of the Bible to God's revelation in Jesus Christ was to be maintained in its truth.[4]

Nor are such *gravamina* confined to individuals, perhaps isolated or in some way atypical. At the time of the promulgation of the Assumption dogma, the Evangelical-Lutheran faculty of theology in the University of Heidelberg issued a joint statement to the effect that the Catholic Church now claims in practice:

> to be able to generate apostolic teaching, whereas its official commission is meant to be simply to guard and interpret historically transmitted apostolic teaching in its purity.[5]

---

[3]In R. P. C. Hanson and R. Fuller, *The Church of Rome. A Dissuasive* (London 1948), p. 84.

[4]Ibid., p. 102.

[5]Cited by Heiler in his 'Das neue Mariendogma in Licht der Geschichte und im Urteil der Oekumene, 2' in *Oekumenische Einheit* II. 3 (1951), pp. 240–55. On the

Put positively, in the context of ecumenism, the same problem presents itself as an invitation to the other historic churches to share the Christian religion in a fuller form, a form which amplifies but does not distort what we may call 'New Testament religion'. The ecumenical importance of the theme of development has been well expressed by the American Jesuit John Courtney Murray, best known for his part in the marking of the Second Vatican Council's declaration on religious freedom. Murray wrote:

> I consider that the parting of the ways between the two Christian communities [he is speaking of Catholicism and Protestantism] takes place on the issue of development of doctrine. *That* development has taken place in both communities cannot possibly be denied. The question is, *what* is legitimate development, what is organic growth in the understanding of the original deposit of faith, what is warranted extension of the primitive discipline of the church, and what, on the other hand, is accretion, additive increment, adulteration of the deposit, distortion of true Christian discipline? ... Perhaps, above all, the question is, What are the limits of development and growth – the limits that must be reached on peril of archaistic stuntedness, and the limits that must not be transgressed on peril of futuristic decadence?[6]

It was in this more limited context of justifying – whether defensively, in apologetics, or, more eirenically, in the ecumenical context, specifically Catholic doctrines (and

controversy aroused by the preparation of the dogma, see H. Hammans, *Die neueren katholischen Erklärungen der Dogmenentwicklung* (Essen 1965), pp. 7–9: much more fully: A. G. Aiello, *Sviluppo del dogma e tradizione. A proposito della definizione dell'Assunzione di Maria* (Rome 1979); and, from a Protestant perspective *(Auctores varii) Die Geschichtlichkeit der Kirche und ihrer Verkündigung als theologisches Problem* (Tübingen 1954), pp. 44–5.

[6] J. Courtney Murray S.J., *The Problem of God Yesterday and Today* (New Haven 1964), p. 53; cited in J. Pelikan, *Development of Christian Doctrine. Some Historical Prolegomena* (London 1969), p. 1.

practices) that the theme of doctrinal development first emerged into the full light of intellectual day in the middle of the nineteenth century. John Henry Newman's *Essay on the Development of Christian Doctrine* of 1845 is the first full scale treatise devoted to the concept, though there are earlier hints at a notion of development in patristic and mediaeval writing. Newman's essay coincided with an awakening of interest in the theme in Germany, among the theologians of the Catholic Tübingen school, and also, though to a lesser extent, at Rome – in the Roman college of the Society of Jesus.[7] The emergence of interest in the topic in three widely dispersed centres – England, Württemberg, Rome – each in independence of the other seems to call for some explanation.

A sufficient explanation can be offered by pointing to two factors. First, by the mid nineteenth century, the Catholic Church was undergoing a marked revival in comparison with the low ebb to which it had sunk during the years of the Revolutionary period. As a result of this renaissance, Catholics were more willing to put forward their claim to be, in some unique sense, the Church Christ founded. Secondly, the nineteenth century was not only a century of advance in historical studies but a century which naturally thought in an historical manner. People regarded historical explanations as, of all explanations, the most illuminating where ideas, events or institutions were concerned. The combination of the Catholic revival and this historical mind-set led, in predictable fashion, to an apologia for Catholicism by appeal to the idea of development.

So much for the more limited segment of discussion in which concepts of doctrinal development are important. The wider context to which the theme belongs concerns, not the

---

[7]For the work of the Tübingen school, see, above all, J. R. Geiselmann, *Die katholische Tübingen Schule: ihre theologische Eigenart* (Freiburg 1965); its chief theorist of development was Johann Adam Möhler, on whom see H. R. Nienaltowski, *Johann Adam Möhler's Theory of Doctrinal Development. Its Genesis and Formulation* (Washington 1959), For the Roman teaching, see especially J. B. Franzelin, *De Traditione at Scriptura* (Rome 1882³), pp. 263–315; and, more widely, W. Kasper, *Die Lehre von der Tradition in der Römischen Schule* (Freiburg 1962). In his foreword to this study, Geiselmann declared that in Franzelin, Möhler had been present at the First Vatican Council, ibid., p. viii.

justifying of specifically Catholic doctrines, but of the entire *ensemble* of mainstream historic Christianity as a religion genuinely founded on the original message of Jesus. Here what is in question is the whole pattern of faith, ethics, worship and Church order on which all historic Christian churches are agreed. Who are the groups that constitute such 'historic Christian churches'? They are all those who accept that the original Gospel is found today in a visible community, defined dogmatically by the faith of the general councils of the undivided Church, worshipping through liturgical forms with a strong family resemblance amongst themselves, and governed through a three-fold ministry of bishops, priests and deacons in an historic succession from the apostles. All such churches, and above all the Catholic and separated Eastern churches, but also Old Catholics, together with the 'high church' portions of Anglicanism and Lutheranism, share a fundamental perception of the nature of Christianity. The religious structure which emerged in the patristic period is, they hold, that structure which was intended by Jesus Christ and his apostles, so that, between the original Gospel preaching and the Church that emerged from the somewhat obscure period known as the 'sub-apostolic tunnel', there is, fundamentally, continuity and not discontinuity.

The belief that between Jesus and the later Church there stretches a basic continuity was rudely shaken by the exegetical and historical enquiries of later nineteenth century scholars, especially in Germany. The 'History of Religions' school, found in a number of German universities as the nineteenth century drew to its close, approached the study of Christian origins in a purely scientific, value-free, spirit – or, at any rate, this was their methodological ideal. Many of their results were at variance with the traditional picture of Jesus and the primitive Church. The encounter between this radical exegesis and historiography on the one hand, and traditional orthodoxy on the other, provoked, once transferred to the Catholic environment, that crisis which would soon be notorious as 'Modernism'.

Modernism's characteristic tendency was to use the idea of

doctrinal development so as to justify the emergence from primitive Christianity of the classical Christian pattern of the patristic era and beyond, but at the same time to suggest that what had once changed so drastically might well change drastically again. So far as the Catholic authorities were concerned, neither the Modernists' manner of defending the Great Church of late antiquity, nor their proposals for an imminent transformation of Catholicism were acceptable. Nevertheless, the scholarly charge that the religion of Jesus and the primitive community was very different from later Christianity still stood, mulishly refusing to go away, and continuing to provide the wider context in which notions of doctrinal development retain their importance today.

It may be useful at this point to give some idea of what those alternative accounts of Christian origins were, or are, to challenge the historic Christian churches' self-understanding so profoundly. Four principal contending versions may be mentioned, all produced, it is perhaps worth noting, by German or Swiss-German scholars.

First in time comes that of Adolf von Harnack (1851–1930), probably the most eminent patristic scholar of his time, especially in matters of the ante-Nicene Church.[8] After holding chairs at various German universities, Harnack became professor at Berlin in 1889, director of the Prussian *Staatsbibliothek* in 1905, and in 1910 president of the *Kaiser Wilhelm Gesellschaft* for the promotion of learning and science. A founder of the important series *Texte und Untersuchungen zur Geschichte der altchristlichen Literatur*,[9] he used his own numerous contributions to the series in order to compose his great *Lehrbuch der Dogmengeschichte*, Englished as the *History of Dogma*,[10] which traces the history of Christian doctrine as far as the Reformation, but with emphasis on the late antique age. For Harnack, dogma is 'a creation of the Greek spirit added to the apostolic faith'.[11] What the Gospel would look

---

[8] For his life, see A. von Zahn-Harnack, *Adolf von Harnack* (Berlin 1951[2]).

[9] 1882 ff.

[10] 1886–9; ET *History of Dogma* (London 1894–99).

[11] P. Schrodt, *The Problem of the Beginning of Dogma in Recent Theology* (Frankfurt am Main 1978), p. 3.

like once shorn of patristic doctrine, he attempted to show in his *Das Wesen des Christentums*, in English, *What is Christianity?*[12] which, by its overwhelmingly ethical presentation of Christianity, attracted more popular attention. His mature views on the emergence of doctrine were summarised in *Die Entstehung der christlichen Theologie und des kirchlichen Dogmas.*[13]

Harnack stressed that the earliest Church preached a message of salvation to which the appropriate response was an act of faith, expressed in a new way of life. But, in superfluous, indeed damaging, addition, the Church soon acquired a formulated doctrine, assent to which was deemed a necessary condition of her membership. Referring to the dogmas of the Incarnation and the Trinity, Harnack wrote:

> In these later dogmas an entirely new element has entered into the conception of religion. The message of religion has been clothed in an understanding of the world, and of the ground of the world, which has been obtained in advance without any reference to the Christian proclamation. Thus religion has become a doctrine which takes its certainty from the Gospel but only part of its content.[14]

Or, as he put it pithily by way of summing up: 'Dogma in its conception and construction is a product of the Greek spirit on the soil of the Gospel'.[15] If Gnosticism represents an acute form of the invasion of Christianity by Hellenism, the Church's orthodoxy implies a more gradual and low-grade infection by the same germ. In the official Church, reliance upon the Spirit of Jesus and his unpredictable gifts was replaced by dependence on a machinery of episcopal government. The Gospel was not, however, fully lost to view: at the Reformation, as events proved, it could be

[12] 1900: ET *What is Christianity* (London 1901; New York 1957).

[13] 1927.

[14] Cited H. E. W. Turner, *The Pattern of Christian Truth A Study in the Relations between Orthodoxy and Heresy in the Early Church* (London 1954), p. 17.

[15] A. von Harnack, *Dogmengeschichte* I. p. 20.

recovered. But it was deeply damaged by philosophically-derived formulations which wove into its fabric many of the preoccupations of contemporary secular thought. In particular, through the work of the early Christian Apologists, the Greek philosophical idea of the *Logos* was assimilated to the person of Jesus.[16] The attraction of this was that the *Logos* concept hypostatised God's creative rationality without endangering his unity: it allowed him to be active in the world without calling into question his transcendence. But the price was too high. When, on the analogy of the divinity of the Son, Godhead was also ascribed to the Spirit of Jesus, the resultant doctrine of the Triune God was nothing but a *Begriffsphantaise*, 'conceptual fantasy', the result of wild and whirling speculation, uncontrolled by historical reference.[17]

The second radically heterodox but highly influential construal of Christian origins which should be mentioned here is that of Martin Werner (1887–1964). In his *Die Entstehung des christlichen Dogmas*, Englished as *The Formation of Christian Dogma*,[18] Werner began by accepting Albert Schweitzer's account of the original Gospel, namely, that the preaching of Jesus was through and through eschatological. According to Schweitzer, Jesus had predicted the imminent end of the present world-order and went to his death believing that his sacrifice on the Cross would bring this about. The earliest disciples lived, therefore, in the kind of immediate expectation of the Parousia which Paul's First Letter to the Thessalonians exemplifies. When hope of the Second Coming faded, the Church, according now to Werner's book, pushed through a process called by him *Enteschatologisierung*, 'de-eschatologising', which turned Christianity into a totally different kind of religion. Later orthodoxy, therefore, has little or no continuity with the faith of the New Testament. Thus the Father of the original

[16]Ibid. I. p. 346.

[17]Ibid. II. pp. 292–3.

[18]*Die Entstehung des christlichen Dogmas* (Berne 1941); Et *The Formation of Christian Dogma* (London 1957). On this writer, see M. U. Balsiger, 'Un thélogien méconnu: Martin Werner', *Etudes théologiques et religieuses* 64.1 (1989), pp. 23–44.

preaching became the Absolute of Greek philosophy; the Son of Man, a supernatural angelic agent, was transmuted into the divine Logos, the substantial 'Word' produced by the Absolute. The New Testament Christ, a victor over hostile cosmic powers, became the agent in the creation of a tame universe. The New Testament idea of salvation as incorporation into a community of elect persons who only will be safe when the turn of the ages comes was replaced with a theory of redemption by deification operating through sacraments. The formless charismatic community of the apostolic Church became a hierarchically ordered and hierurgically orientated society. Thus the Christian Church became what Werner calls

> a Hellenistic-syncretistic Mystery religion, laden with the decadence of post-classical religiosity, strutting about in Christian dress.[19]

A third theory of Christian origins subversive of traditional faith is that of Rudolf Bultmann (1884–1976). The two principal texts to be considered are his *Theologie des neuen Testaments* rapidly translated as *Theology of the New Testament*, and the slightly later *Das Urchristentum im Rahmen der antiken Religionen*, Englished as *Primitive Christianity in its Contemporary Setting*.[20] Bultmann's theory is, in different respects, both more radical and less radical than those of Harnack and Werner. It is more radical in that, for Bultmann, the invasion by alien elements of the original message about Jesus – the proclamation of a new quality of existence made possible by the Easter events – has already taken place in the New Testament itself. Gnosticism, according to Bultmann, antedates the New Testament, and the trace-elements of its cosmological and cultic concerns have sullied the waters at their source. However, Bultmann's account is less radical in that, unlike at any rate Werner, he did not subscribe to the

[19]*Die Entstehung des christlichen Dogmas*, op. cit., p. 725.

[20]*Theologie des neuen Testaments* (Tübingen 1948–53); Et *Theology of the New Testament* (New York 1951–55); *Das Urchristentum in Rahmen der antiken Religionen* (Zürich 1949); Et *Primitive Christianity in its Contemporary Setting* (London 1956).

view that the primary religious declaration of Christianity – its *kerygma* – was ever wholly dominated by alien factors. Rather did the two struggle together for mastery. Though the process of transition, through the New Testament writings, to the life, teaching and organisation of the later Church was outwardly smooth, inner continuity with the original Gospel was at all times under threat. The Church, the bearer of the Gospel, had but a fluctuating hold on her own spiritual treasure. While she might damage the Gospel by the inappropriate forms of expression which she used to communicate her message, she did not, however, wholly destroy it.

Finally, there is the theory of Walter Bauer in his study *Rechtgläubigkeit und Ketzerei in ältesten Christentum* which English-speaking readers may consult under the title *Orthodoxy and Heresy in Earliest Christianity*.[21] Bauer's study is the most erudite and detailed of the four, at least as regards the patristic material under consideration. Basically, Bauer maintains that in the first two centuries there was no clear cut distinction between orthodoxy and heresy. Both orthodoxy and heresy arose simultaneously in the Church, and the traditional view is mistaken in regarding error as later than orthodoxy. Should orthodoxy be understood in any formal, or self-conscious, sense, it was, if anything, subsequent to heresy. Bauer held that formal orthodoxy began as a splinter group under episcopal leadership, only slowly achieving a dominant position in the life of the Church. It was the Roman see which imposed its own standard of orthodoxy on the rest, using the church of Corinth as its spring-bread. Such churches as those of Syria and Alexandria were to begin with quite heterodox, and only gradually did they come to accept the belief-system later hailed as true Christianity. Bauer himself, so it has been suggested, regarded the unity of primitive Christianity as sheer, simple relationship with the one Lord.[22]

[21] *Rechtgläubigkeit und Ketzerei in ältesten Christentum* (Tübingen 1934); Et *Orthodoxy and Heresy in Earliest Christianity* (Philadelphia 1971).

[22] W. Schneemelcher, 'Walter Bauer als Kirchenhistoriker', *New Testament Studies* 9 (1962), pp. 11–22.

> Bauer assumes that the essence of the Christian faith is a principle beyond history and speech: once this 'transcendental' reality is 'categorically' expressed and apprehended, it is *mis*apprehended, and the more thoroughgoing the articulation, the graver the distortion ... He is still bound up in a philosophical world where 'inner' truthfulness is perenially at odds with and at risk from the deceitfulness of material history, and still disposed to see the heart of Christianity as a supernatural – non-worldly, non-historical – still point, to which the contradictory and compromised phenomena of time (persons, words, institutions) are related in an inexpressible or inscrutable way.[23]

Giving such a primacy to the existential over against the historical links Bauer's theory, evidently, to that of Bultmann.

All four theories postulate a marked contrast between the original gospel message and the faith of the fourth century golden age of the patristic Church, although they disagree about the point at which the rupture between the Gospel and the later Church occurred. The assessment of these theories will depend to a large degree on exact scholarship: for instance, on what one thinks of Werner's understanding of New Testament Christology, or again whether one can believe Bauer's re-construction of the early Alexandrian church. In so far as detailed scholarship turns out to destroy their theories, then the problem they create disappears with them. But on the other hand, to the extent that their writings are based on what look like facts, we do have a real problem on our hands, namely that of describing the kind of continuity which may be said to link the original Gospel to the Great Church of later centuries. And for this task we need some view of doctrinal development.

To sum up, the two great questions which cannot be answered without some consideration of doctrinal development are: How is the confession of the Catholic

[23]R. Williams, 'Does it make sense to speak of pre-Nicene orthodoxy', in idem. (ed.), *The Making of Orthodoxy. Essays in Honour of Henry Chadwick* (Cambridge 1989), pp. 4–5.

Church to be justified, vis-à-vis other Christian churches, and how is the primitive Creed, the Creed of the early Church, to be justified, over against alternative readings of Christian origins. Newman and his contemporaries considered largely the first issue; the Modernists, and their rivals the Neo-Thomists, chiefly the second, though, naturally, the two contexts are to be found intersecting with each other from time to time. Those contemporary or near-contemporary writers who have contributed to the debate, such as Schillebeeckx, Congar and Rahner, were more or less equally concerned with both. This is because, as scholars, they knew that the wider question of justifying historic Christianity is still urgent, while as pastors they were also concerned with ecumenism, and hence with the problem of commending specifically Catholic doctrines to other main-line Christians.

From this account of what seems important in the issue of doctrinal development it is possible to construct a picture of the course we shall be following. Essentially, this study is a history of the problem of doctrinal development from the 1840's to the present day. As such, it will fall into four sections. First, we will look at the full-scale emergence of the idea of development in Newman. Secondly, we will examine a variety of attitudes to development among the Modernist writers. Thirdly, we will investigate the Neo-Thomist – or, more widely, Neo-Scholastic – theory of doctrinal development as well as a 'sport' in the orthodox reaction to Modernism, the lay theology of Blondel. Finally, our focus will be upon a number of authors who, from the 1940's onwards, have contributed to the construction of a theological synthesis on this issue in near-contemporary Catholicism. Though the approach is primarily historical, the aim is to identify elements of enduring value in the writers discussed. An 'epilogue' to the story will suggest how, in the wake of the Second Vatican Council, the play of three notions – *pluralism, hermeneutics* (or interpretation theory) and *reception* – has so widened its scope as to imperil the admirably balanced position which immediately pre-conciliar theology so painstakingly occupied, and the Council itself, in the Dogmatic Constitution *Dei Verbum*, on Divine Revelation, beautifully mirrored.

In recent years, the existence, within Catholicism, of theological voices raised in commendation of a wide latitude for that trio of revisionist concepts has given to some commentators the hope – or fear – that this communion is in process of abandoning that strongly (but not exclusively) intellectual understanding of doctrine so deeply entrenched in its tradition and implied at all points in the operation of its teaching authority, or magisterium. Thus Paul Avis, a member of the Church of England's commission for doctrine, draws attention to these three key notions, as handled by Karl Rahner, Edward Schillebeeckx and Yves Congar in their post-conciliar writings (as also by other Catholic divines such as Bernard Lonergan, Hans Küng, Charles Davis), to support the claim that, in the less epistemologically benighted reaches of the Catholic Church, such a de-construction is underway, bringing with it, he rejoices to expect, the end of the magisterium as we have known it.[24] By this he means not simply the curtailment of this or that formal procedure of doctrinal evaluation but the abandonment of the claim to a unique supernatural revelation, whose content is, at least in part, inaccessible by any other means to human subjects; the surrender of the conviction that the community of faith, thanks to the economies of the Son and the Spirit, can determine with both certainty and clarity the truths comprised in a 'deposit of faith' (if not exhaustively, and in all respects); and the demise of the theological belief, canonised in the Dogmatic Constitution on Divine Revelation of the Second Vatican Council, that the Church progresses in her grasp of the truth, seeing it, over time, more lucidly than she did before. As one of his witnesses, Charles Davis, triumphantly sums up, in relation to the theme of *praxis*, so important to much contemporary hermeneutics:

> Since the identity and truth of a tradition cannot be established theoretically, the religious structure we refer to as orthodoxy is rendered impossible.[25]

[24]P. Avis, *Ecumenical Theology and the Elusiveness of Doctrine* (London 1986).
[25]C. Davis, *Theology and Political Society* (Cambridge 1980), p. 8.

But as orthodoxy is nothing other than the right rendering of public doctrine, any question of the *legitimate* development of that doctrine – as distinct from the mere happenstance of a multiplicity of trajectories for *praxis*, is here ruled out of court.

Avis' account is, in part, an *apologia* for what he takes to be the typical, and permanently valuable, reverent agnosticism of Anglicanism on all matters involving inerrancy and infallibility. The Catholic view that revelation permits the definitive distinguishing of truth and error in a way which is determinative for all succeeding generations, as for all contemporary cultures, is, he tells us, profoundly inimical to the Anglican tradition. In this regard, he finds a

> significant affinity between the instincts of Anglicanism and the position worked out by the Roman Catholic Modernists.[26]

It is not, perhaps, for a Catholic author to question the reading of Anglican sources made by so highly placed an Anglican theologian. Yet *prima facie*, the notion that such foundational doctrines of Christianity as the Incarnation and the Trinity would have been regarded by central figures in the Anglican tradition, from the English Reformers to the late Arthur Michael Ramsey, as simply interpretative models whereby constructive theological reason offers a tentative or exploratory reading of the tacit dimension to the Jesus event, seems little convincing.

More widely, Avis' criticism of the agreed doctrinal statements produced by bilateral dialogue between the Anglican and Roman Catholic communions is based upon a particular epistemology, which plays off imagination – with its own distinctive resources of mythopoeic story-telling, symbolisation and concrete image, against intellect in its propositional mood. 'The more precise and formalised statements become, the less they tell us.'[27] But this is a false

---

[26]P. Avis, *Ecumenical Theology and the Elusiveness of Doctrine*, op., cit., pp. 56–7.
[27]Ibid., pp. 26–7.

dichotomy: it does not identify a choice which needs to be made. Imagination plays a vital rôle in our grasping the event of revelation, and as such is necessarily prior to the rational interpretation and, in part, justification of that revelation.[28] Yet as Dr Julius Lipner has pointed out, by way of reviewing Avis' book:

> It is the glory of human consciousness that its tacit dimension can come to fruition in propositions, in articulated meanings which can be true or false.[29]

The story of the idea of doctrinal development from Newman to Congar shows an oscillation between an exaggerated respect for the non-intellectual factors in faith among the Modernists, to a over-enthusiastic embrace of the intellectual elements on the part of the Neo-Scholastics. But the position which Catholic divinity reached on the eve of the Second Vatican Council was well-tempered not least because its best practitioners – the Rahner, Schillebeeckx and Congar of that period – were sensitive to the demands both of imagination and of reason in the formulation of what it is, on the basis of a revelation which is at once trancendent beauty and divine action, that the Church knows to be true.[30]

[28]See especially on this J. McIntyre, *Faith, Theology and Imagination* (Edinburgh 1987).

[29]Cited from *New Blackfriars* 68. 804 (1987), pp. 203–4.

[30]In this formulation I intend to refer to the theological trilogy of 'theological aesthetics', 'theological dramatics' and 'theological logic' produced by this century's greatest Catholic theologian Hans Urs von Balthasar (1904–88).

2

John Henry Newman

Life and work

John Henry Newman was born in London on 21 February 1801 to an Anglican family whose Christianity he later described as 'Bible Religion'. This 'national religion of England' consisted:

> not in rites or creeds, but mainly in having the Bible read in Church, in the family, and in private.[1]

It framed the life of a prosperous London family: Newman's father was a banker, his mother the daughter of a paper-maker of enterprising Huguenot stock. But in the financial collapse which followed on the ending of the Napoleonic Wars in 1815, Newman's father lost his money, and the family crisis coincided with a serious illness for the adolescent boy. Disoriented, his spirit sought solace and found it in a Calvinistic Evangelicalism which, however, he never embraced wholeheartedly, though remaining grateful to it for his first intimations of the fundamental Christian doctrines. Through its instrumentality, he

[1] J. H. Newman, *An Essay in Aid of a Grammer of Assent*, ed. I. T. Ker (Oxford 1985), p. 43. For Newman's life, there is the classic biography by W. Ward, *The Life of John Henry Cardinal Newman* (London 1912), mainly on his Catholic period, Meriol Trevor, *Newman: The Pillar of the Cloud*, and *Newman: Light in Winter* (London 1962), which is not so strong on his thought; the little gem by C. S. Dessain, *John Henry Newman* (London 1966; 1980³), and now *John Henry Newman. A Biography* by Ian Ker (Oxford 1989), with excellent summaries of the main works.

17

fell under the influences of a definite Creed, and received
into my intellect impressions of dogma, which, through
God's mercy, have never been effaced or obscured.[2]

At the same time, he read Isaac Newton's commentaries on
the prophetic books of Scripture, from which he picked up
the belief that the Roman pope was the Antichrist, a
'doctrine' which, he confessed, 'stained (his) imagination' up
to the year 1843.[3]

In 1817, Newman was matriculated in the University of
Oxford; he became a fellow of Oriel College – then the
centre of a miniature intellectual renaissance of Broad Church
or Latitudinarian Anglicanism, the 'Noetic School' – in 1822;
and took major orders in the Anglican Church in 1824. In
1828 he succeeded a Latitudinarian luminary as vicar of the
prestigious 'University church' of St Mary the Virgin. A year
later, amid the combination of pastoral and academic duties,
he felt

> more strongly than ever the necessity of there being
> men in the Church, like the R Catholic friars, free from
> all obstacles to their devoting themselves to its defence.[4]

In 1833 he embarked on an ambitious tour of southern
Europe. In the Eastern Mediterranean, the memory of the
voyages of St Athanasius, that Alexandrian stalwart for
Christ's divinity, moved him to write some verses which
began with a prayer for an Anglican counterpart to the great
Eastern doctor:

> When shall our northern Church her champion see
> Raised by high heaven's decree To shield the ancient
> faith at his own harm?[5]

[2] J. H. Newman, *Apologia pro Vita Sua*, ed. M. J. Svaglic (Oxford 1967), p. 17.
[3] Ibid., p. 19.
[4] C. S. Dessain et al., (eds.), *The Letters and Diaries of John Henry Newman*, vols. i–
vi (Oxford 1978–84); xi–xxii (London 1961–72); xxiii–xxxi (Oxford 1973–77); ii.
p. 150.
[5] Ibid., iii. pp. 155–6.

In Rome, he felt confused. At High Mass in the pope's presence at the Dominican church of St Maria sopra Minerva, he began

> to think that it was a sin, as such, in the Church's uniting itself with that enemy of God, who from the beginning sat on her seven hills, with an enchantress's cup, as the representative and instrument of the Evil Principle.

But, as he looked on

> and saw all Christian acts performing the Holy Sacrament offered up, and the blessing given, and recollected I was in church, I could only say in very perplexity my own words, 'How shall I view thee, Light of the wide west, or heinous error-seat?'[6]

As a human environment, however, he found Rome much like Oxford – 'calm, quiet, so dignified and beautiful'[7] – an intimation, perhaps, that the economically unadventurous government of the *papa-re* had something to commend it. In Naples, he read in the newspapers of the Whig government's Irish Church Temporalities Bill, suppressing ten bishoprics of the (Anglican) Church of Ireland. This was an affront in the eyes of Newman's clerical friends – John Keble, Hurrell Froude, E. B. Pusey – for whom the Church was not the State's creature since she had her own God-given dignity. On his return, he became deeply involved with the 'Oxford Movement', alias the Catholic Revival, in the Church of England, then beginning. His sermons in the University Church, published as *Parochial and Plain Sermons* (1834–42) had a profound effect on the religious sensibility of educated Englishmen. 'A shrewdly practical psychology informs a highly idealistic spirituality', is the judgement of Newman's most recent biographer, Father Ian Ker.[8] That spirituality

[6]Ibid., iii. pp. 267–8.
[7]Ibid., iii. p. 273.
[8]I. Ker, *John Henry Newman*, op. cit., p. 94.

was based on a close study of the Church Fathers, which had
borne fruit in *The Arians of the Fourth Century* (1833), whereas
the 'Tracts for the Times' (1833–41), twenty-four of which
came from his pen, were more wide-ranging, polemical
statements of his religious position. Directed simultaneously
against 'Popery' (Roman Catholicism) and 'Dissent'
(Protestant Non-conformity), they defended the thesis of the
via media – his conviction that the Church of England held an
inter-mediate position between modern Romanism on the
one hand and modern Protestantism on the other, and
represented, in so doing, the patristic tradition itself.

This conviction received more systematic expression in his
*Lectures on the Prophetical Office of the Church viewed relatively
to Romanism and Popular Protestanism* (1837), and again, vis-à-
vis one particular doctrinal theme, in the *Lectures on
Justification* of 1838. Meanwhile, however, his continued
delvings into the patristic past were unsettling this confidence
in the 'apostolicity' of Anglicanism. His study of the
Monophysite crisis brought him face to face with a pope Leo
upholding the Catholic belief, whilst heretics divided into an
extreme and, more threatening for Newman's approach
hitherto, a *moderate* party.

> My stronghold was Antiquity; now here, in the middle
> of the fifth century, I found, as it seemed to me, the
> Christendom of the sixteenth and the nineteenth
> centuries reflected. I saw my face in that mirror, and I
> was a Monophysite. The Church of the Via Media was
> in the position of the Oriental communions; Rome was
> where she now is; and the Protestants were the
> Eutychians.[9]

(In his editing work on the texts of Athanasius, he was
tempted by a similar comparison for the Church of the fourth
century: there the Via Media was the way of the Semi-
Arians.)[10] In the famous *Tract 90*, published in 1841, Newman

[9]*Apologia*, p. 108.
[10]Ibid., p. 130.

advocated an interpretation of the founding Thirty-Nine Articles of the Church of England in a sense which would harmonise them, to the greatest degree possible, with the (Roman) Catholic faith. 'Apostolical' Anglicans had no duties to the framers of the articles, whose uncatholic positions were well known, whereas they *did* have an obligation, both to the Catholic Church and to their own, to 'take our reformed confessions in the most Catholic sense they will admit'.[11] This tract precipitated a violent controversy, drew down the formal censure of the Vice-Chancellor of the University, its Heads of Houses and Proctors, and was condemned in the pastoral charges of a number of individual bishops, leading Newman's own bishop, Bagot of Oxford, to seek to impose silence upon its author. From 1839 onwards, Newman had in any case harboured doubts about the tenability of the Anglican position, and after 1841 began to shed his official rôles as a minister of the established Church. From 1842 on, he lived in a semi-monastic establishment in the village of Littlemore, outside Oxford: a life of withdrawal, study and prayer with a few friends. A sharply-felt blow was Anglican collusion with the pan-Protestant scheme whereby Frederick William IV of Prussia, desirous to introduce episcopacy into his mixed Lutheran-Calvinist church, proposed the experiment of a joint Anglo-Prussian (and so Anglican-Protestant) bishopric in Jerusalem: a project supported by Evangelicals and Latitudinarians for its anti-Tractarian potential. In 1845 Newman was received into the Church of Rome by the Italian Passionist priest Dominic (later, blessed Dominic) Barberi. Almost immediately afterwards, he issued his *Essay on the Development of Christian Doctrine* (1845) by way of defence of his change of ecclesiastical allegiance. The work was not, however, a full statement of his reasons for becoming a Catholic. Of the latter he would write:

You cannot buy them for a crown piece . . . You cannot get them, except at the cost of some portion of the trouble I have been at myself.[12]

[11]Re-printed in *The Via Media of the Anglican Church* (London 1877), II. pp. 344–6.
[12]*Letters and Diaries*, xi., p. 110.

Once ordained priest in Rome, Newman followed the advice of his new ecclesiastical superior, Nicholas Wiseman, vicar-apostolic of the Midland District, and sought out the Oratory of St Philip Neri as an appropriate context for his future activities. This community of secular priests living under a rule, but without the vows of traditional Religious, offered opportunities for scholarship as well as for pastoral work. (Moreover, Philip Neri reminded him of Keble.)[13] He founded his own Oratory in Edgbaston, then just outside the large industrial city of Birmingham, Wiseman's centre. In 1851, he was appointed Rector of the newly-announced and, as things proved, short-lived 'Catholic University of Ireland', in Dublin. The occasion gave him the opportunity to offer his vision of what University education should be, in a Catholic Christian perspective. The 'Discourses on the Scope and Nature of University Education: Addressed to the Catholics of Dublin' take as their simultaneous targets the 'Utilitarian criticism of liberal education within a confessional religious framework' and 'a defensive clerical Catholicism'.[14] Here the burden of Newman's song was, the unity, for the Church's mind, of all human understanding.

All branches of knowledge are connected together, because the subject-matter of knowledge is intimately united in itself, as being the acts and the work of the Creator.[15]

If the Catholic faith is true, Newman went on, then a University cannot exist outwith the Catholic pale, for 'it cannot teach Universal Knowledge if it does not teach Catholic theology'.[16] More widely, Newman praises liberal education, while reminding it of its moral and religious limitations.

[13]Ibid., xii, p. 32.

[14]I. Ker, *John Henry Newman*, op. cit., pp. 382–3.

[15]These 'Discourses', combined with his collected 'Lectures and Essays on University Subjects', were subsequently published as *The Idea of a University*. In the critical edition by I. T. Ker (Oxford 1976), this work is cited here at p. 94.

[16]Ibid., p. 184.

On his return to England, full-time, in 1858, Newman became editor of *The Rambler*, a lay-controlled periodical of distinctly anti-Ultramontane cast. The delation of his article 'On Consulting the Faithful in Matters of Doctrine' by one of the English bishops, together with his criticism of the pope's temporal power (which Pius IX, and Ultramontanes generally regarded as a *sine qua non* of the spiritual freedom of the Holy See) led to strained relations with Rome in the years that followed.

In 1864, a controversy with the Broad Church Anglican Charles Kingsley led to the writing of his *Apologia pro vita sua*, a religious autobiography which, by its combination of frankness and delicacy won him the sympathy of Catholics and non-Catholics alike.[17] One major theme, heralding his mature ecclesiology, is that authority and reason are healthily sustained by conflict with each other.

It is the vast Catholic body itself, and it only, which affords an arena for both combatants in that awful, never-dying duel. It is necessary for the very life of religion ... that the warfare should be incessantly carried on ... Catholic Christendom is no simple exhibition of religious absolutism, but presents a continuous picture of authority and private judgement alternately advancing and retreating as the ebb and flow of the tide. It is a vast assemblage of human beings with wilful intellects and wild passions, brought together ... as if into some moral factory, for the melting, refining, and moulding, by an incessant, noisy process, of the raw material of human nature, so excellent, so dangerous, so capable of divine purposes.[18]

The latter 1860s were dominated by the thought of the

[17]The full title ran: *Apologia pro Vita Sua: Being a Reply to a Pamphlet entitled 'What, Then, Does Dr. Newman Mean?'*. The second edition, appearing in 1865, omitting the first two polemical sections, replaced by a preface, and with a re-worked appendix, was called *History of My Religious Opinions*. In 1873 the original title returned, the preface was re-written and extra notes added.

[18]*Apologia*, op. cit., pp. 224–6.

forthcoming ecumenical Council, convoked by Pius IX. Newman opposed the definition of papal infallibility, prepared while he was publishing his long-distilled fundamental apologetics, the *Essay in Aid of a Grammar of Assent* (1870). Since, however, he had regarded that definition as rather inopportune than unfounded, he was able, unlike some Catholics hostile to the Ultramontane revival, to accept it on the discovery that the episcopate, at least in dispersion if not at the Council itself, were, in practice, morally unanimous for its ecumenicity. In any case, he thought, the Council had only taught a moderate Ultramontanism, not an extremist one. Catholic theologians had long held

> that what the Pope said ex cathedra, was true, *when* the Bishops had received it – what has been passed, is to the effect that what he determines ex cathedra is true *independently* of the reception by the Bishops – but nothing has been passed as to *what is meant* by 'ex cathedra' – and this falls back to the Bishops and the Church to determine quite as much as before. Really therefore nothing has been passed of consequence. Again, the decree is limited to 'faith and morals' – whereas what the Ultra party wished to pass was political principles.[18a]

In 1875, an attack on the dogma by the British prime minister, the High Anglican William Ewart Gladstone, enabled Newman to state his own view of the matter, with the nuances which such extreme Ultramontanes as his fellow-convert, Cardinal Henry Edward Manning of Westminster had left out. As the Newman scholar Paul Misner described the resultant *Letter to the Duke of Norfolk*:

> In a sovereign display of learning and sweet reason he defended the doctrinal import of the new dogma of papal infallibility from the exaggerations of Manning on the one side by refuting the parallel exaggerations of Gladstone on the other.[19]

[18a]*Letters and Diaries* xxv, p. 224

[19]P. Misner, 'The "Liberal" Legacy of Newman', in M. J. Weaver, *Newman and the Modernists* (Lanham, Maryland 1985), pp. 3–26, and here at p. 10.

In 1877 Newman was elected an honorary fellow of Trinity College, and in that sense returned to the Oxford he had never left in spirit. In 1879, the new pope, Leo XIII, made him cardinal deacon of S. Giorgio in Velabro.

My cardinal (exclaimed the pope to a Catholic peer, Lord Selborne)! It was not easy, it was not easy. They said he was too liberal, but I had determined to honour the Church in honouring Newman. I always had a cult for him. I am proud that I was able to honour such a man.[20]

By a strange coincidence, Newman, in his 'biglietto' speech made on receiving, at Rome, the official communication of his election, devoted his response to a protest against liberalism in religion. He described the struggle against such liberalism as the principal leit-motif of his own life:

For thirty, forty, fifty years I have resisted to the best of my powers the spirit of Liberalism in religion. Never did Holy Church need champions against it more sorely than now, when, alas! it is an error overspreading as a snare, the whole earth; and on this great occasion, when it is natural for one who is in my place to look out upon the world, and upon Holy Church as in it, and upon her future, it will not, I hope, be considered out of place, if I renew the protest against it which I have made so often.[21]

Evidently, two senses of 'liberalism' are involved here. It is not too much to say that, in the space between them, the quest for an authentic Catholic equilibrium in nineteenth (and in twentieth century) theology was pursued – and nowhere more clearly than in the idea of the development of doctrine. Newman died on 11 August 1890.

[20]Cited C. S. Dessain, *John Henry Newman*, op. cit., p. 165.
[21]Cited W. Ward, *The Life of John Henry Cardinal Newman*, op. cit., II. p. 460.

Newman's significance for ideas of doctrinal development is now generally accepted as decisive. So I propose to devote three sections to his thought. The first will consider his writings relevant to the issue before his conversion to Catholicism. The subsequent section will look at the *Essay on the Development of Christian Doctrine* as, in a qualified sense, an apologia for that conversion. The last will focus on his ecclesiological writings after the *Essay*, especially those prompted by the definition of papal infallibility in 1870. Taken together, these should give us a satisfactory overview of his contribution to our topic.

The Anglican writings

The relevant texts in the period before his conversion are *The Arians of the Fourth Century*, written in 1833, the *Lectures on the Prophetical Office of the Church*, produced in 1837, and a small number of sermons from the years 1839 to 1843. *The Arians of the Fourth Century* (henceforth 'Arians') represents Newman's discovery of the patristic period, and his turn against what he called 'Liberalism' in religion. By 'Liberalism' Newman meant the attempt to re-construct the Christian religion in terms of the *Zeitgeist* of a given age, its particular concerns and convictions. In studying the Fathers, Newman came to reject the Liberal idea that Christianity is a religiosity, or existential stance, which can in principle be united with any set of philosophical or theological tenets. Instead, he saw Christianity as a revealed content, which is supernatural in origin and so has the right and duty to criticise the world-views it encounters. In *Arians*, Newman's specific aim is to argue that Arianism developed out of Antiochene Christology and not out of Alexandrian theology. But in the course of arguing this (perhaps mistaken) thesis, Newman has much to say about what he takes revelation in the Church to be, as that is disclosed in the age of the Fathers. Before outlining this fundamental theology, it may be helpful to note what Newman has to say about *Arians* in the *Apologia pro vita sua* since his remarks there give us an important clue to how he approached the issue of doctrinal development.

In the *Apologia* Newman explains why as a young man he

was attracted to the early Christian Church. That Church, he claims, saw both nature and the sacramental economy as symbolic mediations of a truth which cannot be adequately expressed in language or, indeed, by any means, until the end of time.[22] The mysteries of the Church are 'but the expression in human language of truths to which the human mind is unequal'.[23] This notion of the intrinsic inadequacy of theological language is clearly relevant to an assessment of doctrinal assertions and so of doctrinal development.

We move on, then, to *Arians* itself, where Newman's earliest remarks of interest for this topic concern theological epistemology – the conditions of a right knowledge of God. And first of all, Newman makes clear his belief that there is some kind of correlation between doctrinal orthodoxy and holiness. Growth in holiness is a necessary condition of growth in the knowledge of God, while decline in holiness brings doctrinal error in its train. As he writes:

> When the spirit and morals of a people are materially debased, varieties of doctrinal error spring up as if self-sown, and are rapidly propagated.[24]

Secondly, Newman asserts that secular modes of human reasoning are inadequate in clarifying the content of Christian revelation. As he puts it:

> Then ... as now, the minds of speculative men were impatient of ignorance, and loth to confess that the laws of truth and falsehood which their experience of this world furnished, could not at once be applied to measure and determine the facts of another.[25]

Thirdly, Newman regards the drawing up of formal doctrinal statements as evidence that something has gone wrong in the life of the Church. They are a signal that there is a threat to what he calls 'tradition'. He writes:

[22]*Apologia pro Vita Sua,* op. cit. pp. 36-37
[23]ibid., p. 37
[24]*The Arians of the Fourth Century* (London 1833), p. 20.
[25]Ibid., p. 37.

If I avow my belief that freedom from symbols and articles is abstractedly the highest state of Christian communion, and the peculiar privilege of the primitive Church, it is not from any tenderness towards that proud impatience of control in which many (i.e. the Liberals) exult as in a virtue; but first, because technicality and formalism are in their degrees, inevitable results of public confessions of faith; and next, because when confessions do not exist, the mysteries of divine truth, instead of being exposed to the gaze of the profane and uninstructed, are kept hidden in the bosom of the Church, far more faithfully than is otherwise possible.[26]

A sound understanding of Christian revelation, then, depends on growth in holiness, is not accessible to secular reasoning, and exists as an internal tradition within the Church, taking the form of an articulated Creed only in some doctrinal emergency.

Newman now goes on to deny that such sound understanding of Christian revelation is communicated directly by the biblical text. He says:

Surely the sacred volume (i.e. the Bible) was never intended, and is not adapted, to teach us our Creed; however certain it is that we can prove our Creed from it when once it has been taught us .... From the very first (the) rule has been, as a matter of fact, that the *Church* should teach the truth, and then appeal to

---

[26]Ibid., p. 41. With this we may compare the words of a contemporary theologian of the Tübingen school, Walter Kasper; commenting on the Nicene resolution of the Arian crisis:

Of course, the price to be paid for this conceptual clarity also became clear in the course of time. This consisted in the increasing danger that the abstract conceptual formulas would become independent and lose their character as interpretations of the historical action of God through Christ in the Holy Spirit. The vital historical faith of Scripture and Tradition threatened to rigidify into abstract formulas which are materially correct but which, isolated from the history of salvation, become unintelligible and functionless for an existential faith', *The God of Jesus Christ* (ET London 1984), p. 260.

Scripture in vindication of its own teaching. And from the first, it has been the error of heretics to neglect the information thus provided for them, and to attempt of themselves a work to which they are unequal, the eliciting of a systematic doctrine from the scattered notices of the truth which Scripture contains.[27]

However, Newman holds that individual theologians, such as the Alexandrian fathers to whom he was devoted, may be able to appropriate the meaning of Scripture, through their special gifts, more deeply than the general run. As he puts it:

> It is surely no extravagance to assert that there are minds so gifted and disciplined as to approach the position occupied by the inspired writers, and therefore able to apply their words with a fitness, and entitled to do so with a freedom which is unintelligible to the dull or heartless criticism of inferior understanding.[28]

Thus at the end of the first hundred pages of *Arians*, Newman's 1833 position on how Christian revelation is mediated in the Church is beginning to emerge in its main lines. Revelation exists as an inner tradition, not in and of itself credally formulated. While the Bible does not constitute this tradition considered as an active teaching, it does corroborate it. Thus when, under pressure from pagans or heretics, the Church formalises her tradition in a Creed, this Creed can be proved from Scripture though not produced out of Scripture. The condition of a sound grasp of the inner tradition is holiness, purity of heart. From this it follows that secular reasoning alone is insufficient for the articulation of doctrine. Nevertheless, theologians who are both intellectually gifted and graced with particular qualities of piety play a special part in establishing the meaning of Scripture and so contribute to the expression of tradition.

Newman proceeds to consider in this perspective an

---

[27] *The Arians of the Fourth Century*, op. cit., pp. 55–6.
[28] Ibid., p. 70.

example of what is involved in the entertaining of doctrinal propositions: and his example is the Holy Trinity, a crucial one since numerous modern writers consider the doctrine of the Trinity to be the supreme instance of the Hellenisation of the New Testament, whether by introducing an alien metaphysic (Harnack), or by removing the eschatological heart of primitive Christianity (Werner), or by introducing Gnostic concerns (Bultmann), or by a group of bishops arbitrarily imposing one interpretation on the Church (Bauer). Newman begins by remarking that the New Testament does not yield that doctrine in any straightforward way.

> As regards the doctrine of the Trinity, the mere text of Scripture is not calculated either to satisfy the intellect or to ascertain the temper of those who profess to accept it as a rule of faith.[29]

How then is the doctrine of the Trinity to be justified? Newman asserts that although the *doctrine* of the Trinity is not taught in Scripture, what he calls 'practical devotion to the Blessed Trinity' *is* taught and exemplified by the New Testament. He places this 'practical devotion' under the heading of 'moral feelings', which feelings, he explains, do not directly contemplate the reality that inspires them. Thus, for instance, an animist in obeying his conscience worships, practically speaking, the one true God, though this God is not a theoretical Object before his mind. Or again, an infant feels 'affectionate reverence' towards its mother or father, even though it cannot discriminate between itself and its parents in words or concepts. But after a point, the infant's reason begins to open. The child inquires after the ground of its own emotions, and finds this ground in the attitudes of its parents towards it. Furthermore, the child can reflect on these attitudes and eventually ascribe them to the *ontological* relationship (not Newman's term) which subsists between parent and offspring. And then:

[29]Ibid., p. 158.

the child's intellect contemplates the object of those affections, which acted truly from the first, and are not purer or stronger merely for this accession of knowledge.[30]

Applying this comparison to theological faith in the Trinity, Newman writes:

As the mind is cultivated and expanded, it cannot refrain from the attempt to analyse the vision which influences the heart, and the Object in which that vision centres; nor does it stop till it has in some sort, succeeded in expressing in words what has all along been a principle, both of its affections and of its obedience.[31]

Notice here that Newman considers the result of this process to be an increase in understanding, but not a difference in underlying relationship with the reality thus better understood. The doctrine of the Trinity as found, for instance, in the Creed of Nicaea-Constantinople, simply expresses what had 'all along' been a principle of the religious lives of ante-Nicene believers.

Newman now goes on to limit the sense in which the doctrine of the Trinity does bring the Church a genuine increment in understanding. He does so by reference to the principle mentioned in the discussion of *Arians* in the *Apologia*: namely, the inbuilt inadequacy of religious language.

The Object of religious veneration being unseen, and dissimilar from all that is seen, reason can but represent it in the medium of those ideas which the experience of life affords.[32]

Moreover, Newman points out the dangers contained in such conceptual articulation of practical devotion. The danger he has in mind at this juncture is that of formal error.

[30]Ibid., p. 159.
[31]Ibid.
[32]Ibid.

Unless these ideas, however inadequate, be *correctly* applied to it, they re-act upon the affections and deprave the religious principle.[33]

So Newman sums up, in a passage with strong Platonist overtones:

> Thus the systematic doctrine of the Trinity may be considered as the shadow, projected for the contemplation of the intellect, of the Object of Scripturally-informed piety, a representation, economical; necessarily imperfect as being exhibited in a foreign medium, and therefore involving apparent inconsistencies or mysteries; given to the Church by tradition contemporaneously with those apostolic writings which are addressed more directly to the heart; kept in the background in the infancy of Christianity, when faith and obedience were vigorous, and brought forward at a time when, reason being disproportionately developed, and aiming at sovereignty in the province of religion, its presence became necessary to expel a usurping idol [i.e. Arianism] from the house of God.[34]

The value of doctrinal articulation, so Newman continues in this passage, lies in its function of excluding heresy but also, and here he speaks more positively than hitherto, in its capacity, when done well, to stimulate the Christian spirit to worship and obedience.

But how do we know that such doctrinal formulation *has* been carried out well, correctly, by the Church? Writing in 1833 Newman has as yet no concept of infallibility. He argues simply that the Church cannot escape articulating doctrine in certain circumstances and that therefore she must do her best.

> If the Church would be vigorous and influential, it must be decided and plain-spoken in its doctrine.[35]

[33]Ibid.
[34]Ibid., pp. 150–60.
[35]Ibid., p. 162.

Thus the Church's bishops must carry out the unenviable task to the best of their abilities:

> Though the discharge of this office is the most momentous and fearful that can come upon mortal man, and is never to be undertaken except by the collective illumination of the heads of the Church, yet, when innovations arise, they must discharge it to the best of their ability; and whether they succeed or fail, whether they have judged rightly or hastily of the necessity of their interpositions, whether they devise their safeguard well or ill, draw the line of Church fellowship broadly or narrowly, countenance the profane reasoner, or cause the scrupulous to stumble – to their Master they stand or fall, as in all other acts of duty, the obligation to protect the faith remaining unquestionable.[36]

Though Newman nowhere speaks in *Arians* of the development of doctrine, a phrase which no doubt he would have rejected at the time, the book is evidently moving in the precise area which that phrase will later mark out. Believing that the classical Christian doctrine of the patristic period could not simply be read off from the Bible by an automatic process, Newman spoke of the same revealed content as being expressed in two ways. To begin with, it is expressed as practical devotion, what might nowadays be termed 'orthopraxy', though one should note that, for Newman, the production of the text of Scripture is the supreme exemplification of such practical devotion. Later, however, the 'grounds' or essential relationships underlying Christian life and devotion in the Church's inner tradition may be excogitated in conceptual form. Though Newman sometimes speaks of this conceptual articulation of revelation as given orally to the apostles but withheld from public discourse through the 'discipline of the secret', his more fundamental thought appears to be that doctrinal articulation must be worked out in fear and trembling by the later

[36]Ibid., p. 164.

Church. Gifted and holy theologians, fathers or doctors of the Church, may help in this task but in the last resort it is the Church's episcopal heads who must decide, for good or for evil.

The Prophetical Office of the Church (henceforth 'Prophetical Office') was written in 1837. Newman's aim in this book was to provide Anglicanism with an adequate and appropriate ecclesiology. The suppression of ten bishoprics in Ireland by the British government four years earlier had driven Anglicans to 'contemplate our own position, and to fall back upon first principles'. Newman's defence of Anglicanism takes the form of an assertion that it is a *via media* between Protestantism and Catholicism, a 'middle way' in the same sense as, for Aristotle, a virtue is a 'mean' between two extremes. For Aristotle, a courageous man is someone who stands at the mean between the two extremes of cowardice and foolhardiness. The man at the mean is not, therefore, someone who is both moderately cowardly and moderately foolhardy. Such a person would not be virtuous, but a vacillating idiot. Applying this principle to the Church: Newman does not argue that Anglicanism is both moderately Protestant and moderately Catholic. He proposes instead that it represents the mean between Protestantism and Catholicism each of which is an erroneous deviation from classical Christianity.

Against Protestantism, Newman's argument is that its special doctrines, such as justification by faith alone, cannot be defended by reference to Scripture. He writes:

> We accord to the Protestant sectary that Scripture is the inspired treasury of the whole faith, but maintain that his doctrines are not in Scripture.[37]

Against Catholicism, Newman's argument is that its special doctrines cannot be defended by reference to Christian antiquity, to the Church of the Fathers and Councils. Newman's claim is that Catholic doctrine cannot be sound because it is innovatory. As he puts it:

---

[37] *The Prophetical Office of the Church* (London 1837), p. 47.

(The Roman Catholic's) professed tradition is, not really such . . . It is a tradition of men . . . It is not continuous . . . It stops short of the apostles . . . The history of its introduction is known.[38]

Romanism is, therefore, what he calls, and here the famous term 'development' at last makes its appearance, 'an unnatural and misshapen development of the truth'. By developing innovatory doctrines, Rome has corrupted the Creed.

But so far this is mere assertion. How does Newman propose to show that Rome's is 'historically an upstart tradition'? First, by offering a criterion for what counts as the teaching of antiquity, and secondly, by showing not only that many Catholic doctrines are ruled out by this criterion, but also that, implicitly, Catholic spokesmen themselves acknowledge this. The criterion is the rule or canon found in the *Comminotorium Primum* of Vincent of Lérins, a fifth century treatise on heresy.[39] The Vincentian canon lays down that only what has been taught 'always, everywhere and by everyone' can be regarded as apostolic. Or as Newman puts it in an interpretative paraphrase:

Catholicity, apostolicity and consent of fathers is the proper evidence of the fidelity or apostolicity of a professed tradition.[40]

And Newman points out that Roman apologists profess to accept this criterion just as much as Anglicans. 'Both the Roman school and ourselves maintain it'. In fact, in Newman's own lifetime Catholic theology in Rome itself was moving to a more nuanced position on the Vincentian canon, under the pressure of historical scholarship. The Catholic apologists known to Newman were chiefly those of the late sixteenth and early to mid seventeenth centuries, Counter-Reformation divines like Robert Bellarmine. In the seventeenth century it was still possible for such Church

---

[38]Ibid., p. 48.
[39]*Comminotorium* II. 3.
[40]*The Prophetical Office of the Church*, op. cit., p. 63.

historians as Cesare Baronio to maintain that all Catholic doctrines and practices were known to the early Church. But this position had become increasingly indefensible, as was shown by the recourse of such eighteenth century apologists as the Vatican librarian Emmanuel de Schelstrate, to the idea of the discipline of the secret. These writers maintained that while all Catholic doctrines and practices were familiar to the early Church, owing to the operation of the *disciplina arcani* there was no evidence to prove this. But by the mid-nineteenth century, Roman theologians such as Johann Baptist Franzelin were arguing that the Vincentian canon must be understood 'affirmatively, but not exclusively'. That is, all of what was taught always, everywhere and by everyone in the early Church must be Christian truth, but not all of Christian truth has been so taught. The aim of this distinction was to make room for legitimate additions to the corpus of Christian doctrine, made under the authority of the Catholic Church.

Since Newman was unaware of this shift in Catholic theology, at least at Rome, he cannot be blamed for regarding the Vincentian canon as the main commonly accepted rule-of-the-game on both sides. Newman accepts that the application of the canon to the history of doctrine is not easy. But he argues that we can do it if we call to our assistance the maxim of the eighteenth century moralist Joseph Butler that 'probability is the guide of life'. As he writes:

> What degree of application is enough must be decided by the same principles which guide us in the conduct of life . . . . which lead us to accept Revelation at all, for which we have but probability to show at most.[41]

Newman proposes, then, to identify apostolic tradition by applying to the history of doctrine the Vincentian canon using as a practical aid Butler's principle of probability. He also suggests some hermeneutical sub-principles which will enable us to carry out this task. Thus, for instance, if two

[41]Ibid., p. 69.

early Councils disagree, we should follow that Council whose members:

> speak one and all the same doctrine, without constraint, and bear witness to their having received it from their fathers having never heard of any other doctrine . . . .

We should *not* follow a Council whose members fail to

> profess to bear witness as a fact, not merely to deduce from Scripture for themselves, besides or beyond what they received from their fathers.[42]

Similarly, we should rate highly an individual father who presents himself as a universal spokesman for a doctrine that historians cannot show to have been introduced at some particular (post-apostolic) time. We should, on the other hand, pay no regard to an individual father who simply offers an opinion on some point. It is in fact by using this 'sub-principle' that Newman is able to discard patristic texts like Gregory the Great on Purgatory, Ephraim on prayer to Mary and so forth, and thus insist that the Church of Rome has added to, and thereby corrupted, the original deposit of faith, turning private theological opinions into doctrines incumbent on all believers.

It is noteworthy that in the *Prophetical Office* Newman does not think of applying to these specifically Catholic doctrines the principles he worked out in *Arians* with regard to the doctrine of the Trinity. That is, he does not consider that the Roman doctrines may have existed in the apostolic period as 'moral feelings' among the faithful just as, on his own showing, the doctrine of the Trinity existed in the ante-Nicene Church as a 'moral feeling': a 'practical devotion towards the Blessed Trinity'. Why does Newman fail to consider this possibility? One obvious reason is that to do so might undermine the Anglican position Newman is expounding. But another, and this second candidate is

[42]Ibid., p. 64.

founded in what Newman actually says, is that he believed
he already had a perfectly good explanation for Roman
additions to the Creed. This explanation was the notion of an
infallible magisterium. According to Newman, the theory of
the Pope's primatial authority in teaching Christian doctrine
was itself an extravagant or improbable reading of the
patristic evidence. But after Trent this theory had been ever
more inflated until it had become a fully-fledged doctrine of
the infallibility of the episcopate *cum et sub Petro*, 'with and
under' the Pope. So much was this so that the infallibility of
the contemporary Church had become the real foundation of
Catholic doctrine. As a result, it was enough for a theological
opinion to be taught by the Roman Church at any point for
it to be regarded as an essential feature of apostolic tradition.

> Whatever principles they (the Roman Catholics) profess
> in theology resembling or coincident with our own, yet
> when they come to particulars, when they have to prove
> this or that article of their Creed, they supersede the
> appeal to Scripture and Antiquity by putting forward
> the infallibility of the Church, thus solving the whole
> question by a summary and final interpretation both of
> Antiquity and of Scripture.[43]

Newman was not far wrong in detecting the existence of
such a tendency in Catholic theology, especially in the Jesuit
school. For instance, in the late seventeenth century Cardinal
John de Lugo had argued that any Catholic doctrine may be
adequately defended by reproducing the following syllogism:

> What the Catholic Church teaches with the assistance of
> the Holy Spirit must be true; But the Catholic Church
> teaches X. Therefore X must be true.

And Lugo did not hesitate to regard conciliar definition as
fresh revelation given to the post-apostolic Church.[44]

[43]Ibid., p. 60.
[44]See O. Chadwick, *From Bossuet to Newman* (Cambridge 1987²), p. 43, with

Likewise, in the eighteenth century Isaac Berruyer, another theologian of the Society, had argued that theological epistemology requires nothing more than the affirmation that the Incarnate Word of God has founded an infallible Church. On this basis it can be known *a priori* that whatever is found in Scripture and Tradition must be conformable to the teaching of the present magisterium.[45] Yet Lugo's theory is scarcely compatible with the idea that revelation comes to its definitive climax and goal in Christ and his apostles, whilst Berruyer's theory collapses all distinction between the magisterium and its sources, as well as between solemn, binding exercises of that magisterium and its more lowly and dispensable activities. All major Catholic theories of development after Newman will be concerned to show how the magisterium can render a development official without actually claiming thereby to constitute its legitimacy.

In the *Prophetical Office*, then, Newman was convinced that the Roman Church had distorted the Gospel by ascribing to it ideas which had simply recommended themselves in the course of history to the Roman pontiffs and their fellow hierarchs. Rome's doctrine of infallibility was 'an effort, presumptuous and unwarranted, as well as founded in error, to stem the tide of unbelief'. By its habitual appeal to the existing Church, Catholicism stood self-condemned. It was powerless to show that its own teaching was founded in that of the apostles and Fathers. Forty years later, in the third edition of the *Prophetical Office* Newman would argue against his earlier self that the Christian is in a poor way if his only guide for interpreting Scripture and Antiquity be the Vincentian canon. A revelation, he wrote in an 1877 footnote, is intended to reveal. The difficulty of operating the canon, even with the help of Newman's additional recommendations in 1837, is

reference to Lugo's *De fide*, disputatio II. 2, 2, and his *De virtute fidei divinae*, disputatio I. 13, 1. I trust that the author of this distinguished study will forgive my imitating, by sincere flattery, the title of his book in that of my own.

[45]O. Chadwick, *From Bossuet to Newman*, op. cit., pp. 70–3, with reference to Berruyer's manuscript 'Réflexions sur la foi', a copy of which exists at Stonyhurst College, Lancashire, as MS A. III. 27.

a reason against (its) being the divinely appointed
instrument by which revelation is to be brought home
to individuals.[46]

In 1837, however, Newman held that the canon enables us to
grasp the substance or 'great outlines' of apostolic revelation
as that was indefectibly preserved in what he called 'the
Church Catholic . . . in all its branches'.[47]

I turn now from the *Prophetical Office* to Newman's
sermons, and especially to the 1843 sermon entitled 'The
theory of developments in religious doctrine'.[48] This sermon
continues a line of thought worked out in five homilies on
the relation of faith and reason preached before Oxford
University between 1839 and 1841. In those five sermons
Newman had drawn a distinction between what he termed
'implicit' and 'explicit' reason. Implicit reason is the
spontaneous interpretation of experience. Explicit reason is
the analysis of this spontaneous operation into formal
procedures of induction and deduction, so far as the nature of
the case admits. Newman proposed that implicit reason is the
more fundamental, because it considers the evidence for a
conclusion in terms of an entire experiential field or flow. In
this total experiential field many considerations occur to the
mind which are lost to view when explicit reason takes over,
isolating items of evidence and submitting them to a formal
process of investigation. In the 1843 sermon on development
in religious doctrine, Newman applies these ideas to
revelation. What he had called implicit reason here becomes
man's original grasp of revelation, his 'impression' of the
revealed 'idea'.[49] What corresponds to explicit reason is the
mind working over this impression, investigating it, reflecting
on it and thus drawing out the idea, divine revelation,
into propositions. In this, Newman found the Blessed Virgin
Mary as presented in the Lucan infancy narratives to be

[46] *The Via Media of the Anglican Church*, op. cit., I., p. 56.

[47] *The Prophetical Office of the Church*, op. cit., pp. 232–4.

[48] *Newman's University Sermons. Fifteen Sermons Preached Before the University of Oxford, by John Henry Newman* (London 1970), pp. 312–51.

[49] Ibid., pp. 176–311.

the model and image of the Church. Pondering the mysteries of revelation kept in her heart, she is:

> our pattern of faith, both in the reception and in the study of divine truth ... (who) symbolises to us, not only the faith of the unlearned, but of the doctors of the Church also, who have to investigate, and weigh, and define, as well as to profess the Gospel.[50]

As in *Arians*, Newman argues that representation of the original impression in propositional form, in a Creed or dogmatic definition, is not strictly necessary for the authenticity or perfection of our grasp of revelation. Implicit judgements about the idea (i.e. revelation) may exist for centuries and guide souls quite adequately without any corresponding explicit formulae.

What is especially interesting about the 1843 sermon in relation to the *Prophetical Office* which preceded it by six years is that Newman illustrates his thesis by doctrines that emerged *after* the patristic period – at least by his own account. Thus for instance he argues that the doctrine of the unity of the divine nature was not enunciated until the thirteenth century (and notably at the Fourth Lateran Council of 1215). Yet this did not prevent it being held throughout the earlier Church in the form of an unconscious impression. It is not too much to say that with this sermon Newman abandoned the main argument against the Roman Church in the *Prophetical Office*, namely, that many of its doctrines were incredible since post-patristic in formulation. At this very time, indeed, he was writing to a friend:

> I am very far *more* sure that England is in schism than that the Roman additions to the Primitive Creed may not be developments, arising out of a keen and vivid realising of the Divine Depositum of faith.[51]

[50]Ibid., p. 313.

[51]Letter of 11 May 1843 to Maria Giberne, cited I. Ker, *John Henry Newman*, op. cit., p. 274.

Yet in the 1843 sermon Newman specifically excluded all consideration of who is to be the judge of dogmatic inferences. He did not try to identify the authority which may finally judge whether a given doctrinal proposition is faithful to the original apostolic impression or not. By 1845, the year of writing the *Essay on the Development of Christian Doctrine*, Newman would consider that the Catholic position could not be defended by the simple acceptance of the principle of development. It was necessary to argue as well for the 'antecedent probability' that a divine revelation would bring with it a divinely protected institution capable of interpreting that revelation aright – and so capable of determining which developments were legitimate.

Newman's personal theology, at any rate, was developing at an accelerating pace, as the internal contrasts within the Anglican works betray. The *Prophetical Office* had contended that the process of credal articulation described in *Arians* stops with the end of the patristic period when Christianity took on its definitive form, and that this is the point of all appeal to the *consensus patrum*. Moreover, Newman had there argued that by applying the Vincentian canon, traditionally accepted by Catholic spokesmen, the Church of Rome can be shown to have exceeded the proper limits of doctrinal articulation and so corrupted the Gospel. The 1843 sermon on development in religious doctrine, however, by applying the distinction between implicit and explicit reason to the entire history of Christian thought effectively abandons the Vincentian canon as a sufficient guide to sound doctrine. Christian revelation is an inexhaustible, living, concrete idea; this idea was impressed on the corporate mind of the apostolic Church which received it by an implicit judgement. Over the centuries, reflection or explicit reason then works over this impression, drawing out from it what we know as the dogmas of the Church. Which Church this is, i.e. in which Christian confession or confessions the one Church now exists, Newman does not as yet consider.

Newman's Anglican period may thus be divided into three

stages, so far as his ideas on doctrinal historicity are concerned. In sum: first of all, in *Arians*, he argues that the classical Christian doctrine of the patristic period cannot simply be inferred from the New Testament. However, the New Testament does express 'moral feelings' or 'practical devotion' which are capable of being further analysed. Using the example of the child discovering the reasons for its feeling towards its parents, Newman suggests that the Church too can come to describe the grounds or underlying relationships of its own inner life. This process of conceptualisation takes the form of the gradual definition of doctrine. Though the practical importance of this for the individual believer is limited, this crystallisation of doctrine defends the Church's inner tradition against heretics. Yet Newman implies that there is no advance guarantee that the bishops of the Church will formulate doctrine well. They may do it well or badly.

In the second stage, that of the *Prophetical Office*, Newman refuses to apply these ideas beyond the patristic period. That period saw the definitive emergence of Christian dogma. Any addition to the body of doctrine after that time can only be corruption. Newman holds this as a principle because, firstly, the Anglican divines of the seventeenth century 'golden age' of the Church of England held it, and secondly, because Roman Catholic controversialists themselves appealed to the 'consensus of the fathers' as authoritative for determining doctrine. Thus the appeal to antiquity provides common ground on which the case as between Anglicanism and Rome can be fought out. However, in Newman's own time, the Vincentian canon, with its rule that Christian truth consists solely of what has been believed always, everywhere and by everyone was ceasing to be used in an exclusive way by Catholic theologians, at least in Rome. In order to defend the legitimacy of post-patristic doctrinal formulation, it was now being said that while all that the canon includes is true, not all that is true is included by the canon. This shift was unknown to Newman. Newman argued that the 'substance' or the 'great outlines' of the faith could be identified by applying the canon in a sensible way, appealing to Butler's axiom that 'probability is the guide of life'. This substance is, Newman considered, infallibly preserved in the Church Catholic according to Christ's promise. That it is not infallibly preserved in the Roman Church in particular is clear from Rome's obscuring of the 'great outlines' by novel doctrines. The substance of the faith is most clearly preserved in Anglicanism, through the via media, that is, the avoidance of either Protestant or Catholic deviation from Gospel truth. This second stage in the development of Newman's ideas on development may perhaps be called a regression, since it largely consists in limiting the operation of the ideas on development he put forward in the first stage.

Finally, the third stage in Newman's Anglican period is represented by the sermon on the theory of developments in religion. Here Newman re-expresses the 1833 idea that the patristic definitions of doctrine are the conceptual elaboration of the ontological grounds of the moral feelings or practical devotion contained in the Bible. Newman invokes here a distinction between implicit reason, the spontaneous interpretation of experience and explicit reason, the analysis of spontaneous interpretation into discursive or logical thought. Revelation or the Christian 'idea' impressed itself onto the corporate mind of the apostolic Church. The vocabulary is drawn from the British empiricists, especially John Locke, and the basic metaphor is a seal cutting a design of wax. This original impression is held by the mind implicitly, i.e. by spontaneous interpretation in predominantly non-propositional form. However, by analysing what is grasped implicitly of the idea, revelation, it is possible to explicitate it and draw it out into fuller propositional form. This is what the Church does in constructing a Creed or other forms of dogmatic definition. Newman no longer regards this process as having ceased with the patristic period. One of his main examples is the doctrinal explicitation of belief in the unity of the divine nature, as made at the Fourth Lateran Council of 1215. What Newman left aside, however, was the question, Who is to be the judge of such developments? Who is to decide whether one putative development is legitimate or not?

Yet the importance of these latter questions is obvious. Suppose that there emerges in the Church a consciously entertained moral feeling, which claims to be caused exclusively by the Gospel. An example might be the moral feeling of devotion towards the Mother of Jesus. While one person might go along with this trend, another might deny that such a moral feeling was genuinely the product of the Gospel. Who is to decide? At a rather different level, two people might share such a moral feeling, both believing it to be caused by the Gospel. But these two people might disagree about how the feeling should be conceptually articulated. One person might argue for conceptualisation in terms of a doctrine of Mary's all-holiness, or 'immaculate conception'. Another might object, holding such a doctrine to be excluded by already developed doctrinal belief in the universal need for redemption. Again, who is to decide? This question brings us to Newman's Catholic writings, and notably to the *Essay on the Development of Christian Doctrine*.

The 'Essay on Development'

There are two editions of the *Essay*. The first was written while Newman was in the throes of reception into the Catholic Church in 1845. He offered to submit it to the local Church authority for correction, bearing in mind that he had never studied theology as a Catholic. But, after some hesitation, they refused, considering that the book would have the greater impact if it came from within a purely Anglican theological culture. The edition of 1878 is better organised, and notable for its emphasis that the theory of doctrinal development is not meant to prove the claims of Roman Catholicism. Rather was the *Essay* intended to dispel objections to Roman Catholicism: not at all the same thing. Newman does not assert in the *Essay* that anyone coming with an open mind to the Christian 'idea', the New Testament revelation, should realise, through the arguments of the *Essay*, that this idea now exists in developed form in the Catholic Church of Pope Pius IX. Instead, the *Essay* proposes to show that the claims of that Church to be the Church Christ founded cannot be called unreasonable simply because, in Catholicism, doctrine has been developed beyond the Fathers (as before them), and because certain such doctrinal developments have been imposed as confessional tests by Church authority. As Professor Nicholas Lash has written:

> The fact of the matter is, quite simply, that Newman did not have a 'theory' of development in the sense in which this concept has been employed in twentieth century theology. In our own day, we simply take it for granted that the Church, in its doctrine, life and structure, has in some sense 'evolved', 'developed' or 'changed' throughout the course of its history (however we evaluate the changes that have taken place). Newman did not share this conviction. It was, therefore, the *fact* of development which he offered as a 'theory', an 'hypothesis', as an alternative to 'immutability' on the one hand and 'corruption' on the other.

And Lash explains:

> He took into consideration many widely differing types of 'development' both because the complexity of the historical evidence demanded this, and because his heuristic conception of 'development' as the key to the problem was not further elaborated in the form of any single theoretical explanation in the modern sense, at all.[52]

In the first edition, the modest aim of the *Essay* is already fairly apparent, as when, in the 'Introduction', Newman describes the theory of development as an 'hypothesis to account for a difficulty'. But his description of principles at work in doctrinal development as offering 'tests' for the authenticity of that development gave some readers the mistaken idea that Newman was proposing 'laws' of

---

[52]N. Lash, 'Literature and Theory. Did Newman have a "theory" of development?', in J. D. Bastable (ed.), *Newman and Gladstone. Centennial Essays* (Dublin 1978), pp. 161–2.

development, akin to the biological laws formulated by Charles Darwin in *The Origin of Species*. This in turn suggested to others that, for Newman, the identity of the Catholic Church as the one true Church of Christ could simply be read off from observation of the laws of development in action.

To guard against such misconceptions, Newman emphasised in the second edition that the *Essay* is not meant to constitute a proof of Catholic claims but to dispel certain objections, and notably those presented by the Anglican Newman himself in the *Prophetical Office*. As the 1878 Preface puts it:

> The following pages were not in the first instance written to prove the divinity of the Catholic religion, though ultimately they furnish a positive argument in its behalf, but to explain certain difficulties in its history, felt before now by the author himself, and commonly insisted on by Protestants in controversy, as serving to blunt the force of its *prima facie* and general claims on our recognition.[53]

And to drive home the point, the Newman of 1878 removed the word 'test' from his description of seven principles at work in authentic doctrinal development, replacing it with the less ambitious 'notes'. In other words, he is stressing that the *Essay* does not offer a full criteriology of doctrinal development which will show Roman developments to be the genuine ones. Newman's criteria for authentic development are tentative and self-consciously limited. As we shall see, this fits in with the basic argument of the *Essay*.

I shall now outline the basic structure of that argument, using the 1878 *Essay* since it is much the more coherent and better ordered of the two. The Introduction sums up the argument against Catholicism found in the *Prophetical Office* and describes Newman's own increasing doubts about the validity of that 1837 position. Basically, these doubts were

[53]*Essay on the Development of the Christian Doctrine* (London 1878), p. vii.

twofold. First, why should the process of doctrinal articulation be acceptable before the great Creeds were produced but not after that date? Secondly, since some doctrines in the Anglican formularies, like original sin, resist inclusion within the Vincentian canon even on a probabilistic use of that rule, (for they do not receive the explicit assent of anything like all of the Fathers), how can those doctrines be justified, whilst others, occupying a similar status, such as that of Purgatory, are rejected? The theory found in the *Prophetical Office* will not stand. What is to take its place? To understand Newman's answer, we must bear in mind the purpose of the *Essay* as Newman conceived it. Newman had already come to believe on independent grounds that the Catholic Church was the true Church. He did not himself believe that these grounds could be fully specified. By an act of implicit reason, of the fundamental spontaneous interpretation of reality, he had come to an intuitive conviction that the Roman Catholic Church was, as he put it in some 1850 lectures later published as *Certain Difficulties Felt by Anglicans in Catholic Teaching*, the answer to:

> the simple question ... Where, what, is that thing in this age which in the first age was the Catholic Church?[54]

This united, international communion, internally sure of its doctrine, though externally the object of suspicion and hostility, could not fail to be the Church of Athanasius and Ambrose. Thus the *Essay* is not the foundation of Newman's conversion, although, as Owen Chadwick has pointed out, had its theology been condemned by some infallible, or at least authoritative, act of the Roman church's teaching office, Newman's argumentation in support of his conversion would have disappeared. What is to take the place of the via media of the *Prophetical Office* is, first, belief in the Roman Catholic Church as Christ's Church but, secondly, then, this belief is

---

[54]*Certain Difficulties Felt by Anglicans in Catholic Teaching* (London 1888), I. p. 368; cf. N. Lash, *Newman on Development. The Search for an Explanation in History* (London 1975; 1979). pp. 9–10.

to be defended and corroborated by the thesis of the development of doctrine. This thesis will be applied, as in the 1843 sermon, to the entire history of Christian theology, but it will now include also consideration of these organs in the Church community whereby one putative development is canonised and another rejected.

The Introduction combines *a priori* and *a posteriori* arguments – the methodological hallmark of the *Essay* which is a marriage of deductive (or Scholastic) and inductive (or empiricist) approaches. Newman argues that certain things are probable antecedently: even before we come to look at the facts in a detailed way. But he also argues that certain things are historically the case, that facts can on occasion explode hypotheses and defeat even antecedent probabilities. But, most characteristically, Newman combines these two types of argument, reasoning that if an antecedent probability is established intelligently, it will illuminate the empirical facts, and enable them to yield a meaning or intelligibility which would otherwise be missed.

The rest of the *Essay* consists of twelve chapters whose chief thrust may briefly be set forth. Chapter One deals with the notion of the development of ideas, and, as Paul Misner has written

> perhaps the closest analogy Newman used was that of a cultural development, the way, that is, of an idea or a complex of ideas, in a society.[55]

In the 1878 edition it is made clear that by 'idea' Newman means the self-expression of some rich and complex reality. The ideas he is speaking of represent objects or realities of some peculiarly significant and many-sided kind. Thus an idea is 'commensurate with the sum total of the possible aspects' of the object it expresses. No one aspect can exhaust the contents of an idea. No one proposition can define it. The process of bringing the aspects of an idea into what

[55]P. Misner, *Papacy and Development. Newman and the Primacy of the Pope* (Leiden 1976), p. 68.

Newman calls 'consistency and form' is to be labelled 'development'. In development, these aspects are portrayed on the broad stage of diverse mental operations carried out within a human culture over time. But to be authentic development, they must truly belong to the original idea.

Development has different modes. Modes relevant to the Christian religion are logical, historical, moral and metaphysical development. By 'logical' development; Newman means deduction from known premisses; by 'historical' a better knowledge of the facts; by 'moral', the exploration of the implications of the feelings of the heart; by 'metaphysical' the analysis of the inner relations found within the original 'impression', the first grasping of some rich reality.

In Chapter Two, Newman sets out his *a priori* argument in favour of developments in Christian doctrine. Since Christian revelation is itself a rich and complex reality, the identification of its various aspects will naturally take time. Furthermore, in order to establish which developments in awareness of the original idea are legitimate, it is likely that there will be an infallible organ within the body of the Church, equipped to distinguish authentic development from inauthentic.

> If Christianity be a social religion, as it certainly is, and if it be based on certain ideas acknowledged as divine, ... and if these ideas have various aspects, and make distinct impressions on different minds, and issue in consequence in a multiplicity of developments, true, or false, or mixed, as has been shown, what influence will suffice to meet and to do justice to these conflicting conditions, but a supreme authority ruling and reconciling individual judgements by a divine right and a recognised wisdom? ... If Christianity is both social and dogmatic, and intended for all ages, it must, humanly speaking have an infallible expounder.[56]

In Chapters Three and Four, Newman defends this *a priori*

[56]*Essay on the Development of Christian Doctrine* II. 2. 13; pp. 89–90.

approach to evidence as something required by historical method. You cannot make sense of the facts without some sort of hypothesis.

In Chapter Five, he contrasts authentic developments with corruptions, suggesting seven 'notes' by which genuine developments will tend to show themselves. These are:

1. Preservation of the original type: in effect, preserving the quality of the original impact of some new thing.
2. Continuity of known principles.
3. Power to assimilate alien matter to the original idea.
4. Logical connectedness.
5. Being anticipated early in a partial way here and there.
6. A conserving attitude to the past: taking steps to preserve an old idea in a new form.
7. Chronic vigour: i.e. lasting in a healthy state for a long time.

Though important, these notes or tests are not the true centre of gravity of the *Essay*. The centre of gravity of the Essay lies in the three great church-historical tableaux which Newman paints: the Church of the first three centuries; the Church of the fourth century Arian crisis; the Church of the patristic golden age in the fifth and sixth centuries. Each tableau culminates with Newman drawing a parallel with the nineteenth century Roman communion, showing that the changes brought about by the Tridentine reformation of the Church are insubstantial compared with the overwhelming sameness between the earlier Christians and the modern Roman Catholics. From Chapters Six to Twelve, Newman, bearing in mind the seven 'notes', compares therefore the first six centuries of the Church's existence to modern Catholicism, and concludes that the Church of Rome emerges unscathed from the comparison. *Prima facie*, the developments found in the Catholic Church can be defended with the interpretative assistance of the notes. They enjoy a reasonable claim to be aspects of an authentic re-composition of the original Christian 'idea' into new 'consistency and form'.

Finally, Newman draws the *Essay* to a close with a moving peroration on the chronic vigour of the Church, which he sees as continually dying and rising throughout history in imitation of her Master and Lord. Thinking no doubt more especially of the 'second spring' of Catholicism in England during his lifetime he writes:

> Such has been the slumber and such the restoration of the Church.[57]

which lives out in history a continuity in discontinuity comparable to that of Christ in his death and resurrection.

Since the writing of the *Essay*, a number of objections have been lodged against Newman's account. These objections amount to little more than three forms of the same charge. The accusation is that Newman, despite his best intentions, effectively committed himself to a theory of continuing revelation, whereby the emergence and definition of doctrine grants the Church absolutely new knowledge.[58] And if the propositions in which this new knowledge is couched are imposed on people as 'of divine faith', what else is this but to demand assent to a divine revelation for truths yet admitted to be new, that is, post-apostolic? More than one passage of the *Essay* might, indeed, be construed in this sense. Thus, for example, Newman found himself able to write:

> Supposing the order of nature once broken by the introduction of a revelation, the continuance of that revelation is but a question of degree.[59]

One form in which this objection is raised takes its starting-point from Newman's references to later doctrines as based on earlier 'feelings' in the Church. As we have seen, in *Arians* Newman had used the idea of a moral feeling capable of later explication through reflection on its foundation and implications so as to throw light on the process of credal articulation. The same language is found in the *Essay* in

[57]Ibid., XII. 9; p. 442.

[58]I. Ker, 'Newman's Theory – Development or Continuing Revelation?'. in J. D. Bastable (ed.), *Newman and Gladstone*, op. cit., pp. 145–59.

[59]*Essay on the Development of Christian Doctrine*, II. ii. 10; p. 85.

connexion with, for instance, belief in Purgatory or acceptance of the legitimacy of venerating the saints. But Owen Chadwick maintains that the distance between simple feeling and articulated doctrine is so great that it forces language beyond the limits of credibility to call a later doctrine part of the deposit in such cases as these.[60] It seems, however, that by 'feeling' Newman did not mean mere sentiment, but rather a kind of intuitive knowledge: what in the 1843 sermon he had called an 'impression'. In the *Essay*, both terms – 'feeling' and 'impression' – occur side by side. Arguably, in using the second term, Newman was concerned to make good the epistemological deficiencies of the term 'feeling' by comparing the apostles' grasp of revelation with our awareness of an object through the senses. Just as the unity and distinctiveness of a material object is reflected in the distinctive unity of the impression it makes on the mind through the senses, so the apostles were graced with an intuitive knowledge of the pattern of the revealed object, the Christian idea. Nevertheless, the *Essay* does retain the *Arians* emphasis on moral feelings as a foundation of later doctrine, albeit in a subsidiary role. Newman continued to hold strongly in these contexts for the appropriateness of the word 'instinct' with its connotations of what is inarticulate and sub-conscious. Thus he wrote in an unpublished paper of 1868, *between* the two editions of the *Essay*, that the Church's original hold on revelation was

> a vision of it, not logical, and therefore consistent with errors of reasoning and of fact in the enunciation, after the manner of an intuition or an instinct.[61]

A second way in which the same objection may be expressed holds that to judge from Newman's seven 'tests' or 'notes' of doctrinal identity, he himself did not believe in the substantial immutability of doctrine. The tests do not,

[60] O. Chadwick, *From Bossuet to Newman*, op. cit., pp. 159–60.

[61] C. S. Dessain (ed.), 'An Unpublished Paper by Cardinal Newman on the Development of Doctrine', *Journal of Theological Studies* 9 (1958), pp. 329–55; the same paper was presented by H. M. d'Achaval in *Gregorianum* 39 (1958), pp. 585–96.

apparently, require that a development be somehow contained in apostolic doctrine, but only that it show a general harmony or continuity with what the apostles believed.[62] Though Newman regards a minority of developments as strictly logical in character, and so contained in earlier doctrine as a conclusion in its premises – for instance, he saw the Ephesian dogma of Mary's divine motherhood as no more than a logical explication of the ascription of divinity to her Son at Nicaea – his more general tendency is to see development as non-logical in character, as, in his own words, historical, moral or metaphysical. Many passages in the *Essay* are said to imply a substantial mutability in doctrine.[63] Thus Newman speaks of development as 'the germination and maturation of some truth on a large mental field', and he talks of an idea growing into an

ethical code, or into a system of government, or into a theology or into a ritual according to its capabilities.[64]

It is argued against Newman that in the case of a doctrinal system, the categories of continuing substantial identity (which Newman affirmed) and substantial immutability (which he appears to have rejected) are one and the same.[65] Newman's biological analogy is misleading. An egg can become a bird, a grub a butterfly, but a system of doctrine cannot undergo great changes without losing its identity.

This objection overlooks the fact that, for Newman, the substantial immutability of Christian truth cannot be discovered by comparing doctrinal systems – that is, by

[62]A. A. Stephenson, S.J., 'Cardinal Newman and the Development of Doctrine', *Journal of Ecumenical Studies* 3 (1966), pp. 463–85.

[63]Stephenson remarks appositely in this connexion that 'substantial' may either mean, as in idiomatic use, 'more or less', 'deserving the name in essentials' (a weak sense), or have the more technical meaning, classically expressed by pope John XXIII in his address inaugurating the Second Vatican Council, where the pope distinguished between the immutable 'substance of the ancient doctrine', the *depositum fidei*, and the manner of its expression (strong sense): thus art. cit. at pp. 468–9.

[64]*Essay on the Development of Christian Doctrine* I. i. 4; p. 38.

[65]A. A. Stephenson, S.J., 'Cardinal Newman and the Development of Doctrine', art. cit., pp. 472–3.

comparing different forms of conceptual articulation of doctrine at various stages in the history of the Church. It can only be discovered by considering all such systems in their relation to the original Christian idea. The same immutable revelation inhabits the various doctrinal systems found at different chronological points in the development of the Church's conscious mind under the pressure of particular situations in history. For Newman, we can only be positively certain that this is so through a faith-acceptance, using implicit reasoning, that the present Roman Catholic church is the Church Christ founded, endowed by him with appropriate organs for canonising legitimate explicitations of the original deposit. Yet, negatively, we can clear away objections to this belief by showing how a great idea can only manifest itself in and through development – by appealing, then, to antecedent probability, and also by showing that the actual historical developments found within Catholicism do show symptoms of being authentic development, using the yardstick of the 'notes' to do so.

The third and final ground for the criticism that Newman in effect holds to a 'continuing' revelation, is that he evidently regards the development of apostolic faith into post-apostolic doctrine as sharing the same structure as the development of the Old Testament into the New.[66] According to Newman, the structure of both of these developments consists in a relation between prophecy and its fulfilment. In Old Testament times, the New Testament existed as an 'unfulfilled prophecy'. In apostolic times, the later developed faith of the Church existed in the same way. As Newman explicitly remarks, the 'doctrinal, political, ritual and ethical sentences' of the New Testament are

> parallel to the prophetic announcements (of the Old Testament) . . . and (since they) have the same structure, they should admit the same expansion.[67]

---

[66]Cf. N. Lash, *Newman on Development*, op. cit., p. 111; idem., *Change in Focus. Doctrinal Change and Continuity* (London 1973), p. 93.

[67]*Essay on the Development of Christian Doctrine*, II. i. 10; p. 66.

This citation has been highlighted by Nicholas Lash in his study *Newman on Development*. There Lash argues that if, for instance, the Papacy existed in the early centuries only as a prophecy, we might as well say that it did not exist at all – except as a prophecy.[68] But, in point of fact, Newman qualified the somewhat unguarded statements which gave rise to these comments. Note the implications of the phrase 'on the other hand' in a passage germane to our purpose:

> While it is certain that developments of revelation proceeded all through the old dispensation and down to the very end of our Lord's ministry, on the other hand, if we turn our attention to the beginnings of apostolic teaching after his ascension, we shall find ourselves unable to fix an historical point at which the growth of doctrine ceased, and the rule of faith was once for all settled.[69]

By the words 'on the other hand', Newman marks a distinction between the development of revelation itself, from the Old Testament to the New, and the succeeding development of doctrine, of our understanding of the biblically developed revelation. For Newman, the development of doctrine may have the same structure as the development of revelation, since both are development, but the development of doctrine is not part of the course of history of revelation in the way that the movement from Old Testament to New belongs to that course.

In a comparison suggested by Ian Ker: the development of Sophocles' play the *Antigone* through its five acts is a unique and self-contained development, however much, after seeing the play acted, our own understanding of it may itself develop.[70] The *Antigone* is a finished work of art with its own internal development, yet its 'idea' is constantly finding new expression as people write about it or talk about it, or

[68] N. Lash, *Newman on Development*, op. cit., p. 112.

[69] *Essay on the Development of Christian Doctrine*, II. i. 12; pp. 67–8.

[70] I. Ker, 'Newman's Theory – Development or Continuing Revelation?', art. cit., p. 156.

even write new plays based on it like the Existentialist version by Jean Anouilh.

In the last resort, the *Essay* is a difficult work to interpret, so much so that we may be tempted to apply to it J. A. Froude's description of history: 'a child's box of letters with which we can spell any word we please'.[71] Thus, just as orthodox Scholastics in the wake of the Modernist crisis claimed it as supporting their notion of 'homogeneous' development, the Modernists themselves were no less enthusiastic in its praise. The French Modernist Alfred Loisy's first essay on the relation of history and dogma was stimulated by receiving a copy of the *Essay* from the 'English' Liberal Catholic, Baron Friedrich von Hügel. Newman, he declared, had been 'the Church's most open theologian since Origen' – a not entirely unmixed compliment given the condemnation of certain Origenist theses by the Second Council of Constantinople! Likewise, the Anglo-Irish Modernist George Tyrrell would write:

> Just those Catholics for whom Newman would have felt the utmost antipathy – those, namely, who, in spite of the *Syllabus*, entertain sanguine dreams of 'coming to terms' with the modern mind – have learnt to look to him and his methods as the sole hope of their cause.[72]

Lash, while regarding the Modernist crisis as muddying the waters of Newman interpretation, for the 'complex and ambiguous relationships' which both united and separated it from the work of the Modernists would ensure that no 'objective and dispassionate study of the *Essay* would be possible for several decades', also gives grounds for supposing that the exegesis of the *Essay* will ever be a disputed affair.[73] In his contribution to the symposium *Newman and Gladstone*, he points out, first, that, just because Newman had described

---

[71]J. A. Froude, *Short Studies* I., cited J. Kenyon, *The History Men. The Historical Profession in England since the Renaissance* (London 1983), pp. 120–1.

[72]G. Tyrrell, 'Preface', to H. Bremond, *The Mystery of Newman* (London 1907), p. xii.

[73]N. Lash, *Newman on Development*, op. cit., p. 147.

revelation, the Christian idea, as a reality so irreducibly complex that it cannot be directly stated, he is obliged to concede that, *a fortiori*, the development of that idea will not be governed by any one principle which can be stated in rigorous theoretical form. And secondly, Newman's method (whatever Tyrrell may have meant by that word) was, in a musical metaphor, 'fugal'. It consisted in the near-simultaneous highlighting of a variety of aspects. Newman's main analogies for development – logical, biological, psychological – are fundamentally, so Lash holds, metaphors. He points out that for Newman the organic analogy, for instance, is related to such biblical images as the parables of the growth of the Kingdom and the Johannine symbol of the Vine. The logic of the *Essay*, in other words, is a logic of metaphor. Newman set out to show how a number of different features of the Church's development are coherently inter-related, not only with each other but with the primitive deposit. Yet he found that he could only state these relationships 'allusively, delicately, by metaphor'. And so the way was left open for differing and indeed conflicting uses of the *Essay*. As Tyrrell put it in his customary forthright way:

> Of his personal sympathies there can be no doubt. He had no quarrel but every sympathy with the dogmatic intransigence of Scholastic theologians ... (His) incontestable abhorrence of doctrinal liberalism does not at once prove that he may not be the progenitor of it ... He whose whole career was a combat with latitudinarian tendencies forged one or two weapons against them which have since (whether fairly or unfairly) been actually turned to their service. . . . [74]

Before looking at the Modernists' attitude to the theory of development, however, an account of Newman's ideas on this subject would not be complete without saying a word about his relations with the local church of Rome in his day: both with Roman theologians, and with the desire of Pius

[74]G. Tyrrell, 'Preface', art. cit.

IX for a definition of papal infallibility at the First Vatican Council, the most controversial doctrinal development to come to the full term of solemn promulgation in his lifetime.

Newman and Rome

In this last section on Newman, it remains, then, to consider his relations with Rome. I have in mind two aspects: first, the reception of his theory of development at Rome and secondly, how Newman reacted to the test-case of the growing desire in many quarters for a dogmatic definition of papal primacy and infallibility – what Karl Rahner would call 'the most acute case of doctrinal development that there is'.[75] *The Essay on the Development of Christian Doctrine* could easily be invoked to justify extreme Ultramontanism, yet in a series of writings Newman attempted to limit in regard to the new dogma the operation of a principle he himself had stated more fully than anyone else.

First, then, the reception of Newman's thesis of development at Rome. Here what concerns us is Newman's correspondence with Giovanni Perrone, at that time the leading theologian of the Collegio Romano. In 1847, Newman sent Perrone a Latin *précis* of his *Essay* which Perrone returned with his comments, the whole constituting what is known as the 'Newman-Perrone Paper on Development'. To understand the points at issue it is necessary to look more widely into Perrone's work, since his contributions to the Paper are often extremely short. For instance, in Chapter III, Newman had written,

> It can happen that, with regard to one or another part of the deposit, the Church might not be fully conscious of what she felt about a thing.[76]

To this Perrone simply adds the comment, *Hoc dicere non auderem*: 'I would not dare to say that'. Looking more widely

[75]K. Rahner, 'Papst', *Lexikon für Theologie und Kirche*[2] VIII., 46: 'Die beschärfste Frage der Dogmenentwicklung überhaupt'.

[76]T. Lynch (ed.), 'The Newman-Perrone Paper on Development; 1847', *Gregorianum* 16 (1935), pp. 402–47.

afield means in practice a perusal of Perrone's *Praelectiones Theologicae*, his textbook on fundamental theology. Allen Brent has usefully compared the relevant sections of this work and concludes, fundamentally, that Newman and Perrone were much wider apart than might at first sight seem the case.[77] Perrone had already read Johann Adam Möhler's *Symbolik*, a work which tries to justify specifically Catholic doctrines for a German Protestant audience. As a result of the evidence Möhler brought forward, Perrone accepted that some growth in the body of Catholic doctrine had taken place since primitive times, and he likewise accepted the distinction between the implicit and the explicit as a proper way of presenting such growth. But while both of these concessions brought him closer to Newman, his actual understanding of the implicit-explicit distinction was very different from that of the English theologian. For Brent, Newman's primary comparison for the explicitisation of the implicit was the growth of a human mind, itself compared to biological development. For the child, the same reality exists as intuition, instinct or feeling which in the adult is a conceptualised, theoretical affirmation of how things are. Perrone's picture, however, was not like this at all. Perrone saw the deposit of faith as given once for all in a quite conscious way – but scattered by the apostles among the local churches of the primitive *oikoumenē*. In the disposition of the apostolic patrimony, some churches acquired one article of the Creed and others another. And this for Perrone explains the hesitations of the universal Church on certain points of doctrine, and the consequence need to consult and to hold councils. As he wrote:

It was not possible for either individual bishops or particular churches from whom the Church universal was being composed to reach agreement all at once about those things which the apostles had committed to bishops or churches either orally or in individual writings.[78]

[77]A. Brent, 'Newman and Perrone: unreconcilable theses on development', *Downside Review* 102, 349 (1984), pp. 276.

[78]Cited ibid., p. 282.

The explicitisation of doctrine takes place when articles of faith are collected up from local churches and brought together at the centre. This centre may be a moving centre: the conciliar institution; or it may be a fixed centre: the Papacy. When the scattered articles are thus brought together and promulgated with authority, they are said by Perrone to move from a state of implicitness to one of explicitness. Thus for Perrone the fact that doctrine has a history does not follow from the very nature of revelation, as Newman held. Rather does it derive from the quite contingent facts of the missionary situation facing the apostles. As a college they divided and went their separate ways. They created churches with different needs and interests. As a result of the combination of these two factors, the whole deposit of faith was not communicated in every single successor church, though the entire deposit *was* communicated to the *sum* of successor churches. Thus, if anyone in the ante-Nicene period believed in the Son's co-eternity and co-equality with the Father, they believed a doctrine which materially speaking, in point of fact, had been passed down as a doctrine by an apostle or a group of apostles. But since the Church as a whole had not yet taken cognisance of this doctrine, it was not formally speaking a part of the explicit faith of the Church.

On Perrone's account, once the bishops of the Church have gathered together the *disjecta membra* of the apostolic deposit, they will have, in effect, the premisses of a theological conclusion. Thus if they gather together on the one hand belief in the unity of God, and on the other belief in the divinity of the Son, then they have before them the premisses of a theological deduction, namely that the Son is *homoousion* with the Father. In other words, once the bishops have brought together the geographically scattered pieces of the mosaic, what they actually do with them, fundamentally, is to carry out a logical procedure. Dr Brent points out that Newman was out of sympathy with giving this kind of weight to the rôle of logic in the making of doctrine. This was not because he disputed the soundness of traditional logic as such. Rather was it because he saw imaginative sensitivity

as more important than logical analysis where the expression
of revelation was concerned. As a Christian Platonist, he held
man's understanding of sensuous particulars to be necessarily
fragile and ambiguous. As a dogmatic theologian he adopted
a position consonant with this metaphysical outlook: the
human grasp on the finite vehicles of divine revelation
requires no less strenuous sensitivity of an imaginative kind –
and not simply, then, the making of syllogisms.

But Newman's crossing swords with Perrone did not leave
any painful scars. Newman was not to be accused or
erroneous teaching at Rome until twelve years later, when in
1859 his article 'On Consulting the Faithful in Matters of
Doctrine' was delated. Oddly enough, Newman had thought
that, in that article, he had achieved a *rapprochement* with
Perrone on at least one major factor in doctrinal development,
namely the 'sense of the faithful'. In this period, Catholic
theologians had been under pressure to work out a rationale
for the definition of the doctrine of the Immaculate
Conception, proclaimed by Pius IX in 1854. Perrone proposed
that the *lacunae* in patristic testimony to that belief could be
filled in by appealing to the sense of the faithful, their feeling
for or sensitivity towards the content of doctrine. Newman
imagined that Perrone saw this feeling or sensitivity in the
way he had himself: in other words, as an inner instinct,
imperceptibly growing more self-conscious in the minds of
the faithful. But Perrone seems to have regarded the sense of
the faithful as what we might term 'behavioural' in character.
It was comprised from earliest times in ritual or devotional
practices; it was not a gradually unfolding intuition. More
widely, it is unlikely that the Roman theologians of the
period would have wished to construct an entire theory of
doctrinal development on the basis of the factors involved in
the 1854 dogma. They regarded the latter as an exceptional
case in the general history of dogma. It was, they thought
uniquely difficult to justify as continuously held teaching and
therefore required a special line of defence all its own, and
not to be made general.

Turning now to the matter of Newman's attitude to the
definition of papal primacy and infallibility, a doctrine which

in the eyes of many extreme Ultramontanes was meant to provide the basis for a whole succession of further doctrinal proclamations through *ex cathedra* papal pronouncements: how did Newman view this, sometimes regarded since as the classic case or problem for the theory of development?

In the 1845 *Essay*, Newman discussed the emergence of the papal office as an example of the theory of development. Though not central to the argument of the *Essay*, it illustrates Newman's notion of antecedent probability in relation to the workings of divine revelation in the Church. It is antecedently probable that the Christian society, the Church, will have one supreme pastor who can act as the centre of unity for all.[79] Newman confines himself to linking the papal office with the Church's unity, not with her infallibility. In the *Essay* he made no explicit statements about the seat of infallibility, simply arguing that there were grounds for accepting the one communion on the face of the earth which claimed to exercise this so necessary teaching authority.[80] Though he himself held to the pope's infallibility as a private theological opinion, it was a *theologoumenon* little favoured among English Catholics at the time of his reception into the Church. Secondly, in the *Essay* Newman had proposed that the papal office was a partial fulfilment of Old Testament prophecy about the Kingdom of God.[81] The Old Testament prophesies a future spiritual kingdom, a spiritual monarchy governed by a spiritual dynasty, and in the New Testament, Newman suggests, Christ fulfilled this prophecy by his promises to Peter. However, as Newman went on to admit, in point of fact we do not see this Petrine office in its fully-fledged form within that apostolic period. Its complete emergence is a development: a development not within revelation, as from Old to New, but a development of the completed revelation, the Christian idea.[82] *How* is the Papacy

[79]Cf. *Essay on the Development of Doctrine*, IV. iii. 8; pp. 154–5.

[80]Ibid., II. ii. 12; pp. 88–9.

[81]Notably in the first edition: thus P. Misner, *Papacy and Development*, op. cit., p. 4; pp. 50 ff.

[82]This typology, relating the Kingdom of God to an 'imperial Church' already appears in *Parochial and Plain Sermons* II. pp. 232–54 in 'The Kingdom of the Saints'

a development of the completed revelation? In one of two ways. Sometimes, Newman speaks of Christ as founding the Papacy by promising its *eventual* emergence; at other times, he speaks of a latent papal principle at work in the Church from the moment of the Ascension and Pentecost, but not manifesting itself openly until the time was ripe. The second and third centuries were when time was unripe for the papal principle to come out of its latent stage, because they were centuries characterised by the sporadic persecution of widely scattered communities. But when conditions allowed a papacy to appear, it did appear. In the revised edition of the *Essay* it is this dormancy theory and not the prophecy theory which Newman favoured, possibly because he considered it more in keeping with the dogma, which by then had been defined by the First Vatican Council.

In the months immediately before the Council opened, Newman was approached by various individuals for his views on the definability of a *iure divino* papal primacy, and of papal infallibility. Newman's most important response, so far as the idea of development is concerned, is the 'Flanagan Paper' of February 1868. For the benefit of John Stanislas Flanagan, a former Oratorian colleague whose ideas on doctrine were purely 'fixist', Newman stressed one and one only of the models found in the 1845 *Essay*: namely, the psychological model of how the individual mind comes to explicit awareness of truths which have long possessed it at some deep level.[83] This contrast between implicit and explicit states of an individual's memory, which derives from Newman's University sermons, and is already present in the 1843 homily on developments in religion, would be more fully worked out in the *Essay in Aid of a Grammar of Assent*, written during the Vatican Council, and the key to the later Newman's understanding of epistemology. However, this is not to say that he positively repudiated the more varied picture he had offered in the *Essay* on development, as is

---

(1835), and in the 1842 homily 'The Christian Church as an Imperial Power' in *Sermons Bearing on Subjects of the Day*, pp. 218–36.

    [83]C. S. Dessain (ed.), 'An Unpublished Paper . . .', art. cit.

obvious from the modest nature of the revisions he made to the *Essay* in its second edition of 1878. But for Newman, on the eve of the First Vatican Council, the definability of the twin doctrines of the universal primacy, by divine right, of the Roman bishop, and his infallible teaching office, would chiefly turn on the results of an act of corporate introspection by the Church. If her memory of this aspect of her divine foundation (the promises of Christ to Peter) had crystallised sufficiently into conceptual clarity, then she could move to the definition of the dogmas concerned.

However, as is well-known, Newman had grave doubts *both* as to whether the Church's corporate memory was clear enough on the topic for definition, *and* as to the possible harmful effects of a definition which might unbalance the structure of the Church by placing too much emphasis on Pope and curia. In Newman's attitudes to this issue, it is not easy to separate out the autobiographical and theological factors. As Paul Misner has written:

> I have no competence in psychology, but at least superficial notice must be taken of the frustrations that Newman felt in the church of Pius IX and that redoubtable Ultramontane Manning ... I am sympathetic to the view that these frustrations led to a progressively worse depression and disability to cope, even intellectually, with hierarchical authority.

In the middle 1860s, Newman advised those troubled by what they saw as the oppressive course that Roman ecclesiastical authority was following to be silent and submit, until Providence should induce a change of heart and policy in the leaders of the Church or otherwise overrule their faulty aims – for example, by death. But, slowly, Newman came to construct a theological basis for resisting Church authority in limited but significant ways. Two main occasions presented themselves for his thoughts on these matters: the British Prime Minister W. G. Gladstone's pamphlet on the Vatican Decrees in 1874, and the re-publication of the *Lectures on the Prophetical*

Office of the Church, under the new title of *The Via Media* in
1877. However, the *Letters and Diaries* of Newman for the
years 1868 to 1871, as published by Thomas Gornall, S.J., on
behalf of the Birmingham Oratory, show that this topic was
never far from Newman's thoughts. He now began to
elaborate themes new to his readers, attempting to vindicate
the rights of conscience and a certain autonomy for theology
over against the development of papal authority.

By 1870, Newman had become, indeed, quite bitterly
opposed to the dogmatisation of what he held to be
(nevertheless) true *theologoumena* about the Petrine office. The
dogmas would be inopportune, both because they would
force the pace at which the Church's corporate mind was
travelling in the unfolding of its original awareness of the
Petrine office, and because in the hands of the extreme
Ultramontane party, such dogmas would gravely unbalance
the Church's life. As a result, the new doctrines would unsettle
the weak in faith, discourage people interested in becoming
Catholics, and scandalise the Protestant mind. It should be
noted that Newman's opposition to the extreme
Ultramontane party was not based upon a defence of the
rights of the episcopate. Newman did not regard episcopal
authority as an important safeguard against the abuse of papal
authority. His lack of interest in a theology of the episcopate
is one of the factors which makes him what has been called
'an Ultramontane sui generis'.[84]

In his reply to Gladstone, issued in the form of an open
letter to the Duke of Norfolk, Newman was principally
concerned with the kind of obedience which the Pope might
require on the basis of his universal jurisdiction over the
faithful, especially where that might touch the duties of the
citizen, and so the sphere of the State. It was in this context
that Newman made his promise to 'drink – to the Pope, if
you please, – still, to Conscience first, and to the Pope
afterwards'. Though the Pope's commands are to be obeyed
on principle, like those of any other duly established
authority, nevertheless there will also be cases where

[84]P. Misner, *Papacy and Development*, op. cit., p. 136; ibid., p. 150.

consciences must refuse obedience. The heart of Newman's response to Gladstone concerns the proper interpretation of *Pastor aeternus*. Newman argues that even infallible judgements about doctrinal developments, such as he takes *Pastor aeternus* to be, require subsequent theological interpretation. Gladstone had misunderstood *Pastor aeternus*, misled by extreme Ultramontanes like Manning. Though the decree rightly calls papal jurisdiction 'universal' in the sense that it holds sway over every person, and every juridical person in the Catholic communion, it does not mean to teach that the *object* of papal jurisdiction is simply uncircumscribed, such that it can be extended to all matters of personal or public concern. The terms *disciplina* and *regimen* used in the document are technical ecclesiological terms, not

> words of such lax, vague, indeterminate meaning, that under them any matters can be slipped in which may be required for the Pope's purposes in this or that country.[85]

And in a striking sentence Newman concludes from the kind of exegesis he has just been doing that

> None but the Schola Theologorum is competent to determine the force of papal and synodal utterances, and the exact interpretation of them is a work of time.[86]

In this remark, Newman anticipates the last text we must consider, the 1877 'Preface' to the *Via Media*. In that preface, he put forward the principle that in some sense the Church's theologians have the last word in the interpretation of her faith. As he puts it:

> Theology is the fundamental and regulating principle of the whole Church system. It is commensurate with

[85]'Letter to the Duke of Norfolk on the occasion of Mr Gladstone's Recent Expostulation', in *Certain Difficulties Felt by Anglicans in Catholic Teaching* (London 1876), p. 234.
[86]Ibid., p. 176.

revelation, and revelation[87] is the initial and essential idea of Christianity.

Newman insists that, in a certain sense, theology, which he now identifies with the prophetical office itself, has a 'power of jurisdiction' over the regal office, that of Pope and curia, and the sacerdotal office, the priest with his flock. In what sense? In that sense that:

> theologians [are] ever in request and in employment in keeping within bounds both the political and the popular elements in the Church's constitution.[88]

Taken by itself, this passage seems to imply a radical subordination of both ministerial authority and popular faith to the judgement of theologians. But Newman's thought is too balanced and inclusive for this to be his final comment. In fact, his basic idea in the 'Preface' is that in the Church three equally necessary functions operate by continuous interaction. And these are: a theological function, a governing function, and a devotional function – what Von Hügel would later describe as the intellectual, institutional and mystical elements in the Church. It is important to note that Newman's three elements are more fundamentally three functions than they are three sets of people. A bishop, for instance, might well also be a theologian, and he might need to call on his awareness of the irreplaceable rôle and claims of theology in order to relativise his sense of the equally irreplaceable rôle and claims of his own duties in pastoral government. Nevertheless, Newman was indeed stressing that the hierarchy could not dispense with theology, with careful reflection and constant return to the sources of faith in Scripture and Tradition. He saw that the subordination of good theology to the felt needs of hierarchy or people could only be damaging in the long run. Yet, on the other hand, and here, with characteristic elusiveness, he takes back with one hand what he had just given with another, we must also remember that

[87]'Preface; to *The Via Media of the Anglican Church*, op. cit., I, p. xlvii.
[88]Ibid., I., p. xlviii.

theology cannot always have its own way; it is too hard, too intellectual, too exact to be always equitable or to be always compassionate.[89]

And in the closing pages of his 'Preface' he presents examples of how, in Church history, the episcopate, and especially the Papacy, had pushed through measures they held to be obviously good for the Church even though no one could defend them theologically at the time: examples like relaxing ancient prohibitions on readmitting apostates to communion, or setting aside customary denials of the validity of baptism as administered by schismatics. Newman's last word to us on doctrinal development is, then, a complex one. His message is, in part, a sobering warning that the identification and interpretation of doctrinal development requires more discernment and prudence than almost any other action in the life of the Church.[90]

Two final points about Newman by way of conclusion. First, in evaluating the 'Preface' to the *Via Media* we must bear in mind that, in Newman's day, unlike our own, theologians were a conservative force in the Church who looked primarily either to Christian antiquity, or to the Scholastic tradition for their inspiration. Newman invoked them, over against the Papacy, with a view to resisting exaggerated, unilateral or over-hasty developments in official

[89]Ibid.

[90]It is, surely, to this complexity that Owen Chadwick alludes in calling the *Essay* 'that unusual combination, a book unconvincing and yet seminal': *Newman* (Oxford 1983), p. 47. Chadwick sums up the quarter century of his ruminations on the *Essay* by writing:

> The idea of development was the most important single idea which Newman contributed to the thought of the Christian Church. This was not because the idea of development did not exist already. But it was a very restricted idea, so restricted that it posed insuperable problems for anyone who studied history with open eyes. Newman made it wider and vaguer, and thereby far more fertile in conception, and more useful to anyone who cared about intellectual honesty, or the reconciliation of faith with the evidence of the past which history finds. Reviewers dismissed his arguments courteously or contemptuously. But in the long view the *Essay* was more weighty than one man's introspection of his predicament. That predicament happened to be only a single case to illustrate the predicament of Christendom, ibid., p. 48.

teaching and popular practice. Manning, whom one could hardly accuse of an excessive desire to limit Church authority, writing some five years later, describes docility to the common opinion of theologians as an integral feature of obedience to the Church.[91] This is why it is seriously anachronistic to present Newman's 'Preface' as an encouragement to the activities of radically dissenting divines in the crisis of theological faith which has followed the Vatican Council's successor body, the *Second* Vatican Council, in and since the 1960s.[92]

Secondly, there is one vital respect in which Newman's writings about doctrinal development cannot be interpreted in a Modernist sense. Newman regarded every development, once received by the Church, as a 'definitive and irreversible acquisition which could not be abandoned'.[93] This is perhaps the most important sense in which his account of development is rightly called 'organic' – though, as we shall see, the exploitation of the organic metaphor by Modernist writers led the critics of the Modernists to see in that metaphor less auspicious aspects. It is to the Modernists in their relation, at once positive and negative, to Newman that we must now turn.[94]

[91]H. E. Manning, *The Eternal Priesthood* (London 1883), p. 216.

[92]N. Lash, 'Catholic Theology and the Crisis of Classicism', *New Blackfriars* 66. 780 (June 1987), pp. 279–87.

[93]P. Misner, *Papacy and Development*, op. cit., p. 68.

[94]The theme, this, of M. J. Weaver (ed.), *Newman and the Modernists* op. cit.

3

Alfred Loisy

Life and work

Alfred Firmin Loisy was born in 1857 in the village of Ambrières in north-eastern France, the son of a small farmer. At the age of seventeen, he entered the local seminary of Chalons-sur-Marne. In 1875, he decided to transfer to the Dominicans, and was accepted, but the opposition of his family and confessor made him defer a final decision. After ordination in 1879 he spent a year as *curé de village*, an experience which confirmed his view that the parochial ministry was not for him. In 1881, therefore, he received permission to go to the newly founded Parisian *Institut Catholique* for further studies. As it transpired, attendance at the Institut would entail hearing supplementary lectures at the *Collège de France* where the rationalist scholar Ernest Renan, a former seminarian, was lecturing on the Hebrew text of the Old Testament. By Loisy's own account, Renan would influence him considerably.[1]

Once at the *Institut*, Loisy settled down to writing a thesis on the nature of biblical inspiration which his teachers praised but besought him not to publish. Entitled *De divina Scripturarum inspiratione quod doceant ipsae Scripturae et patres antiqui*, it set forth Loisy's idea of the 'relative truth' of the Bible. The Bible has, he maintains, a 'relative value' vis-à-vis the Word of God which it both manifests and conceals, thus generating a 'relative truth'. This idea might carry an orthodox sense, but the staff of the *Institut* felt they had

---

[1] A. F. Loisy, *Mémoires pour servir à l'histoire de notre temps* (Paris 1930–31).

already been exposed to too much publicity where
adventurous scholarship was concerned, thanks to their
association with the Church historian Louis Duchesne.
Duchesne's method in Church history has been described as
a methodological naturalism somewhat akin to Descartes
'methodical doubt'.[2] As a student, Loisy was not untouched
by Duchesne's example. Yet, however novel Duchesne's
sense of historical method, his actual conclusions were
hardly likely to disturb faith – unless faith is to turn on
the veracity of the biography of pope St Linus in the *Liber
Pontificalis* or the historicity of the foundation of the diocese
of Sens by one of Jesus' seventy-two disciples. Nevertheless,
Duchesne's Sorbonne doctorate on the *Liber Pontificalis* had
in fact been denounced to the Congregation of the Index
by the bishop of Angers. Duchesne was reproved by both
the Jesuit dogmatician cardinal Johann Baptist Franzelin, and
his Benedictine confrère, the antiquarian Jean-Baptiste Pitra,
the latter for 'an excessive liberty of thought and expression
in what touches the sovereign pontiffs and the decisions of
the Church'. His criticism of the traditional ascription of
the evangelisation of Gaul, and the concomitant founding
of the French dioceses, to the immediate disciples of Jesus
particularly irritated the local episcopate.

Duchesne's difficulties, and even more those of his
conservative pupil Pierre Batiffol (1861–1929) who would
head the so-called 'right-wing' succession from Duchesne,
as Loisy the left, showed the problem Church authorites faced
in this period in distinguishing responsible historical
theologians from iconoclasts, inessential matters from
essential, modernisers from Modernists. It is hardly surprising,
then, that Duchesne warned a certain promising biblical
student that the spiritual climate in the Catholic Church was
not ripe for an attempt to reconcile the Bible with historical
science. In a letter of 1885 to the baron von Hügel, Duchesne
expressed his belief that, nonetheless, the fate attempt would
be made.

[2] E. Poulat, 'Mgr Duchesne et la crise moderniste', *Modernistica* (Paris 1982),
pp. 137–160.

Catholic exegesis is on the eve of a transformation.
We must avoid giving this transformation the appearance
of a revolution.[3]

In the same year, 1885, the young abbé Loisy began teaching
Hebrew at the *Institut Catholique*, in 1889 adding thereto the
more controversial material of a course entitled 'introduction
to the Bible'. Within a few years, and as predicted by
Duchesne, the sky had begun to darken.

The cloud, no bigger than a man's hand, appeared when
M. Icard, the superior-general of the prestigious seminary of
Saint-Sulpice, forbad his students to attend Loisy's courses, an
action which had been the prelude to the troubles of Duchesne.
In January 1893 the rector of the Institut, Maurice d'Hulst, tried
to defend his protégé by an ill-conceived article in *Le
Correspondant* on the disputed questions of inspiration and
inerrancy.[4] Loisy complained that d'Hulst had misrepresented
his views and set them forth in a moderate article in
L'Enseignement Biblique, a review he had himself founded.[5] But
the fat was already in the fire. The Holy See had been apprised
of the dangerous views circulating in Paris. The French
bishops, who were the founders and governors of the Institut
Catholique, closed down *L'Enseignement Biblique* and Loisy
was asked to resign from his post: a move evidently designed
to protect the fledgling institute. Within a few months, there
followed pope Leo XIII's encyclical on the authority of the
Bible: *Providentissimus Deus*. [6]Loisy at once wrote to the pope
promising his adhesion to its teaching and received a warm
reply. For the moment Loisy withdrew into a form of pastoral
work, becoming chaplain to a Dominican convent school at
Neuilly-sur-Seine. However, in 1896 he re-emerged to found a
second review, the *Revue d'histoire et de littérature religieuse*.

[3]Cited ibid., p. 142.

[4]For 25. 1. 1893.

[5]'La question biblique et l'inspiration des Ecritures'; *L'Enseignment Biblique*
(November–December 1893), pp. 1–16.

[6]'De la croyance à la foi', in E. Poulat, *Critique et mystique. Autour de Loisy, ou la
conscience catholique et l'esprit moderne* (Paris 1984), pp. 14–43, and here at p. 16.

The following year, 1897, Loisy's interest in the question of doctrinal development was aroused by receiving a copy of Newman's *Essay* from the hands of the baron von Hügel.[7] This stimulated him to write a series of articles from 1898 to 1900, known as the 'Firmin articles' from the pseudonym he employed and which were, as we shall see, a radicalising of Newman's thought in a way that was, in part, questionable. Meanwhile, following a breakdown in his health in 1899, Loisy had gone to live in Bellevue, in the Parisian *banlieue*. He obtained an ecclesiastical permission to celebrate Mass in his private residence – thanks to the good offices of a bishop sympathetic to scholarship, the 'Erasmus of Modernism', Eudoxe-Irénée Mignot of Albi. He also sought and obtained a lectureship at the prestigious Ecole Pratique des Hautes Etudes, a State institution. He owed this post principally to the excellence of his technical work on the growth of the biblical canon as expressed in his *Histoire du canon de l'Ancien Testament* of 1890, and its successor volume on the New Testament, published in 1891. Althought some Churchmen considered the acceptance of such an academic honour as a passing over to the camp of the enemy (these were the years of increasing tension between Church and State which would lead to the expulsion of the Religious Orders in 1902, and the abrogation of the Concordat in 1905), Loisy's name was put forward, unsuccessfully, for the episcopate by Prince Albert of Monaco.[8]

But Loisy first came to widespread public notice through his reply on behalf of the Catholic Church to Adolf von Harnack's evocation of Christian origins and identity, *Das Wesen vom Christentum*, a reply which came out under the title *L'Evangile et l'Eglise* in 1902. Loisy's apologia defended Catholicism, over against liberal Protestant scholarship, as a justified transformation of the original Gospel. Though the work was sharply criticised by the archbishop of Paris and other French hierarchs, the Papacy refrained from intervening. In the next year, 1903, Loisy published a study

[7] *Mémoires* op. cit., I. pp. 285–301.
[8] L. R. Kurtz, *The Politics of Heresy. The Modernist Crisis in Roman Catholicism* (Berkeley 1986), p. 65.

of the principles and methods he had drawn upon in composing his apologia: *Autour d'un petit livre.* A commentary on John, *Le quatrième Evangile*, appeared almost simultaneously. The latter was something of a turning point in the *affaire Loisy* in that it caused considerable anxiety among Loisy's earlier defenders. The English New Testament scholar William Sanday, Lady Margaret Professor of Divinity at Oxford from 1893 to 1920, declared in his essay 'An Anglican View of M. Loisy' that Loisy's criticism of the Fourth Gospel's lack of historicity was so radical that Christian doctrine seemed left 'suspended in the air', unable to show any historical continuity previous to the early second century.[9] Pope Pius X, who had just arrived on Peter's chair, evidently agreed with Sanday since, in December 1903, he placed five of Loisy's works on the Index. [10] In the face of the pope's action, Loisy made a reluctant formal submission in 1904, resigned his secular teaching post and retired to his beloved native countryside. He seems to have abandoned the exercise of his priesthood at some point in 1906. But meanwhile he was becoming a crucial figure in a loose network of writers and thinkers who were becoming known as 'Modernists' – a term that appears to have been first used in Italy in 1904.[11] For Friedrich Heiler, the High Church Lutheran historian of Modernism, Loisy was 'der Vater des katholischen Modernismus',[12] and the Dominican exegete Marie-Joseph Lagrange who collaborated with Loisy in his early years held much the same opinion.[13]

There is a long-standing debate about what Catholic Modernism actually was, a debate to which the papal encyclical on the subject, *Pascendi*, is a major but not an all-determining contribution. The account of Modernism in

[9]W. Sanday, 'An Anglican View of M. Loisy', *The Pilot* IX. 201, 23. 1. 1904; cf. L. F. Barmann, *Baron Friedrich von Hügel and the Modernist Crisis in England* (Cambridge 1972), p. 113.

[10]*Index Librorum Prohibitorum* (Vatican City 1948), pp. 286–7.

[11]E. Poulat, *Modernistica* op. cit., p. 137.

[12]F. Heiler, *Der Vater des katholischen Modernismus: Alfred Loisy 1857–1940* (Munich 1947).

[13]M.-J. Lagrange, *M. Loisy et le Modernisme. A propos des 'Mémoires'* (Juvisy 1932), p. 136.

Pascendi may be thought of as a logical or conceptual projection of Modernist tendencies rather than a factual description of their literary actualisation. The appearance of the encyclical, together with the accompanying disciplinary decree of the Holy Office, *Lamentabili*, in 1907, finally ended Loisy's career in the Church. Refusing to submit to the teaching and provisions of these two documents, he was declared *vitandus* in 1908, the most severe canonical penalty available in the canon law of the time. Not only was he excommunicated, but no Catholic ceremony was to be performed in his presence. In a terrible fulfilment of the saying of Jesus about the sword that will divide families, this penalty barred Loisy from attending his sister's funeral, and the weddings of his nieces to whom he was greatly attached. His reply to the Roman action came in his third 'little red book', *Simples Réflexions sur le décret du Saint-Office 'Lamentabili sine exitu' et sur l'encyclique 'Pascendi dominici gregis'*.

Loisy continued to produce erudite works of biblical scholarship, notably his massive two volume *Les Evangiles synoptiques* in 1907–8. In 1909 he was appointed professor of the History of Religions at the Collège de France, a post he held until his retirement from professional life in 1926. His studies of Christian origins became increasingly pessimistic about the possibility of recovering the original features of the Jesus of history: as in, for instance, his *La Naissance du christianisme* of 1933; or *Remarques sur la littérature épistolaire du Nouveau Testament* in 1935; or, again, *Les Origines du Nouveau Testament* in 1936, Especially maverick was *Le Mandéisme et les origines chrétiennes* published in 1934. His personal religion came to assume the form of what he termed a 'religion of humanity': a moral mysticism which combined an idealistic (in the common-or-garden sense) moral philosophy with belief in an indescribable divine mystery behind the world. This found expression in, for example, *La Religion* (1917; 1924²); *La Morale humaine* (1923; 1928), *Religion et humanité* (1926), and *La Crise morale du temps présent et l'éducation humaine* (1937). He moved to the village of Ceffonds, in Haute-Marne, near one of his sisters. In his old age, he devoted considerable energy to attacking supporters of the 'Christ as myth' school, asserting the reality of the Jesus of history and his perennial fascination.[14] But this did not signify anything like a return to orthodox believing, as he made clear in his 1937 essay 'De la croyance à la foi', re-discovered and re-published in 1984. There Loisy testified to having:

> a religious faith, which, if it ascribes to Christianity a pre-eminent place among world religions, recognises as well that all these ancient religions, even the most primitive, played a part in the education of man. All these religions, or so it seems to the present author, must finally merge themselves in one way or another, into a higher religion, adapted to the needs of a spiritually unified humanity.[15]

During the weeks immediately preceding the Fall of France, Loisy became gravely ill. On 16 May 1940, the French government abandoned Paris. Because of the national disruption, Loisy's death a fortnight later, on 1 June, went almost unnoticed. His last words were taken from the book of Job:'Je suis en paix avec le Seigneur'. He was buried as he had wished in the village of his birth. His tombstone bore an inscription he had devised personally. It read:

Alfred Loisy
Prêtre
Retiré du ministère
et de l'enseignement
Professeur au Collège de France
1857–1940
Tuam in votis
tenuit voluntatem

[14]A. F. Loisy, *Histoire et mythe à propos de Jésus Christ* (Paris 1938); *Autres mythes à propos de la religion* (Paris 1939) For the sake of completeness, we should also mention, among the writings of Loisy's last years: *G. Tyrrell et Henri Bremond* (Paris 1936), and *Un mythe apologétique* (Paris 1939).

[15]Cited in E. Poulat, *Critique et mystique*, op. cit., p. 14.

The Latin phrase should probably be translated 'In his heart he always stayed faithful to your will'. It has, however, also been suggested that the *vota* might have referred to his priesthood. After all, he wore clerical black to his dying day.

Loisy's state of mind as a Churchman

It is difficult to interpret Loisy's state of mind as a Churchman. The three main sources are quite notoriously discordant. In the first place, there are his own autobiographical writings, and, in particular, *Choses passées* (Paris 1912–13), translated into English as *My Duel with the Vatican* (!), and the voluminous *Mémoires pour servir à l'histoire religieuse de notre temps: 1860–1931*, a work of over 1500 pages, published in Paris in 1930–31. Secondly, there is the full scale biography by another excommunicated priest-scholar, Albert Houtin, published posthumously in 1960. Lastly, there are a variety of contemporary writings which constitute brief assessments of him by those who knew him, chiefly persons in, or on the edge of, the Modernist circle.[16]

All the sources agree that Loisy underwent a serious crisis in his Christian believing in 1886, when he was 29 years of age. The question on which they differ is, In what sense did he emerge from it? On Loisy's own account, his difficulties with believing had been heavy indeed even before this time. He speaks of the period 1874 to 1878 as 'four years of intellectual and moral torture', and of his ordination to the sub-diaconate in the latter year as 'the great mistake of my life'. [17] But in 1886, to judge by the autobiographical writings, he underwent a yet graver crisis, which can only be described as a loss of dogmatic faith itself, such that for some years after he could explain his continued service of

[16]Further sources for Loisy's life are the letters found in: M. D. Petre, *Alfred Loisy: his religious significance* (London 1944); M. dell'Isola, *Alfred Loisy* (Parma 1957); R. Marlé, S. J. *Au coeur de la crise moderniste* (Paris 1960); and in the *Bullétin de littérature ecclésiastique* for 1966 and 1968 (letters to Mignot). See also: R. de Boyer de Sainte Suzanne, *Alfred Loisy. Entre la foi et la croyance* (Paris 1968). My account of 'Loisy's state of mind as a Churchman' is indebted to that of Dr Alec Vidler in his *A Variety of Catholic Modernists* (Cambridge 1970).

[17]*Mémoires* op. cit., I. pp. 364ff.; quoted in E. Poulat, *Critique et mystique*, op. cit., p. 46.

Catholicism to himself only as a service to a moral agency, whose ethically transforming potentialities are conveyed through its liturgical worship. Loisy held, indeed, that the promises — the *vota* — he had made on entering the priesthood to dedicate his life wholly to the Church remained binding, even though he now saw the Church as herself the agent of the moral education of humanity rather than as the instrument of a supernatural revelation. But around 1900, still following Loisy's own testimony, he recovered his faith in Christianity as a revealed religion, at any rate to some degree. Thus in a letter of 1902 he wrote:

> Either I am quite mistaken about the final result of historical research regarding Christian origins, or the outcome will be a more real, intimate and profound conception of the divinity of Christ, and of his vivifying action, and not the evacuation of Catholic dogma.

But from 1904 onwards, this revived dogmatic faith, stimulated by his contracts with such believing but 'open' Catholic scholars as Von Hügel, was, again on Loisy's own account, undermined by the reaction to his writings of the authorities of the Roman church. The decisive blow was an exchange of letters with Pope Pius X, mediated by the good offices of the archbishop of Paris. In a letter of March of that year, Loisy had offered, as an alternative to outright abjuration of the views he had expressed in the two 'little red books', the abandonment of his lecture courses wherever these were to deal with the delicate interface of history and dogma, as well as the suspension of the scientific publications he had in hand. His letter began:

> Most holy father, I well know your Holiness' goodness of heart, and it is to that heart that I now address myself.

The pope's reply, addressed to the archbishop of Paris, opened in its turn:

I have received a letter from the Reverend Abbé Loisy
in which he appeals to my heart. But this letter was not
written from the heart. . . . [18]

And Pius X went on to require from Loisy an unqualified
submission to the judgement of the Holy See. In *Choses passées*
Loisy described the effect that this letter had on him.

Something gave way within me when I heard the
opening words. The head of this Church to which I had
given my life, for which I had worked so hard for
thirty years past, which I had loved and could not help
loving still, outside of which I had no hopes or
ambitions, could find nothing to say, when I had
responded to absurd demands by a supreme sacrifice,
than the harsh words, 'That letter addressed to my heart
was not written from the heart'. All the same, it was
written from the heart. Pressed into it was the last drop
of feeling left in my Catholic soul. . . .And because I
asked to be allowed to die peaceably in this Church of
my baptism, without being made to lie in order to
remain in it, I was treated contemptuously as a false
martyr.[19]

A completely divergent account from this
autobiographically based version is found in the book by
Houtin, a close friend of Loisy's until his (Houtin's) death in
1926.[20] Houtin depicts Loisy as a pure rationalist during his
years in the Church, hypocritically acting the part of a devout
priest. Houtin described what it was like to visit Loisy in this
biography which he ordered not to be published until after
its subject's death.

[18]Cited A. Vidler, *A Variety of Catholic Modernists* op. cit., p. 54. The entire letter
is reproduced in L. Laberthonnière, *La Notion chrétienne de l'autorité* (ed. L. Canet,
Paris 1955).

[19]*Choses passées*, pp. 295 ff.; the full text of Pius X's letter to Richard for Loisy is
in P. Cenci, *Il Cardinale Raffaele Merry del Val* (Rome 1937), pp. 187–8.

[20]E. Poulat (ed.), A. Houtin (F. Sartiaux), *Alfred Loisy, sa vie, son oeuvre* (Paris
1960).

Whenever you entered the apartment you were at once struck by the idea that the master of the house was a devout priest who, notwithstanding his daring opinions, observed all the rules of the Church and indeed was a faithful disciple of its greatest thinkers. . Splendid engravings of Newman and Fénélon . . .adorned the drawing room. In the dinning room a breviary was placed in a conspicuous position. Over his desk there was a crucifix with which he had himself photographed. In order to drive home the impression these things were calculated to create, he was careful in the course of conversation to mention that, since his deplorable health prevented him from going to the parish church, he said Mass daily at home, thanks to an indult which he had procured. Soon afterwards, he found occasion to add that he hardly ever went to Paris except once a fortnight to make his confession.[21]

Most importantly, Houtin claims that in March 1907, i.e. six months before the condemnation of Modernism, Loisy told him in a private conversation that for twenty years he had ceased to believe in the existence of the soul, free will, a future life or a personal God. The publication of Houtin's work in 1960, through the efforts of the French historian of Modernism Emile Poulat, naturally created a much bleaker portrait of Loisy. But subsequently the trustworthiness of Houtin's life has been challenged. Houtin himself appears to have been a thorough-going and embittered sceptic about human beings at large. In the second volume of his own autobiography, *Ma vie laïque*, he declares his belief that most people, whether religious or not, are frauds.

Personal interest dictates to most men what they dare to call their 'convictions', not only in matters of religion but in every sphere of thought. Just as some people acquire honours and wealth by zealously but insincerely defending the religions in which they were born, so

[21]Cited A. Vidler, *A Variety of Catholic Modernists* op. cit. pp. 27–8.

other people exploit to their profit the ideas of the State
and of the Fatherland, about which they are as sceptical
as ecclesiastics are about religious institutions.[22]

Such being Houtin's considered view, it seems entirely
possible that he interpreted Loisy's descriptions of his crisis of
faith, and difficulties in faith, as a confession of outright
scepticism.[23]

So the tendency of scholars is to seek a *via media* between
Loisy's account of himself. which is clearly in part apologia,
and Houtin's debunking, by appealing to the third set of
sources I mentioned, the judgements of other Modernists or
persons closely connected with Modernism. Especially
noteworthy here is the study of Loisy entitled *Un clerc qui n'a
pas trahi*, written by the Abbé Henri Bremond, the historian
of French spirituality, under the pseudonym Sylvain
Leblanc.[24] Bremond distinguished between 'dogmatic faith'
and 'mystical faith'. He argued that at least until 1904 Loisy
had what might be termed a mystical form of Catholic faith.
That is, he did not accept the Church's dogmas as true in the
sense in which her recognised doctors propounded them.
Nevertheless, in Bremond's words, he adhered with his whole
being to

the invisible realities of which he still believed the
Catholic Church to be the principal and indispensable
guardian. . . From the confused block of his original
beliefs, all the dogmatic element had disappeared; all the
mystical element remained, though it was being more
and more shaken.[25]

The discussion is likely to continue. What seems clear is that
throughout his mature life Loisy had no metaphysics with
which to underpin his faith in God. Nor did he have a definite

[22]Ibid. pp. 25–39.
[23]Cited ibid., p. 32.
[24]Paris 1931.
[25]Ibid., p. 45.

Christology. As the Anglican writer Alec Vidler has put it:

> The real question is...whether his metaphysical
> agnosticism and his lack of a firm and positive
> Christology were tolerable in a priest.[26]

Some light may be thrown onto the mystery of Loisy by
the last circumstantial account we have of him. It dates from
1937, in which year, armed with an episcopal dispensation,
the young Catholic philosopher Jean Guitton – later to be
professor of the history of philosophy at the Sorbonne –
visited him in his country retreat. Guitton describes him in
these words:

> In the house there was nothing which suggested any
> break with the Church. On the walls, I recognised
> Duchesne, Lacordaire, a lithograph of the gentle Fénélon,
> the strange features of Newman. He showed me a bronze
> figure of Christ carrying his cross. He told me that each
> morning a little girl, six years old, came to see him, and
> how she picked up this statuette calling it 'mon Jésus',
> which provided Loisy with the opportunity to give her
> a little catechism on the Passion. Everything was still
> ecclesiastical in this little room at Montier-en-Der... M.
> Loisy was anxious to tell us that he had been obliged to
> quit the Church against his will. When I replied that he
> no longer had the faith to remain legitimately within the
> Church, he said to me: 'My poor friend, what is faith?
> How does one know if one has it or doesn't have it? I
> so loved to say the Mass'. He repeated that he had
> wanted to put questions. 'I was a reformer', he said.

---

[26]A. Vidler, *A Variety of Catholic Modernists* op. cit. p. 51. Cf. the cognate
judgement of the Australian student of Modernism, Valentine Moran, S. J.:
> What strikes one reflecting on the theology of Loisy, its shifts and its
> developments, is not so much what he came to think as the absence of any
> principle, philosophical or theological, which could have given stability to his
> thought. He would always have insisted that religion was a social thing; apart
> from that, there is nothing that he might not have said.
= 'Loisy's Theological Development', *Theological Studies* 40.3 (September 1979),
pp. 411–452, and here at p. 451.

And he added in a lower voice, 'A pseudo-reformer'.
And then he said, 'They threw me out'. [27]

It may be suggested that Loisy wore a mask for so long that
in the end he became that mask. The mask was that of
priesthood: not that of a Christian presbyter in the apostolic
succession, dispensing the dominical Word and sacraments –
for too many ambiguities had clustered in his own mind to
leave him any security as to how much reality lay behind
such terms. Rather, Loisy saw himself as a priest in a wider
and older sense, as a *pontifex* between men and the divinity, a
priest who would bid them come closer to each other in
peace and charity, and worship the one God who had at once
a thousand names and no name at all. Such a priesthood
could take the outward symbolic forms of the Catholic
priesthood of traditional French piety, as well as any other. It
could include it, but need not be confined to it, and so could
survive its forcible removal. It may be instructive to compare
Loisy's case with what the Oxford student of Greek religion
E. R. Dodds had to say about an exact contemporary of
Loisy's who also saw himself on the dividing-line between a
dying traditional Christianity and a new paganism struggling
to be born: the Irish poet W. B. Yeats.

> We have been told *ad nauseam* (wrote Dodds) that Yeats
> wore a mask, and there is a sense in which this is plainly
> true. Yet in fact, with the possible exception of Louis
> MacNeice, Yeats is the only poet I have known or
> encountered who looked just like what he was – no
> mere rhymester,but a *vates,* a poet in the full, ancient,
> arrogant meaning of the term. He behaved like the
> consecrated priest of a mystery – the mystery of words,
> which alone are certain good. Was that simply a piece
> of theatre? Those who knew him best have answered
> 'No'. The mask had consumed the man: he had become
> that which he had chosen to appear as being: in Plotinus'
> phrase, he had carved his own image. [28]

[27]J. Guitton, *Dialogues avec M. Pouget sur la pluralité des mondes, le Christ des
Evangiles et l'avenir de notre espèce* (Paris 1954), pp. 77–99.
[28]E. R. Dodds, *Missing Persons. An Autobiography* (Oxford 1977), p. 57.

Loisy on the idea of doctrinal development

What, then, does Loisy have to say on the matter of doctrinal development? The starting point of an answer must be the six 'articles de Firmin', which appeared pseudonymously between 1898 and 1900, and were intended to lay the foundation of 'a new programme of Catholic renovation'.[29] In the first, Loisy describes Newman's theory of development, in order, in the second, to oppose it to the individualistic theory of religion he found in Liberal Protestantism. In articles three and four he outlines his concepts of religion and revelation respectively. In article five he discusses the authority of revelation, and finally in article six, applies his theory of development to history.

In the first Firmin article, Loisy acclaims Newman as the 'great doctor' which Catholic theology needs in the modern age. Von Hügel had introduced him to Newman's writings, sending him, *inter alia*, as we have seen, the essay on development. As Loisy explains, the aim of the *Essay on the Development of Christian Doctrine* was to show how Catholic developments were indispensable to the preservation of the Gospel and thus as divinely legitimate as that Gospel itself. Indeed, the Gospel cannot be distinguished, *au fond*, from those developments: the single idea lives in its many expressions. Heresy, Loisy suggests, is often born of stagnation, i.e. of an ill-judged conservatism. Moreover, he stresses that the application of Newman's seven 'notes' for authentic development is not left to the arbitration of the individual believer or scholar. True discernment of how to apply them comes about through the religious life of the collectivity of the Christian society. More particularly, legitimate developments need to be guaranteed by a divinely authorised infallible organ. 'Authority and revelation are

[29]These articles were: 'Le développement de dogme d'après Newman', *Revue du Clergé Français* 17 (1898), pp. 5–20; 'La théorie individualiste de la religion', ibid. (1899), pp. 202–215; 'La définition de la religion', 18 (1899), pp. 193–209; 'L'Idée de la révélation', ibid. 21 (1900), pp. 250–271; 'Les preuves et l'économie de la Révélation', ibid. 22, (1900), pp. 127–152; 'La religion d'Israel', ibid. 23 (1900), pp. 337–363. For a full summary, see E. Poulat, *Histoire, dogme et critique dans la Crise Moderniste* (Paris 1979²), pp. 74–88.

correlative terms.' Loisy suggests three lines of research in which Newman's discovery needs to be followed up.

First, it should be extended beyond Christianity to the history of religion from its origins. Via the Old Testament, Christianity is ultimately descended from the (pagan) religion of prehistoric humanity. The great moments of revelation which mark new phases in this development do not, remarks Loisy, undermine that development but rather guarantee it. They are 'regular transformations' in which the work of the past is not destroyed, nor is a new religion introduced. Instead, at these revelatory moments, such as, presumably, the gift of the Torah, the pre-exisiting religious tradition is 'illumined by a new light, increases its vitality, and enlarges its action'. Secondly, Newman's theory needs to be made more precise in relation to Christian origins, i.e. with regard to the way in which the climactic revelation enters into development and attaches itself thereto. Thirdly, Loisy suggests (not very accurately) that Newman tended to reduce Christian development to the movement of ideas. (He is, no doubt, misled here by Newman's referring to the rich and complex reality of revelation as the Christian 'Idea'.) Loisy proposes that, in future, we should distinguish between 'le moment réel' of development, and 'le moment théologique' of the same process. The first of these Loisy identifies with the concrete life of the Church where faith is expressed in liturgy, preaching and devotion. The second comes about when, by reflection on important questions thrown up by this life, theology has its say, thus leading up to 'le moment dogmatique' when a development is canonised by Church authority. Finally, Loisy asks after the status of Newman's theory to which he is here offering what are, in his own mind, refinements. That theory (he points out) is not counted as yet among the official topics of Catholic teaching. But Loisy argues that nonetheless it is

in a very real manner in possession of the tradition, since things have happened *as though* people believed in it, since the Church has not ceased to develop, without hesitation or scruple, in the way Newman describes, since the whole of history is there to give evidence in favour of his theory. Thus the theory has been admitted implicitly, equivalently, the need not yet being felt to formulate it explicitly.[30]

In the second article, Loisy counterposes the theory of the development to the ideas of the enormously influential German scholar Adolf von Harnack and his French counterpart and admirer Auguste Sabatier, dean of the faculty of Protestant theology in Paris. The Harnackians define religion and authority over against each other, opposing to the external authority of Church, tradition and biblical letter the interior light of the spirit discerning in Scripture the Word of God. Loisy argues that, on the contrary, whoever says 'religion' says the opposite of individualism.[31] Religion has always pursued the union of men in God, and so has always been, in some manner or other, an institution. Moreover, *pace* Harnock once again, what is found in the Christian religion, and thus institution, is too rich and complex to be summed up in a single feeling, or defined in a single formula. Christianity may indeed be said to have been realised 'virtually' in the person of Jesus Christ. Its 'virtue', its internal strength or power, was constituted at that historic moment which was the personal biography of Jesus. Yet, Christianity has never been fully realised in any single consciousness, not even in the human mind of Jesus himself. It certainly may not be reduced, Loisy goes on, to the feeling of devout sonship towards God as Father which first emerged with Jesus' self-awareness. This being so, there must surely be mediations of Christianity, finite self-expressions helpful in assisting us to grasp the whole: mediations which will form, then, a developmental line in history.

Harnack and Sabatier had themselves confessed that their 'pure Christianity' is not in fact found unmixed in the Gospel. Concurring, one could even say, remarks Loisy:

[30]Ibid., p. 76.
[31]Ibid., p. 78.

The whole Gospel is Jewish in the sense that it was conditioned by Judaism, being adapted to the milieu where it was preached. It could not have been otherwise without ceasing to be alive, and it could not have remained Jewish without terminating in the place where it was born. But for its life to continue, was it necessary to have ingenious philosophers, who could examine what in the Gospel was 'purely universal' and what was 'purely Jewish', accepting the former and rejecting the latter, re-editing for the benefit of the apostles a little creed which included only the essence of what struck them as perfect religion?

And Loisy answers his own question:

The life of a religion never consists in the search for a quintessence, but in a religion's action upon souls; and everything that helps this action, everything that the religion draws into its orbit and uses for its end, shares in and serves its life. The question, therefore, is not one of knowing how to define the essence of Christianity or of the Gospel. An absolute definition is not possible because Christianity is a living reality and not an intellectual concept ('un concept de l'esprit'). One gets people to understand it by describing it as it is.

And he continues, applying this to the defence of Catholicism:

If all this development is animated by the spirit of the Gospel, if it is necessary for the Gospel's conservation and diffusion, if it is useful in promoting the religion of Jesus, what objection can we have to it? To reproach the Catholic Church for all these things, is not that to reproach it for having lived and for being alive today? And if the Church had not lived, where would the Gospel be now?[32]

[32]Ibid., pp. 78–9.

According to the Harnackians, a threefold revolution had ruined the Church's authority. Luther's revolt destroyed its religious appeal, Galileo's its scientific credibility, and now the revolution of the historical method was destroying the foundation of its dogmas. Each showed in its own way that while authority was essential to Catholicism, it was not essential to the Gospel. Thus the Gospel and the Church can be seen to be radically distinct and even mutually opposed. Dogma being the highest and most characteristic product of authority, the status of Catholic dogma had naturally become the crucial point in the debate. Loisy argues that although a dogmatic formula may become petrified, the dogma itself is by no means identical with its formulation.

> The Church neither teaches nor thinks that her dogmatic formulae are the adequate and absolutely perfect expression of the supernatural realities they represent. She defines them as the best and indeed the only good ones in the period when she defines and uses them. She does not consider them as being in every repect immutable, incapable of further perfecting, for both in the past and today she constantly makes them more complete, explains them, makes them more precise, illuminates them and improves them by these additions, explications and precisions.

The danger for the Church lies in

> confusing faithfulness to tradition with immobility in tradition, the conservation of the faith with the maintenance of formulae and cessation of reflection on the object of belief, the legitimacy of what is today with the absolute identity of past and present, the interests of religion with the temporal advantages of the hierarchy.

And Loisy concludes:

> It is certain that this danger exists for the Catholic

Church ... The wonder is that by and large she has
escaped it: she has always re-made herself and reformed
herself in time.[33]

In the third Firmin article, Loisy moves on to offer a
concept of religion, which he describes as always constituted
by two components: the social and the individual. The social
dimension guarantees to religion its ability to endure over
time, yet it should not be taken to absorb the individual
entirely. For religion is the concern of the intelligence and
the will, and these can belong only to individual persons. For
our purposes, what is interesting in this article is Loisy's
distinction between religion and religious formulae. As he
writes:

Religious formulae are no more religion than scientific
formulae are science. And yet scientific formulae
contains science and transmit it. In the same way,
religious symbols contain the faith and perpetuate it.
One can correct and improve these symbols, one can
also alter them, but but one can never do without
them. . . They are that relative expression through
which we glimpse the impenetrable Eternal.[34]

In the fourth article, Loisy considers the idea of revelation.
Harnack and Sabatier believed that for Catholic orthodoxy
(and indeed for its Protestant counterpart) revelation is a
once-for-all communication of immutable doctrines. This
definition they hold to be traditional yet insupportable. Loisy
agrees that it is insupportable but denies that it is traditional.
The mistake of the liberal Protestants lies in their failure to
distinguish between truth and doctrine. Doctrine has as object
the truth which it aims to grasp and express, a truth which
(however) always transcends it. The idea of revelation,
according to Loisy, signifies this unbreakable duality. All
religion regards itself as revealed religion because it believes

[33]Ibid., p. 79.
[34]Ibid., pp. 80–1.

itself to have received a divine truth, expressed in human terms. In fact, the divine Absolute is not communicable or intelligible to us except through human concepts. But these concepts should be seen as symbols of a reality infinitely surpassing every created intelligence. Moreover, these symbols do not present themselves in the first instance as speculative thought: neither Judaism nor Christianity possessed, to begin with, a Creed. Dogma, that is the conceptual elaboration of the symbols, only develops out of religion if a faith happens to be embodied in a philosophical or scholarly environment. In such a case, believers will naturally want to make the religious conception of the universe, man and life agree with the scientific conception of these same objects. The function of dogma is therefore to maintain a harmony between religious belief and scientific development, and in that sense between faith and reason. Loisy sees then, two aspects in which doctrine is limited. First, it is limited over against the transcendent truth which it tries to express. Secondly, it is limited by the conditions of intellectual life in the society where it is formulated. Loisy hastens to add that this should not dismay us. Since no idea exhaustively expresses life, we cannot expect ideas to express exhaustively a divine and eternal life. And furthermore, Loisy insists that these built-in limitations of dogma do not justify us in removing the doctrinal content of Christanity and replacing it with mere feeling. One cannot but think back to Newman's 'Biglietto speech' on receiving his cardinalate, and how he had on that occasion declared liberalism to consist in regarding revealed religion as 'but a sentiment and a task'.[35]

In the fifth Firmin article, Loisy stresses that a revealed religion postulates an infallible Church. *Prima facie*, there is a conflict between a religious faith demanding absolute adherence – the Gospel – and the inevitable relativity of its symbols. Moreover there is a *prima facie* contradiction between the individual's faith-commitment and the indispensable social or community context of belief. To

[35]W. Ward, *The Life of John Henry Cardinal Newman, Based on his Private Journals and Correspondence* (London 1912), II. p. 466.

overcome these contradictions there must be a teaching authority which can defend personal faith against the tendency of doctrine to petrify and become a dead letter, namely by developing doctrine, while at the same time protecting the beliefs of the community against the anarchy which would result from letting everyone express their faith in whatever way they wanted – namely through the criticism by Church authority of individual expressions of doctrine. As Loisy puts it:

> A church which allows its authority to fall continues to exist only in appearance.[36]

In the sixth and last Firmin article, Loisy tries to apply these ideas to biblical history, and more specifically, to the development of Israelite religion. It was this article, the application, and not the first five, the principles, which led to the condemnation of the 'Articles de Firmin' by cardinal Richard, archbishop of Paris: a condemnation grounded on the incompatibility of their teaching with that of the First Vatican Council's Constitution *Dei Filius* and Pope Leo XIII's encyclical letter on the inerrancy of Scripture *Providentissimus Deus*. In 'La religion d'Israel', Loisy argues that we know virtually nothing of the state of Hebrew religion before Moses. The opening chapters of Genesis do not intend to teach how man and religion entered this world, and how men lived in prehistoric times. Rather:

> they simply want to make us understand that man appeared on this earth by God's will and power, that he was from the start a disobedient and morally unbalanced creature, that nevertheless God watched over humanity in those far distant times as later and governed it in his justice and mercy.[37]

As to tracing the primitive development of religion, modern

---

[36]E. Poulat, *Histoire, dogme et critique dans la Crise Moderniste* op. cit., p. 84.
[37]Ibid., p. 85.

scholars can do this in a way less extraordinary and more human than that found in conventional apologetics, but which is still *au fond* the same, 'being at every point a history which is divine'. And Loisy goes on to suggest that in the Old Testament we see, under divide guidance, a gradual purification of religious symbols which, at first, in the patriarchal period, were polytheistic, and perhaps even animistic or fetishistic. Loisy counsels his readers to discount any feeling of repugnance towards such notions.

> The idea of God might have humble origins without being for all that a great thing... Even the fetish is a sign of the divine presence...There is no religion without images and symbols. The highest thought that man can have of God is still no more than an image, an 'idol' in the original sense of that word, where he tries to lodge the infinite.[38]

It is noteworthy that, in this article, Loisy does not commit himself to the common idea of nineteenth century social anthropology that religious history follows an iron law of progress. So-called 'laws' of religious evolution are, he maintains, at least at present mere hypotheses.

It is time to attempt an evaluation of these essays in the light of our theme. Loisy's *articles* possessed a considerable degree of maturity, and even of balance, which is surprising when one thinks how little Catholic theology had as yet to do with such new disciplines as sociology, cultural anthropology, the history of religions and indeed, for the most part, critical exegesis itself. He understood Newman fairly well. Yet the signs of serious trouble to come are apparent in the fourth article, on revelation. For, firstly, Loisy shows a marked tendency to confuse revelation with inspiration, itself the subject of his doctoral thesis at the Institut Catholique. The two most popular notions of inspiration among thoughtful Catholic writers in Loisy's time were illuminationism (associated with M.-J. Lagrange, O.P.)

[38]Ibid., p. 87.

and directionalism (associated with E. Lévesque, P.S.S). In inspiring, God illuminated the mind of the biblical author to enable him to judge in a way that corresponded to the divine judgement of things, and he directed the author's will so that he wrote with that purpose which reflected God's own. Loisy's notion of revelation seems to be that in these two ways God at a certain point 'inspired' a religious community, enabling them to see already existing realities in a new light, and to draw from them a new purpose. Now a concept of revelation is always going to be of crucial importance for a concept of doctrine, since doctrine is nothing other than an effect of God's self-revealing action. Is, then, the concept of revelation which Loisy offers here acceptable in the context of special, supernatural, distinctively Christian revelation to which he wishes to apply it?

If we regard the primary locus of revelation as being the humanity assumed by the Logos, a humanity whose unique significance is further interpreted by the Spirit sent forth jointly from the Father and the Son-made-man, then Loisy's idea of revelation in these articles will not suffice. The Christian revelation follows from the intersection of the eternal Trinitarian relationships with historical human relationships, and this is not simply a new 'light', or a new 'direction', but a new *reality* entering human history. In partial extenuation of Loisy, it may be noted that Thomas Aquinas (on whom most contemporary Catholic accounts of inspiration drew in some way) did himself tend to align the concept of inspiration with that of revelation: both were forms of 'prophetic' knowledge. Yet Thomas, thanks to his largely Cyrilline Christology, for which the prophetic intellect of Jesus Christ was a unique mind, being the human mind of the Logos itself, was able to preserve the difference in kind between Christian revelation and not only natural revelation but the revelation found in the Old Testament too. As we shall see, those critics of the Modernists who defined their position broadly in terms derived from Thomas, would find strategies for saving a notion of revelation-as-inspiration from the vagueness which afflicted it in Loisy.

Secondly, and not unconnected with this, there is a

weakness in Loisy's account of the relation between doctrinal symbols and God. Loisy has only two terms: (i) the ineffable God, and (ii) imperfect doctrinal statements about (i), whereas in reality there should be three: (i) the ineffable God, (ii) Christ as divine-human mediator, and (iii) imperfect doctrinal statements. The imperfection of doctrine will clearly be less radical if doctrine is in large part a reflection or interpretation of the words and deeds of one who was not only God but man and so inherently intelligible to human beings.

But, thirdly, Loisy already shows signs of a Christology so low that it cannot play its proper part in a Christian account of revelation and doctrine. Crucial here is Loisy's statement that Christianity was not actually realised in the consciousness of Jesus. The term 'Christianity' is elusive, but let us suppose that basically it may mean either of two things. Either, it means the entire historical complex of institutional forms, manners of worship, modes of thought and action which comprises Church history. Or it means the revealed content specific to the Christian economy, Newman's Christian 'Idea'. If Loisy means the first and is maintaining simply that Jesus did not actively envisage the emergence of monsignori, the Litany of Loreto, St Thomas Aquinas' *Summa Theologiae*, and the Catholic Mothers' Union, all is well, or may be well. But, if Loisy believes that the revealed idea of Christianity was not itself fully entertained by the human mind of Jesus, then he is leaving the way open for the notion that the religious creativity of the later Church has added to the deposit of faith beliefs that Jesus never dreamed of.

Fourthly and finally, it may be said that the difficulty of knowing quite what Loisy means by 'Christianity' is linked with another drawback of his idea of development. That idea is much too general and indiscriminate. Loisy lumps together institutional, doctrinal and cultural developments in the Catholic Church and requires us to take or leave the whole lot, *en bloc*, as a package. For institutional, doctrinal and cultural developments have it in common that all have helped to keep the Gospel alive and to extend its action. But the point of doctrinal development is that, unlike institutional and cultural development in the Church, it cannot be left behind in history. In principle, vicars-apostolic and classical polyphony can be left behind, but a legitimate doctrinal development cannot, since, of its nature, it is a true insight into the original revelation, and therefore is as precious and as permanently valid as that revelation itself. Loisy tries to prove too much, or, rather, tries to prove too much at a level of seriousness significantly lower than what the Catholic view of doctrinal development requires.

Bearing in mind the strengths and weaknesses of the *articles de Firmin*, we shall be well-placed to assess those of Loisy's more celebrated (and certainly fateful) *L'Evangile et l'Eglise*. In the introduction to this work, Loisy offers an outline of his aims. He explains that he is not offering an apologia for Catholicism or for traditional dogma. Were this his aim, his book would be highly defective, especially as regards Christ's divinity and the authority of the Church. He will not attempt here to demonstrate the truth of Catholic Christianity, but merely to show what he calls the historical bond that unites Catholicism with the earliest Gospel. Correctly, Loisy represents Harnack's *The Essence of Christianity* as taking for the heart of the Gospel message faith in a merciful God, revealed by Jesus. Loisy asks whether it is plausible to suppose that a great religion, which has managed to transform human culture, could consist in only one thought? Harnack must surely have simplified history in the interests of a theory – in which there is little to choose between him and the more hidebound conservative theologians among the orthodox. And so Loisy pleads:

> The gospel has an existence independent of us. Let us try to understand it in itself, before we interpret it in the light of our preferences and our needs.[39]

To determine as historians the essence of Christianity, it is no use asking what aspect of Christianity we today regard as vital. Rather, we must ask what Jesus regarded as vital; what

[39] *L'Evangile et l'Eglise* (Paris 1902); Et *The Gospel and the Church* (London 1908²), p. 8.

the primitive Church regarded as vital; and, finally, what each successive epoch in the Church's life regarded as vital. By comparing the results of these enquiries, we can determine whether Christianity 'has remained faithful to the law of its origin', or whether, by contrast, the Gospel light was darkened for most of Church history, being rescued only in the sixteenth or nineteenth century, as orthodox and Liberal Protestantism respectively, would maintain.

> If any common features have been preserved or developed in the Church from its origin till today, these features constitute the essence of Christianity. At least, the historian can take account of no others.[40]

Loisy goes on, in the rest of his introduction, to suggest a number of methodological principles against which Harnack has erred. Firstly, there is no logic in regarding as the essence of a religion the points that distinguish it from another – though Harnack had tried to define the Gospel by excluding from it everything Jewish.

> The essential *distinction* between religions lies in their differences, but it is not solely of their differences that they are constituted.[41]

Secondly, the essence of the Gospel can only be determined by a critical discussion of all the relevant Gospel texts, not just of a selection. But Harnack's reconstruction of the primitive Gospel rests fundamentally on only two texts, the Lucan 'The Kingdom of God is within you', and the so-called 'Johannine thunderbolt' in Matthew 11:

> No one knows the Son except the Father and no one knows the Father except the Son, and those to whom it pleases the Son to reveal him.

[40]Ibid., p. 9.
[41]Ibid., p. 10.

And this will not do: it is much too limited and selective. Thirdly, tradition, in the ordinary sense of that word, is the means by which we know whatever we do know about Jesus.

> Whatever we think, theologically, of tradition, whether we trust it or regard it with suspicion, we know Christ only *by* the tradition, *across* the tradition, and *in* the tradition of the primitive Christians. This is as much as to say that Christ is inseparable from his work, and that the attempt to define the essence of Christianity according to the pure gospel of Jesus, apart from tradition, cannot succeed, for the mere idea of the gospel without tradition is in flagrant contradiction with the facts submitted to criticism. This state of affairs, being natural in the highest degree, has nothing in it disconcerting for the historian; for the essence of Christianity must be in the work of Jesus or nowhere . . .[42]

Fourthly, Loisy holds that we must not begin our search by assuming that the essence of Christianity is something unchangeable. To assume this is to transform Christianity 'into a metaphysical entity, into a logical quintessence'. Harnack fears that his essence of Christianity would be spoiled if he introduced into it 'any idea of life, of movement and development'. Here our crucial term re-appears, and we must pause to consider more fully what Loisy has to say by means of it in his case against the German theologian.

Harnack had described Christianity, in somewhat Hegelian-sounding terms as 'the one absolute religion'. Though he refused to capture its essence in a theoretical definition, he believed he had succeeded in describing it in terms of a sentiment – the feeling of filial confidence in God as merciful Father. The continuing self-identity of this one sentiment in Jesus and in Christians constitutes for Harnack the continuity of the Christian religion and the unchangeableness of its

[42]Ibid., p. 13.

essence. Loisy's argument against this proceeds in two stages. First, he allows for the sake of argument that Christianity's essence may lie, as Harnack maintains, in faith in the divine mercy. But then:

> Is this essence, even in these reduced proportions, actually unchangeable, and why should it be? Has the divine mercy been understood in absolutely the same way by the apostles and by Herr Harnack?[43]

If the understanding of the divine mercy has changed, so then has the form of the sentiment Jesus inspired. Only the 'final direction' of this sentiment will stay unchanged, since it preserves the original impulse given by Christ. But second, if we thus admit that the form of something inspired by Christ can change whilst leaving intact its basic impulse, why cannot we extend this principle to other 'sentiments'? What for instance, asks Loisy, of such matters as the hope for an eternal kingdom, or devotion towards Christ's person, that Christ 'who has never ceased to occupy the thought of the Church from the beginning'.

> All these elements of Christianity in all the forms in which they have been preserved, why should they not be the essence of Christianity? Why not find the essence of Christianity in the fullness and totality of its life, as something which shows movement and variety just because it is life – even if, as life, proceeding from an obviously powerful principle it has grown in accordance with a law which affirms at every stage the initial force which brought it into being.[44]

At this juncture, Loisy institutes a lengthy comparison, familiar to readers of Vincent of Lérins, between the Christian tradition, and a seed that grows into a tree, or a living being which 'remains the same while it lives and to the extent that

[43]Ibid., p. 15.
[44]Ibid., p. 16.

it lives'. By contrast, Harnack does not conceive Christianity as 'at first a plant in potentiality, then a real plant, identical from the beginning of its evolution to the final limit', but as:

> a fruit, ripe, or rather, overripe, that must be peeled, to reach the incorruptible kernel; and Herr Harnack peels his fruit with such perseverance that the question arises if anything will remain at the end . . .[45]

So much for the long and important methodological overture to *L'Évangile et l'Église*. Passing on to the substance of the book we find five sections on, respectively, the Kingdom, the Son of God, the Church, Catholic dogma and Christian worship. Clearly, our interest lies mainly in the penultimate of these, on dogma, but the three previous sections provide the important immediate context for what Loisy has to say on our topic. In his account of the Kingdom, Loisy argues against Harnack that, though rooted in interiority and requiring a moral conversion, the Kingdom in the preaching of Jesus is eschatological, collective or corporate, and historically real – that is to say, to be realised in the public space of a shared world of events. He warns in this connexion against 'modernising' the idea of the Kingdom to suit contemporary taste. In his section on 'The Son of God', Loisy takes issue with Harnack for his view that filial feeling towards the Father was the chief constituent of Jesus' consciousness. Though the gospels do not permit a psychological analysis of the religious consciousness of Jesus, they do suggest that its central feature was, rather, his sense of his own providential world-historical rôle, a rôle tied to the hope of the Kingdom which his ministry announced. Loisy considers that Jesus propounded no doctrine concerning his own person and mission. Nevertheless, Jesus did regard his own person and mission as intimately bound up with the Kingdom. No one could believe in Jesus' message without believing in his mission and so in Jesus himself. Harnack, in his re-construction of Jesus' preaching of the Kingdom, had

[45]Ibid., p. 19.

made the Kingdom consist in a purely interior relationship between the soul of Jesus and the Father. As Loisy puts it, he had wanted to save the Absolute by snatching it from history. Yet, Loisy contends, it was the flux of history which prepared the way for Jesus, just as it was through that flux that the image of his life comes down to us. And Loisy concludes his central Christological chapter with a passage relevant to his view of the development of doctrine:

> Everything that entered into the Gospel of Jesus has entered into the Christian tradition. What is truly evangelical in today's Christianity is not that which has never changed for, in a sense, everything has changed and has never ceased to change. What is truly evangelical today is that which, despite all external change, flows from the impulse Christ gave, is inspired by his spirit, serves the same ideal and the same hope.[46]

This is, one can note, a statement so general that it may mean a very great deal, or almost nothing at all.

On the Church, Loisy opens by pointing out that the Gospel is not an abstract doctrine, directly applicable to all men in all periods by its own immediate power. Rather is it a living (and thus concrete) faith, to be incarnated in different ways in different periods within the human milieu. For this very reason, *development* must be its inner law and not its progressive degradation. In this light, the Church can be seen to be necessary to the Gospel. By forming a limited, centralised, hierarchical inner group within the wider fraternity of his disciples, Jesus foresaw the diffusion of the Gospel in the present world and thus prepared the Kingdom to come.

> Jesus announced the Kingdom, and it was the Church that came[47]

[46]Ibid., pp. 115–16.
[47]Ibid., p. 166.

– a statement which Loisy did not intend to be ironic, though it has been treated as ironic by many since who have not troubled to read his book. Since Jesus' time, Loisy goes on, our perspective on the Kingdom of God has been broadened and modified, and its definitive advent pushed forward in time. Nevertheless, the Church remains ordered to the hope of the Kingdom, educating and organising with this goal in mind. The long life of Christianity, its *durée*, is what has caused its evolution. And Loisy suggests that, just as the earthly sojourn of the embodied soul makes that soul more capable of seeing God in the beatific vision, so the Church's earthly pilgrimage prepares her more fully for the final Kingdom. Loisy follows up this statement with a potted history of the Church. He sees that history as a flawed but fundamentally successful attempt in a changing world to dominate the flux of events and fulfil the mission confided to her. This is not to say that she must drag everything about that past into her future. For instance, Loisy suggests that, however useful the theocratic forms of the mediaeval papacy were in their time, popes in the future may cease to be great personalities on the stage of world politics, and in their manner of treating others will seek procedures more fitting to the spirit of Christian brotherhood.

And this brings us to the subject of Christian dogma, since, according to Loisy, the development of dogma is an aspect of the growth of the Church. The primitive Gospel was, and could only be, Jewish. Its Hellenisation was a spontaneous effort of faith which had to define itself *vis-à-vis* the Greek culture in which the Church found herself. From the historian's viewpoint, the Trinity and the Incarnation were Greek dogmas, unknown to Jewish Christianity. Greek culture provided their conceptual building blocks, their theoretical components. Nevertheless, the actual way in which those components were synthesised in the great conciliar dogmas and the spirit which animated them did not derive from the secular world. Dogmas, declares Loisy, are divine as to their origin and substance, but human in their structure and composition. They are not truths fallen from heaven and preserved by the religious tradition in the precise form in which they appeared.[48]

Their formulation is the fruit of a laborious theological effect, the condensation phase of a ceaseless activity of interpretation and elaboration. Their future, Loisy predicts, will surely conform to their past, following that perpetually changing condition of human intelligence to which the Church has always known how to adapt herself. One notices here that Loisy omits the careful qualifications he made in the Firmin articles as to how such future changes will only 'alter' in the sense of 'improving' the formulation of doctrine.

Loisy goes on to maintain that in the unity of the same Creed there is kept together an infinite diversity of nuances. With considerable disregard for history, Loisy insists that, in the past, Church teaching has been 'constantly flexible'. This was because, though faith needs the mediation of formulae, the Church knows that all such formulae are necessarily inadequate. Loisy explains that there are two ways in which to abuse dogma. One is by refusing to think about it, what he calls having 'the faith of the charcoal-burner', the superstitious illiterate. The other way of abusing dogma is to suppose that it constitutes the whole truth, 'la vérité intégrale'. This he terms 'le rationalisme des théologiens'. We notice that Loisy does not seem to think it is possible to abuse dogma by deforming it, misrepresenting it or denying it. Sins against dogma, in Loisy's mind, are always conservative sins. However this may be, Loisy's conclusion on dogma is unexceptionable. He points out that, by its very nature, Christian doctrine is a necessary but inadequate instrument of revealed truth. As such it requires a perpetual effort of appropriation, both personal and corporate, carried out within tradition and so within the Church, the religious society which assures tradition's permanence. In the conditions in which the Gospel lives in this world, it needs masters to propagate it and a doctrine in which to express itself. A major change in the state of 'science' – that is, of philosophy,

[48]Ibid., p. 210.

and of secular knowledge at large – can render necessary a new interpretation of the ancient formulae. Progress in doctrine takes place against resistance, but is achieved through an accommodation with what preceded it. It is characterised by the attainment of a balance of antinomies: for instance, there is only one God, yet Jesus is God; salvation is entirely from God, yet man is responsible for his own salvation; doctrine is guaranteed by the Church's infallible authority, yet its formulae are affected by the relativity of history. So Loisy concludes that in its *ensemble* doctrinal development has served the cause of the Gospel, which was itself unable to subsist as a pure essence. In his own day, he thought, the efflorescence of the Gospel in dogmas may seem withered up. But there is no reason to proclaim the end of dogma: the fecundity of Christian though is not exhausted, even if the Catholicism of his contemporaries is too cautious in its regard.

In attempting to evaluate *L'Evangile et l'Eglise* in terms wider than the occasional critical aside I have offered so far, it will be desirable to bear in mind the judgements upon it by the ecclesiastical magisterium. Two months after its appearance, the book was censured by the archbishop of Paris. This was on quite general and formal grounds, namely that it had been printed without an imprimatur, and was, moreover, likely to disturb the faith of ordinary believers. But, as we have seen, when Loisy proceeded to publish his explanation of the principles he had used in writing *L'Evangile et l'Eglise*, namely the second little red book *Autour d'un petit livre*, the newly enthroned pope, Pius X, stepped in and placed both books on the Index along with some of Loisy's more detailed exegetical works. As such, this action does not tell us what the Holy See found wrong with the books. For that we have to wait until 1907 as did, indeed Loisy himself. The decree *Lamentabili* of that year cited in all 13 propositions from *L'Evangile et L'Eglise* in order to condemn them as views inappropriate for a Catholic scholar to hold. However, the precise degree of reprobation attaching to each condemned proposition was not noted: it might have ranged from outright heretical to simply dangerous to faith, and this must be borne in mind in evaluating the Holy Office's action. Although the 13 propositions were immediately recognisably paraphrases of Loisy's text, his name was nowhere mentioned, either in *Lamentabili* or in the encyclical *Pascendi* which was shortly to follow.[49] Lagrange considered that in this policy of citing no names, the Holy See wished to avoid the controversy over 'droit' and 'fait' which had so prolonged the Jansenist crisis: Jansenists and their sympathisers accepting the papal condemnation of the content of Jansenist theses but denying that they were actually found in Jansenist authors.[50] In *Lamentabili*, only two condemned propositions concern the nature of dogma in any explicit way: these are nos. 22 and 60. The first of these states:

> The dogmas which the Church presents as revealed are not truths fallen from heaven but rather an interpretation of religious facts which human intelligence has acquired by laborious effort.

Loisy had written in *L'Evangile et l'Eglise*:

> The conceptions which the Church presents as revealed dogmas are not truths fallen from heaven, and preserved by tradition in the precise form in which the first appeared. The historian sees in them the interpretation of religious facts, acquired by a laborious effort of theological thought.

In his *Simples réflexions*, thoughts on the papal decrees, Loisy remarks that, in proposition 22, the Holy Office was contrasting two admittedly irreconcilable views of dogma's nature. One is rationalist, and regards dogma as a product of the human spirit; the other is Catholic, which sees it as a truth man cannot reach by his own powers. But Loisy explains that he was not himself speaking of the nature of dogma, but about the genesis of dogmatic formulae on the

[49]Cf. ibid., pp. 214, 221–2; 225.
[50]M.-J. Lagrange, O. P., *M. Loisy et le Modernisme*, op. cit., pp. 154–5.

empirical plane of their expression and communication. He had not intervened in a controversy between positivist philosophers and orthodox theologians, but had tried to describe as an historian how dogma had come to receive its formulation. In the second edition of *Simples réflexions*, he added:

> As soon as one speaks of a human effort, the theologians imagine that one is denying the divine action.[51]

It is useful to recall here as well the affirmation of what can be called a 'divine-human asymmetry' in the formation of dogma in *L'Evangile et l'Eglise* 4, where Loisy calls 'dogma divine as to its origin and substance, human as to its structure and composition'. I describe this as an *asymmetrical* account of the divine-human character of dogma because it seems to give the greater rôle to divine initiative as surely one must do if doctrine is truly the crystallisation of revelation.

The other condemned proposition relevant to Loisy's view of dogma was *Lamentabili's* no. 60.

> Christian doctrine in its beginnings was Jewish, but it became, through successive evolutions, firstly Pauline, then Johannine and finally Hellenic and universal.

This is a condensed form of a longer passage in which Loisy recognised his own thought, but with the exception of one significant modification. As he wrote in *Simples réflexions*:

> I said Christian *thought* (*la pensée chrétienne*), not *doctrine* (*la doctrine*).

And he goes on to explain the difference:

> I had in mind the form of belief, not its fundamental principles (*la forme de la croyance, non ses principes fondamentaux*)[52]

---

[51]*Simples réflections sur le décret du Saint-Office 'Lamentabili sane exitu' et sur l'encyclique 'Pascendi dominici gregis'* (Paris 1908), p. 64.

[52]Ibid., p. 117.

– its conceptual idiom, as we might gloss this, not the affirmations expressed via that idiom. M. Emile Poulat has drawn attention in his *Histoire, dogme et critique dans la Crise Moderniste* to the crucial importance of these two propositions in the debate between Loisy and Rome – the other eleven condemned propositions following straightforwardly from this basic disagreement in fundamental theology. Poulat puts it like this. Rome proceeded from defined doctrines to the biblical text, Loisy from the text to the doctrines.[53] What was in dispute was the relationship, then, between the primitive documents and the doctrines recognised as belonging to the apostolic deposit. Rome regarded this relation as being 'immediate': that is, if Loisy's historical exegesis did not in and of itself yield the full Catholic doctrine it was defective. Loisy, on the other hand, held that the relation between the primitive documents and the doctrines recognised as belonging to the deposit was not immediate but, rather, mediate. That is, only the lapse of time, allowing for further Christian experience and reflection, could draw from the primitive documents the doctrines of the patristic Church. This explains why, in his third little red book, *Simples Réflexions* ... Loisy agreed that Rome had by and large represented his exegesis correctly, but denied that he was on that account guilty of the doctrinal reductionism ascribed to him.

We are here, I believe, at the heart of the Modernist crisis. To try to get a firmer hold on the issues involved, it may be useful to remind ourselves of Newman's approach to the same problem in *The Arians of the Fourth Century*. There Newman had argued that the doctrine of the Trinity cannot be directly inferred from the New Testament. To this extent, Newman and Loisy concurred. Yet Newman had gone on to say, as Loisy significantly did not, that nonetheless the doctrine of the Trinity was present in the New Testament in the form of practical devotion. Patristic doctrine is a conceptual transposition of what we can term the *latent*

[53]E. Poulat, *Histoire, dogme et critique dans la Crise Moderniste* op. cit., pp. 111–12.

intelligible content of the New Testament, and, in particular, of Jesus' own words and deeds, in the flesh and in his risen glory. But the authors of *Lamentabili* had a different position again. So far as one can see, their view was that patristic doctrine, the doctrine recognised in the patristic Church as belonging to the apostolic deposit, is a conceptual transposition not just of the latent intelligible content of the New Testament, and notably of the words and deeds of Jesus, but, more than this, of the actively taught content found in those sources or *loci*. The same active teaching is found in the work of Jesus, in the New Testament writers and in the patristic Councils, though it may be expressed in different ways. This is most evident in the condemnation of proposition 31:

> The doctrine concerning Christ taught by Paul, John and the Councils of Nicaea, Ephesus and Chalcedon is not that which Jesus taught but one which the Christian consciousness formed about Jesus.

The intention behind the proscription of this proposition is obvious: the doctrinal authorities wished to assert in the area of Christology the substantial identity which holds between the original revelation and the same revelation in the mode of transmission. They wanted to insist that the revelation given once for all remain substantially the same when the Gospel is passed on in the Church. But does this very laudable intention really require that we exclude the kind or real movement from latency to explicitness which Newman believed he had found in the relation of the Scriptures to the doctrines?

> No one will ask you to say (wrote Duchesne to Loisy in early 1903) that, at his first meeting with St Andrew and St Peter, our Lord gave them a visiting card which said, 'Jesus Christ, the eternal Word, consubstantial with the Father'. Considerable development may be, and is, allowed.[54]

[54]Letter of 15 January 1903, cited in A. Loisy, *Mémoires*, op. cit., II., pp. 191–2.

And if there is such a real movement, if doctrine has a genuine history, then the elements of Christian experience and reflection which Loisy regarded as vital in the making of doctrine can be restored. This is not to say, however, that they should be restored in the way in which Loisy presented them. For Loisy did not teach such a substantial permanence of revelation in the transmission of the Gospel in the Church, but had recourse to vague language about the preservation of the Gospel spirit, the Gospel ideal, the Gospel hope or the Gospel's direction.

But here the friends of Loisy may reasonably interject a word in his defence. Loisy himself consistently maintained that he was not writing as a theologian, for a Catholic audience, but as an historian for an audience of Protestants and non-believers. In *Autour d'un petit livre*, his constant cry is that the intention of his book has been misconceived. People have regarded as a theological system what is only 'un modeste essai de construction historique'. In *L'Evangile et l'Eglise* there would have been no point in invoking the Catholic dogmatic tradition directly: Harnack and other non-Catholic readers would have rejected that as a way of arguing. May it not be, then, that in the real movement from latency to explicitness which joins Jesus and the New Testament to the later Church, the substantial permanence of revelation in its transmission was not theologically denied by Loisy but simply left unasserted on the grounds that a historian as such could not prove it? Here we come to that aspect of Loisy's work shortly to be stigmatised by Maurice Blondel as 'historicism'. Is it possible for the believer, when speaking as an historian, effectively to deny what he would affirm when speaking as a theologian? In *Autour d'un petit livre*, Loisy states that the Catholic dogmatic tradition, as a source for the authoritative interpretation of the original Gospel, 'is not receivable in the order of historical investigation'. There is surely *a* sense in which this is true. Were it possible to read off the entire Catholic dogmatic tradition from the evidence of the New Testament considered historically, then we would need no special Church organism for transmitting and canonising the meaning of the original Gospel in each generation. Historians, working with their proper tools on the texts of the Bible, could themselves prove to us the truth of everything the Catholic Church teaches. But then Loisy goes on to say:

> The historical study of religious facts and their religious appreciation are wholly distinct things.[55]

Here Loisy has gone too far. How can the historian's understanding of such religious facts as the life and teaching of Jesus, be *wholly* distinct from the believer's appreciation of those facts? The believing or theological evaluation of the facts is not compatible with any and every reconstruction of them by the historian, no matter how reductionist. There are some historical portraits of Jesus which, if true, exclude his being a divine legate, a figure endowed with unique authority. Dogmatic Christology cannot survive unless it is given a suitable basis in the historical portrait of Jesus offered with the help of exegetes in apologetics or what would now be termed fundamental theology.

This will be one of the principal concerns of the Pope's encyclical *Pascendi*, published some weeks after *Lamentabili*, as it will of Blondel's 'History and dogma' and of Batiffol's essays on the methodology of Church history. Here three points will be established. First of all, between history and dogma there cannot be a double truth, any more than in St Thomas' quarrel with the Latin Averroists he could allow a double truth as between philosophy and theology. Reason and faith must be compatible and complementary, and therefore so must historical reason and dogmatic faith. Secondly, where the work of Christian scholars is concerned, the material object of both historical investigation and doctrinal exploration is the same: the single revelation as given by the Mediator, the single Lord Jesus Christ. This is true, even though their formal perspectives on that object, and thus their concrete methods of approach, may differ. This means that the exegete must always be concerned to show

[55] *Autour d'un petit livre* (Paris 1903), p. 215.

how his texts might yield that further meaning which the dogmatician finds in them. Thirdly, the possession of dogmatic faith should be regarded not as a disadvantage, but as an enabling advantage for the historian or exegete, precisely in their own work. Dogmatic faith does not make it more difficult to practise the historical study of Christian origins; it makes such study easier, by giving one clearer light in which to see one's subject.[56]

In conclusion, and to get a sense of the positive vision which Loisy hoped to substitute for that of classical Catholic teaching, we can turn to the letter on dogma found within *Autour d'un petit livre*. Loisy's apologia for *L'Evangile et L'Eglise* had been constructed in the form of seven open letters, and the penultimate one of these is directed to 'un jeune savant sur les dogmes'. Loisy argues here that his approach is more authentically Catholic than that of his episcopal opponents, at least according to his understanding of what the word 'Catholic' means.

> Catholicism consists in receiving, as emanating from an authority divinely established, that interpretation of the Gospel which the Church gives now (*actuellement*) . . . Whoever calls himself a Protestant implicitly affirms the sufficiency and immutability of the Gospel revelation. Whoever calls himself Catholic implicitly denies that absolute sufficiency and immutability.[57]

And, repudiating the (Eastern) Orthodox conception of 'the Church of the Seven Councils' as at an antipodean extreme from the Catholic view, Loisy calls the rule of faith 'a living reality like faith itself'. Not only is this the authentic Catholic sentiment, but it opens the way for an accord between dogma and learning. Thus, by insisting on their a-historical approach to doctrine, the Church's pastors are for Loisy theologically unfaithful to the essential principle of Catholicism – and at the same time imprudent in removing from beneath their

[56]Cf. P. Toinet, 'Le Verbe de Dieu en condition de temporalité', in idem., *Pour une Théologie de l'exégèse* (Paris 1983), pp. 61–91.

[57]*Autour d'un petit livre*, op. cit., pp. 205–6, 208.

own feet the basis for Catholicism's intellectual self-defence. Yet in point of fact, has not Loisy returned to that defence of Catholicism by the eighteenth century Jesuit Isaac Berruyer already rejected by Church authority in the 1760's? In effect, Loisy uses the idea of doctrinal development to say that the contemporary Church and its magisterium have a blank cheque to re-define the Gospel in terms they find pastorally useful in any given age, without any intellectual care for the continuity, indeed identity, of contemporary confession with the apostolic deposit. The essential difference from Berruyer's position was that Loisy, as historian, did not in fact believe that Jesus of Nazareth had instituted the Church and its magisterium. Both the community and its ministerial authority were simply positive, *de facto*, reactions to the career of Jesus. This is why, though episcopate and papacy bear a pastoral responsibility for adapting the Gospel to the needs of each age for the sake of the spiritual and moral education of humanity, they have for Loisy no supernatural rights vis-à-vis the intellectual convictions of believers, and, in particular, the intellectual convictions of believing scholars.

Did the body of Newman, resting in the peace of the Warwickshire countryside at Rednal, turn a little in its grave? Perhaps the truest judgement on Loisy is that of Jean Guitton in his *La Pensée de M. Loisy*, where he speaks of the 'interior instability' which afflicted his thought from the moment when he lost the idea of the *donné*, the revealed 'given', an idea essential to Catholicism.[58] Dismissing the idea of an apostolic deposit, a determinate revealed datum, Loisy exalted the Church while trivialising the Gospel, defending the institution while minimising its founder. Just as, Guitton says, the eighteenth century knew *le faux dévot*, ours produced in Loisy the model of *le faux croyant*. Having cut the roots of faith, why, then, did Loisy desire so fervently to remain in Catholic communion? Basically, because he saw the Catholic Church as the only religious society in the world capable of uniting men to each other and to the divinity, thus raising

[58] J. Guitton, *La Pensée de M. Loisy* (Aix 1936), in E. Poulat, *Critique et mystique*, op. cit., p. 129.

their moral and spiritual level to its highest limits. His final 'religion of humanity' was, Guitton maintains, 'la transposition laïque du catholicisme'.[59] This is a paradigm of 'development' which, among liberal spirits in the age following the Second Vatican Council' would still find implicit support. It might usefully be compared, for instance, with the most radical varieties of liberation theology. As Guitton concludes:

I have sometimes wondered if Loisy's mistake was perhaps that, by a secular transposition of the typical temptation of ecclesiastics, he sought too enthusiastically a triumph of the Church in the world.[60]

[59]Ibid. (i.e. Guitton's book), p. 121.
[60]J. Guitton, *La Vocation de Bergson* (Paris 1960), p. 192.

4

George Tyrrell

The development of Tyrrell's theology

George Tyrrell was born in 1861, the son of a Dublin journalist.[1] His family were Low Church Anglicans. In search of a type of Christianity with what he deemed greater intellectual coherence, he entered the Roman Catholic Church in London in 1879, and the following year became a novice in the English Province of the Society of Jesus. His 'first period', from 1880 to 1896, was characterised by militant Thomist orthodoxy, and is reflected in (the bulk of the) essays re-published later as *The Faith of the Millions*.[2] As philosophy professor in the Jesuit studentate (at Stonyhurst, Lancashire) from 1894 to 1896 he berated the 'Baroque' Scholasticism of the Society's favoured theologian, Francisco Suárez (1548–1617), advocating a return to the historical St Thomas. He saw no disadvantage in Pope Leo XIII's attempt to impose a single common master on the Catholic schools, describing the pro-Thomist encyclical *Aeterni Patris* as 'a blow against sectarian narrowness and in favour of a Catholic and liberal uniformity'.[3] By this, he appears to have meant a uniformity of method and terminology which might

[1]For Tyrrell's life, the chief sources remain his autobiography, as edited by M. D. Petre, and the latter's biography which picks up the story where Tyrrell left off, in 1884, and bases itself on his letters and her reminiscences. See M. D. Petre, *Autobiography and Life of George Tyrrell* (London 1912; two volumes). Cited hereafter as ALGT utilising hitherto unpublished material is N. Sagovsky, *'On God's side? A Life of George Tyrrell* (Oxford 1990).

[2]*The Faith of the Millions. A Selection of Past Essays* (London 1901: 'First Series', 'Second Series'). Here cited as FMI and FMII.

[3]J. Crehan, 'Tyrrell in his Workshop', *The Month* 2, 3 (N.S., 1971), p. 111.

create a context of clear communication for the critical assessment of all other systems.[4]

However, he was accused of turning young Jesuits into Dominicans and removed from his post. In retrospect he commented on his choice of theological mentor:

> The fact is that Aquinas represents a far less developed theology than that of the later Scholastics, and by going back to him one escapes from many of the super-structures of his more narrow-minded successors, and thus gets a liberty to unravel and reconstruct on more sympathetic lines . . . My feeling is that, under cover of Aquinas, much might have been quietly introduced and assimilated unconsciously that will be opposed if presented in an alien and hostile garb.[5]

The year of his relegation to the *scriptorium* of Farm Street, 1896, also saw the gestation of his first book, *Nova et Vetera*, a devotional work, like much of his output, and the fateful occasion of his first encounter with the Baron Friedrich von Hügel. Von Hügel gave Tyrrell his first taste of the new wine of the historical-critical study of Christian origins which was to burst the old wine-skin of Thomism – at least when considered as a sufficient basis for a contemporary theology.

Thus began Tyrrell's 'second period' which has been described as one of 'mediating' (i.e. mediatory and moderate) liberalism'.[6] The aim of 'mediating liberalism' was to present Catholic Christianity to the modern mind in broad and sympathetic terms as a harmonious body of truth rooted in an objective, supernatural revelation yet welcoming scholarship in its self-presentation. Such a 'change of tactics', as Tyrrell termed it, was directly indebted to J. H.

[4]D. J. Schultenover S. J., *George Tyrrell. In Search of Catholicism* (Shepherdstown 1981), p. 32.

[5]Letter of 6.12.1907 to von Hügel, cited in ALGT II. p. 45. A less manipulative view of St Thomas is found in Tyrrell's early essay 'Aquinas Resuscitatus', *American Catholic Quarterly Review* 16 (1891), pp. 673–90.

[6]ALGT I. p. 99; cf. D. G. Schultenover, *George Tyrrell* op. cit. pp. 44–5.

Newman's biographer, Wilfrid Ward, as Tyrrell freely acknowledged.[7] It formed a judicious compromise between the apologetic assertion of public doctrine and its critical re-appropriation, and held to the Wardian axiom that if scholars exercise caution, ecclesiastical authorities will show moderation. During this second period, Tyrrell wrote a group of articles on the nature of doctrinal development, an inevitable theme for one who had placed himself in a succession consisting of Newman and Ward. Meanwhile, von Hügel had introduced Tyrrell not only to the advanced exegetical studies of the Abbé Alfred Loisy but also to the new 'vitalist' and 'action' philosophies of Henri Bergson and Maurice Blondel.[8] Tyrrell ceased to be content with Ward's ecclesiastically eirenic but intellectually less than perspicuous position. He began to seek for a more radical recasting of theology. In 'A Perverted Devotion', an article criticising pulpit recourse to the doctrine of Hell, he stigmatised the Scholastic interpretation of eschatological dogma as theological rationalism, pleading instead for a 'certain temperate agnosticism' on the ultimate fate of the damned.[9] Though the English Jesuits were prepared to pass this essay, their Roman *confrères* demurred.[10] They rejected Tyrrell's proposal that the human mind, because of its finitude, is

[7]G. Tyrrell, 'A Change of Tactics', *The Month* 86 (February 1896), pp. 215–27, reprinted in FMI, pp. 1–21. Tyrrell's adoption of Ward's programme is found in his review of the latter's *The Life and Times of Cardinal Wiseman* (London 1897), and entitled 'Wiseman: his Aims and Methods', *The Month* 91 (February 1898), pp. 142–50. Reprinted in FMI, pp. 22–39.

[8]See their correspondence as excerpted in M. D. Petre (ed.), *Von Hügel and Tyrrell, The Story of a Friendship* (London 1937).

[9]Originally published in *The Weekly Register* 100 (16 December 1899), pp. 461–73. Reprinted in M. D. Petre (ed.), *Essays on Faith and Immortality* (London 1914), pp. 158–71. 'A certain temperate agnosticism', defended by Tyrrell through reference to the apophatic element in the sermons of Leo the Great, remained a defining feature of Catholic Modernism. See M. D. Petre, *Modernism. Its Failures and its Fruits* (London 1918), p. 207; C. F. Crews, *English Catholic Modernism. Maude Petre's Way of Faith* (Notre Dame, Indiana 1984), p. 88.

[10]For Tyrrell's relations with the Jesuit Generalate, see D. G. Schultenover, 'George Tyrrell: Caught in the Roman Archives of the Society of Jesus', *Proceedings of the Roman Catholic Modernism Working Group of the American Academy of Religion* (1981), pp. 85–114.

incapable of grasping *hic et nunc* what may be the final state of man. As a result, Tyrrell was moved a second time, to the bucolic retirement of a small Jesuit mission at Richmond-in-Swaledale, where he stayed from 1900 to 1905.

These years initiated the 'third period' of Tyrrell's activity and witnessed the emergence of his most characteristic ideas. Before Tyrrell's dismissal from the Society in 1906 he had produced a small library of books, some in his own name and others pseudonymously. For a condensed statement of his approach to theology in this third period one cannot do better than consult his essay 'The Relation of Theology to Devotion', of which he wrote in 1907, the year of his excommunication:

> It is all here – all that follows – not in germ but in explicit statement.[11]

In this brief study, Tyrrell points out that 'theology' may refer in a Catholic context to one of two things. More narrowly, it is the Scholastic tradition currently in possession in institutes of academic and ministerial formation. More widely, it is the attempt to articulate revelation, an enterprise defined by Tyrrell in terms of the unification and elucidation of data provided by Christian experience in the concrete. The applying of philosophical concepts to revelation, as carried out in Scholastic theology, tends like all philosophising to 'excessive abstraction and vague unreality'. It needs to be constantly tested by facts:

> the facts here being the Christian religion as lived by its consistent professors.[12]

Tyrrell draws examples of how Scholastic theology and the lived Christian experience can conflict from the realms of

---

[11] *Through Scylla and Charybdis* (London 1907), p. 86. 'The Relation of Theology to Devotion' was originally printed in *The Month* 94 (November 1899), pp. 461–73. Reprinted in FMI pp. 228–52, and *Through Scylla and Charybdis* (op. cit., cited henceforth as TSC), pp. 85–105.

[12] TSC p. 104.

soteriology, Eucharistic doctrine and Christology. It is characteristic of the unpredictability of Tyrrell's radicalism that in dealing with the Eucharist he draws on such 'experiential facts' to defend the view that the glorified Christ is locally present in the Eucharistic elements as the 'Prisoner in the tabernacle'. But it is in relation to Christology that he introduced what will become his key terms in theological method: *lex orandi* and *lex credendi*. The test of doctrine is, he asserts, whatever spirituality either directly affirms or indirectly requires. Theology stands to religious devotion as art criticism stands to art. Just as the art critic 'formulates and justifies the best work of the best artists', so the theologian must take as his measure the *lex orandi*, the 'devotion of the best Catholics'.[13] Though Tyrrell retains the concept of an aboriginal apostolic 'deposit of faith', he sees that deposit as being a prayerful experience of the heart rather than a communication of beliefs to the mind. In this he announces his secession from the school of Newman and Ward.

Until some point in 1909, the year of his death, Tyrrell adhered consistently to the principles laid down in 'The Relation of Theology to Devotion'. The development of his personal theological life took the form of underpinning these *idées-clés* philosophically by appealing to the pragmatist and voluntarist notions of A. J. Balfour and William James. In *Lex Orandi*, for instance, Tyrrell asks how we know the Creed is true, in whatever sense it may be true. He replies that the Creed is true in that there is a 'certain analogy' between its formulae and 'the eternal realities of the spirit-world'. Here Tyrrell takes the crucial step of extending to credal confession the view of theological language he has hitherto reserved for philosophical theology. He argues that we know the Creed is true (in the sense just outlined) because of its proven value as

> a practical guide to the eternal life of the soul – a proof
> which is based on the experience not of this man or
> that, however wise and holy, but of the whole Christian

[13]Ibid. p. 105.

people and of the Church of the saints in all ages and nations, of the consensus of the ethical and religious *orbis terrarum*.[14]

And in an attempt to explain the genesis of orthodoxy he went on:

It is ... Christian devotion, rather than Christian metaphysics, the need of the soul rather than the need of the intellect, that has selected the orthodox faith in preference to heterodox error.[15]

Such a re-statement of the concepts of catholicity and orthodoxy commits Tyrrell to the view that a Christian belief can be known to be true by being fruitful in practice. But is 'being fruitful in practice' what Tyrrell *means* by 'being true'? Probably not. Tyrrell never embraced a thorough-going pragmatism but he married his tendency to pragmatism with something approximating on occasion to a double standard of truth:

Certain concrete historical facts enter into our creed as matters of faith. Precisely as historical facts they concern the historian and must be criticised by his methods. But as matters of faith they must be determined by the criterion of faith, i.e. by their proved religious value.[16]

Three years after *Lex Orandi*, in a sequel entitled *Lex Credendi*, Tyrrell defended himself against the charge of mere pragmatism, showing that he felt its force.

[14]*Lex Orandi* (London 1903), pp. 57 ff. There is an echo here of Wiseman's appeal to the *orbis terrarum* in his 1839 *Dublin Review* article on Donatists and Puseyites. But whereas Wiseman appealed to the doctrinal judgement of the universal episcopate, Tyrrell appealed to the mystical sense of the *plebs sancta Dei*.

[15]Ibid. p. 153. That popular devotion plays a major part in the historical ascertaining of orthodoxy need not be doubted. See e.g. H. Chadwick, 'Eucharist and Christology in the Nestorian controversy', *Journal of Theological Studies* (N.S. 2, 2; 1951), pp. 145–64.

[16]*Lex Orandi* (op. cit.), p. 164.

A belief which constantly and universally fosters spiritual
life must so far be true to the realities of the spiritual
world and must therefore possess a *representative* as well
as a practical value.[17]

But the objections of Tyrrell's critics could be fully met only
by relating such argument from religious experience to some
wider account of knowledge and reality. This Tyrrell was
unable or unwilling to do.[18]

Meanwhile, Tyrrell's public tone was becoming ever more
strident, especially in the wake of the (remarkable
intransigent) joint pastoral letter of the English bishops, 'The
Church and Liberal Catholicism' which had appeared in early
1901.[19] Whereas Loisy was stressing the compatibility
between traditional Catholic doctrine and the new biblical
and historical sophistication, Tyrrell was underscoring their
incompatibility – in order, it seems, to bring the crisis over
doctrine to a head. In the pseudonymous *The Church and the
Future*, he rejects Loisy's proposal that traditional dogma
might be re-interpreted in a sense compatible with the results
of criticism. Christ's teaching was not dogmatic but
prophetic: a 'vividly realised intuition of the coming
Kingdom of God, and of its sovereign earth-and-time
dwarfing importance', differing from other prophetic
utterances only in that its bearer saw himself as 'the King of
that redeemed humanity, through whom their redemption
was at last to be effected'. In regard to this vision, Christ
sought only a *'practical* acknowledgement that he was the
Way'. It is not a body of doctrine that has been committed
to the Church's guardianship but only a 'way' or manner of
life, and in an uncanny anticipation of the contemporary

[17]*Lex Credendi* (London 1906), p. 252.

[18]Ibid. p. 68.

[19]'The Church and Liberal Catholicism', *The Tablet*, 5.1.1901. Dated, in fact,
29.12.1900, it was issued in the name of the cardinal-archbishop, and the bishops, of
the Province of Westminster. This letter elicited from Bernard Ward the comment
that the bishops's attitude to the educated laity was 'Go and see what baby's doing
and tell him he mustn't', M. Ward, *Insurrection versus Resurrection* (London 1937),
p. 135. See further W. J. Schoenl, 'George Tyrrell and the English Liberal Catholic
Crisis 1900–1901', *Downside Review* 92 (1974), pp. 171–84.

Anglican writer Don Cupitt, Tyrrell takes primitive Christianity to be comparable with Buddhism. The theologian's task is to distinguish the *form* of doctrine from its *matter*: its (infallible) truth to the 'spirit of Christ' from the (highly fallible) truth of its constituent philosophical and historical elements to the 'world of man's outer experience'.[20] In *A Much-Abused Letter*, which led to his expulsion from the Society, Tyrrell recognised that the Church authorities were unlikely to embrace his somewhat Pickwickian notion of doctrinal truth. He counselled an academic in intellectual difficulties with faith to abandon the 'officially formulated Catholicism' and adhere instead to the 'as yet unformulated Catholicism' or, rather, the living multitudinous reality thus perversely formulated.[21] And Tyrrell ends by prophesying that the Catholic Church may have to die in order to perpetuate itself in giving its life for what is not itself.

> May not Catholicism like Judaism have to die in order
> that it may live again in a greater and grander form?[22]

In 1907 Tyrrell's career as a 'Modernist' who was also a communicant Catholic was brought to an end by papal action, elicited by the bishop of Southwark but precipitated by Tyrrell's own hand. At the time of the promulgation of the decree *Lamentabili sane exitu* and the encyclical *Pascendi dominici gregis* in 1907, Tyrrell's negotiations with various bishops for incardination as a diocesan priest were on the point of a successful conclusion, thanks to the good offices of Mercier of Malines.[23] Yet if one may believe a letter to the Old Catholic bishop Vernon Herford antedating the Roman documents, he believed Pius X, whose anti-Modernist policies were already clearly signalled, to be in his intransigence both heretical and schismatic.[24] In two letters to *The Times* he

---

[20]'H. Bourdon', *The Church and the Future* (London 1903), pp. 47–9; 73; 89–90.

[21]*A Much-Abused Letter* (London 1906), p. 60.

[22]Ibid. p. 89.

[23]ALGT II. pp. 299–300.

[24]Cited in E. Leonard, *George Tyrrell and the Catholic Tradition* (London 1982), p. 120.

repudiated the papal strictures on Modernism in the style of a Hebrew prophet, thus faithfully echoing the preferred mode of the pope himself.[25] Though only forty-six years of age he had just two years of life left. Unknown to himself, he was in the grip of Bright's disease, an enemy which brought him to his death in ecclesiastically contentious circumstances in the Sussex village of Storrington in July 1909.[26]

Though in a sacramental wilderness, Tyrrell produced a final trilogy. In *Through Scylla and Charybdis* he collected and expanded his mature writings on the nature of revelation, doctrine and theology. He argued that the intellectual crisis of Catholicism could be resolved only if people realised that while theology has a history, doctrine can have none, being simply the stake which marks the presence of revelation, itself a largely ineffable experience of the spiritual world.[27] In *Mediaevalism*, goaded by the pen of his erstwhile protector Cardinal Mercier, he excoriated Neo-Scholasticism, and, mindless of his early enthusiasm for the Neo-Thomist activities of Leo XIII, wrote it off as no more than an Ultramontane papacy's instrument of theological control.[28] In *Christianity at the Crossroads*, published posthumously, what Tyrrell himself described (in part, ironically) as his 'system' seems on the verge of internal collapse. Wholly convinced of the truth of Albert Schweitzer's account of Jesus as an apocalypticist, Tyrrell now declared his attachment to a 'futurist' eschatology, deeming Christianity to be essentially other-worldly and *toto caelo* at variance with any ideology of progress. Resurrecting Newman's language of a continuous Christian 'Idea', Tyrrell proposed that traditional Catholic teaching and piety on 'the Last Things' was simply the apocalyptic vision of Jesus in a new key.[29] But this unexpected turn left intact, indeed strengthened, the paradox that a theologian so concerned to reconcile the Church with contemporary culture was so entirely convinced that history

[25]'The Pope and Modernism', *The Times* 30.9.1907, p. 4; ibid. 1.10.1907, p. 5.
[26]ALGT II. pp. 420–46.
[27]TSC passim.
[28]*Mediaevalism. A Reply to Cardinal Mercier* (London 1908), pp. 143–58.
[29]*Christianity at the Crossroads* (London 1909; 1963), pp. 50–3, 74.

had contributed nothing to the fundmental religious appreciation of the primitive Gospel. How that could be, Tyrrell's changing attitudes to the theory of doctrinal development will show.

Tyrrell and the idea of development

Tyrrell's earliest essay on the theme was prompted by an editorial in the London *Times* during the celebrations for Victoria's Diamond Jubilee.[30] Surveying what it called 'ecclesiastical development' during the reign, *The Times* praised the religious progress which, in all churches save that of Rome, had rendered theology broader and more enlightened. In defence of the role of *some* concept of progress in this context, Tyrrell appeals to Vincent of Lérins' *Primum Commonitorium* as well as to the Council of Florence, arguing that while after Christ and his apostles progress in *objective* revelation ceased (since they represented the 'fulness of time'), revelation can be said to make *subjective* progress by way of addition not to the deposit of faith but to the Church's understanding of it.[31] To explain himself, Tyrrell draws on Newman's analogy in *The Arians of the Fourth Century* between the growth of a child's mind and that of the corporate Church.[32] He also echoes Newman in his concealed citation of the Lucan description of Mary's ruminations on the Finding in the Temple.[33]

> What happens to the individual, happens to the Church as a whole. She holds fast to the form of sound words; she keeps the deposit once and for all delivered to their saints. But more than this, she ponders these words and compares them in her heart; she sees more and more

[30]'Ecclesiastical development in the reign of the Queen', *The Times* 2.1.1897.

[31]'Ecclesiastical development', *The Month* 90 (1897), pp. 380–90 cited below as ED.

[32]J. H. Newman, *The Arians of the Fourth Century* (London 1833; 1871), pp. 143–4.

[33]J. H. Newman, 'The Theory of Developments in Religious Doctrine', *University Sermons* (London 1871³; 1970), No XV, pp. 312–13; Lk 2, 19.

how much they involve; she, as it were, draws nearer and nearer, till details before unnoticed stand out distinctly, and consequences heretofore tangled in their premises are drawn out and separated.[34]

Despite the 'cordial', affective counter-balance of Tyrrell's reference to the Infancy narratives, he sees the process involved as essentially *logical* in character. By skilful Socratic questioning, the entire Roman Catholic faith as believed today could have been elicited from a Christian of the primitive generation. From the words 'This is my Body', such a Christian could have 'inferred the detailed Eucharistic doctrine of the *Lauda Sion*'. Such progress is analysis, not development like that of acorn into oak.

Yet Tyrrell goes on to modify this restrictive statement by appeal to the commonplace Late Scholastic distinction between what is held *de fide divina*, as an intrinsic constituent of divine revelation, and what is believed simply *de fide ecclesiastica*, as part of those infallible teachings which the Church has put forth in the service of the revealed deposit, but by reference to post-apostolic 'science' or 'history'. Thus, we know which doctrines are revealed dogmas, and which councils of the Church are ecumenical, through 'ecclesiastical faith', but, once equipped with this knowledge, we affirm the content of such dogmas and the authority of such councils by 'divine faith', as a direct response to the self-revealing God. It is only where a revealed article of faith has entered into symbiosis with a philosophical truth or historical fact that

we have a true development, by the absorption of extraneous matter, of natural truths and facts, and the consequent increase in bulk of the body of our beliefs.[35]

Failure to observe this elementary distinction between the merely analytic or Socratic progress of dogma, and the

[34]ED p. 382.
[35]Ibid. p. 383.

genuinely developmental increment of such ecclesiastical doctrine accounts, Tyrrell concludes, for the way Catholicism is simultaneously accused *both* of 'wall-eyed rigidity' *and* of 'unwarrantable additions to the faith of the Apostles'.

Yet such a nuanced concept of doctrinal progress is not, of course, that contained in the editorial mind of *The Times*. The latter can blandly advise the churches to 'keep pace with the intellectual advance of the day', since to it the development of Christianity is nothing more than an aspect of the development of culture itself. Whereas *Catholics*

> most thankfully accept, with the limitations already explained, the charge of intolerance and of adamantine immobility. It is perfectly evident to us that Christ came to teach the masses of mankind, and not to argue or plead with scribes and doctors of the law; and that for the masses dogmatic teaching is a necessity.[36]

And Tyrrell goes on to say that it is no less evident that he commissioned the Church to a similar office. Without her authoritative guardianship, the deposit of faith 'must inevitably be lost'.

The publication of an English translation of Auguste Sabatier's *De la Vie intime des dogmes et de leur puissance d'évolution* enabled Tyrrell to return to the subject in the following year, 1898.[37] Tyrrell finds the value of Sabatier's book to lie in the 'clearness of its opposition to Catholic conceptions'. For Sabatier, the Creed is a 'divinely inspired allegory'.

> In the soul of Christ and the prophets and apostles, God causes some strong and unusual spiritual commotion which they of their own ingenuity, consciously or unconsciously, seek to utter and embody in allegories . . .[38]

[36]Ibid. p. 388.
[37]A. Sabatier, *The Vitality of Christian Dogmas and their Power of Evolution: A Study in Religious Philosophy* (London 1898).
[38]'Sabatier on the vitality of dogmas', *The Month* 91 (June 1898), pp. 592–602.

On this scheme, revelation is the arousing of an indistinct apprehension of the divine Object. This apprehension, registered as a sentiment, then seeks its own formulation in a theory or idea. Dogma is, then, the fruit of reflection on religious feeling. The theologian's task is to assist the evolution of such self-expression in the changing conditions of culture. In particular, he should serve as midwife to what Sabatier called 'intussusception', a neologism naughtily explained by Tyrrell as

> to keep to the 'form of sound words', while quietly slipping new meanings under them, and explaining them away as long as they will possibly admit of it, and when this gets too difficult (one) may noiselessly introduce new terminology and suffer the old to retire into its well-earned rest.[39]

Against all this, Catholic theology regards revelation as a 'supernatural instruction of the mind'. Either directly, or through some created agency, God uses those forms and images which constitute the mind's 'language' to express truths not known before, or at least not known in the same way.

Sabatier's description would fit the history of *natural* religion, where just such theoretical and narrative attempts to satisfy and explain religious feeling take place, with what resultant mixture of truth and error, and degeneration of symbolism into mythology, we known only too well. It was to avoid the drawbacks of such 'man-begotten' religions, that the Divinity:

> devised for us the economy of the Incarnation, and in the life of the God-Man and his precursors and followers, uttered Eternal Truth and Love as far as it can be uttered in the enacted language of human life . . .[40]

[39]Ibid. p. 596.
[40]Ibid. p. 598.

In so far as divine revelation is thus embodied in the sacred history it is 'God's language', and, like the language of creation itself, is the same for all men in all ages, however they interpret or misinterpret it. The record of such revelatory events is apostolic tradition, as crystallised primarily in Scripture. The Church's relationship to the primitive tradition is described by Tyrrell in terms of what may be called reflective guardianship. Though the Church does not deny that, were the revelation given today, or had it been communicated in ancient China, the same divine truths 'would sound strangely unlike themselves', nevertheless, in obedience to the dispositions of Providence, she

> treasures the original mind-forms and language in which Divine truth has been committed to her, as it were the perishable earthen vessel in which a priceless gift is contained.[41]

Moreover, the Church 'ponders' that form of words which alone is divinely guaranteed, and over the centuries, by a process as inevitable as men's inclination to 'put their thoughts in order', has embodied her ponderings in what Tyrrell presents as the simple and straightforward idiom of the Schools. The Church 'wisely adopted a philosophy little removed from the first spontaneous efforts of the mind towards unity'. Though not claiming that the Scholastic articulation of dogma is the only one possible, or even the best, she cautions her children that those who venture on other translations of revelation 'do so at their own peril'. The real Christ came to enlighten the mind by truth as well as to sanctify the will by charity, but the Christ of Sabatier is careless of how the mind might explain to itself the feelings he inspires. Stripped of its historical and dogmatic truth-claims, the essence of Christianity survives here only in the continuance of a religious sentiment. Though Sabatier insists that Christ 'is not here: he is risen', having cast aside the 'cerements and grave-clothes of dogmatic statement', Tyrrell

[41]Ibid. p. 601.

feels it would be more frank to say to the mourner at the tomb: 'His disciples have come and stolen him away': 'well-intentioned, no doubt, in their zeal for his reputation; but surely mistaken in their judgment and weak in their faith'.

The first indication of Tyrrell's dissatisfaction with his early, part-Scholastic, part-Newmanian, account of doctrinal development occurs in 'The Relation of Theology to Devotion'. There Tyrrell denies that the Church's guardianship of revelation is reflectively developmental as well as preservative, asserting that human thought and language are so inadequate to revelation that they are more its detritus than its representation.[42] In the *Church and the Future* Tyrrell invokes the language of doctrinal development in a sense quite different from that he had earlier given it. He now speaks of Christ's 'spirit' (or religious attitude) working itself out in the Church, developing as humanity encounters fresh situations and problems. Such development of the spirit brings with it a parallel development in the doctrinal expression of that spirit. This body of doctrine offers us a construing of the eternal realities (the Kingdom) to which we must adjust our lives if we are to live with Christ's attitude or spirit. But such doctrine is unconnected with theological, i.e. intellectual, understanding, being purely of the spiritual order, i.e. the order of a life-transforming contact with transcendent reality.[43]

However, the principal source for Tyrrell's mature view of doctrinal development is *Through Scylla and Charybdis*. He opens by setting forth his main conclusion which will, he predicts, strike his readers as 'entirely reactionary'. It is the desirability of a return to the 'earlier and stricter view as to the unchanging, unprogressive character of the apostolic revelation'. His chief conclusion is to be a repudiation of all attempts to mitigate the supposed difficulties of this severer view by theories of development, dialectical or otherwise. It insists rigorously on the theological contention that the dogmatic decisions of the universal Church do not in any

[42] TSC p. 95.
[43] *The Church and the Future* (London 1903), p. 157.

way add to or amplify the revelation which it is their purpose to safeguard and re-assert; that, whatever be true of the natural light of reason or of theological science, the supernatural Light of the World does not shine more brightly on us today than on the earliest Christian generations. Understanding by 'dogma' a religious truth imposed authoritatively by the Word of God, not as a conclusion of theological reflection, it rejects the very notion of this development, and still more of the multiplication of dogmas, and acquiesces cordially in the patristic identification of novelty and heresy.[44]

Tyrrell's introduction states his chief reason for reverting to J. B. Bossuet's root-and-branch rejection of all notions of progress in doctrine.[45] Theories of development are, he maintains, hypotheses in a state of accelerating breakdown, and so we must 'return to our point of departure'. The 'hypotheses' he has in mind include both Scholastic and non-Scholastic theories of doctrinal development. He points out that the concept of development of doctrine has become a commonplace of Catholic theology, yet cites W. E. Gladstone in support of the view that this constitutes a silent theological revolution in Catholicism during the course of the nineteenth century.[46] Conservatively-minded theologians instinctively distrust the theory of development as not so much explaining, but rather explaining away the traditional 'note' of apostolicity, a vital criterion of revealed truth. Tyrrell declares himself 'fully in sympathy' with their anxieties. Unfortunately, because such conservative theologians have inherited certain mistaken concessions of principle begotten by the 'liberalisings' of bygone days, they have failed to see the issues clearly. By 'liberalisings' Tyrrell makes it clear that

[44]TSC pp. 4–5.

[45]As found, for example, in Bossuet's *Histoire des variations des églises protestantes*, Preface, ii. See O. Chadwick, *From Bossuet to Newman. The Idea of Doctrinal Development* op. cit., pp. 5–13.

[46]W. E. Gladstone, *The Vatican Decrees in their Bearing on Civil Allegiance. A Political Expostulation* (London 1874), p. 6. Gladstone claimed that if the office claimed by the Church is not (principally) 'a witness to facts' but 'a judge, if not a revealer of doctrine', then 'no amount of historical testimony can avail against the unmeasured power of the theory of development'.

he means not just mid-nineteenth century figures like Newman, nor even St Thomas, but the celebrated patristic author of the metaphor of development, *profectus*, himself.[47]

Tyrrell proceeds to state his objections, first to the logical-Scholastic family of theories of development, and then to their (largely) non-logical Newmanian rivals. For the *Scholastic* theorists, apostolic revelation is itself 'a divinely authorised though rudimentary theological system' which expands by two means. Firstly, additional doctrine is developed by a deductive process and confirmed by Church authority. Secondly, philosophical or historical claims presupposed by this original 'system' are identified, and these too are taken to be covered by the sanction of revelation. Thus for the Scholastic theory of doctrinal development, it must be heresy to deny a later deduction from the apostolic deposit, e.g. that Jesus Christ has two natures, human and divine. Similarly, it must also be heresy to deny certain historical facts bound up with the original rudimentary system, e.g. that Peter preached at Rome, and certain philosophical principles entailed by it, e.g. the immortality of the soul. In such ways, Scholasticism generates an entire intellectual structure from out of the apostolic deposit. Unfortunately, this structure can now be seen to conflict at certain points with both science and history. Tyrrell lodges the further objection that, whereas such philosophers as J. S. Mill deny the cognitive value of deduction, the School theologians insist that when we have succeeded in deducing fresh doctrine from the apostolic deposit we genuinely know more. Yet in this case, Catholic Christians today must enjoy a higher degree of enlightenment compared with their fellows in the early Church. But then:

> Must we not regard the apostolic age, when all these deduced dogmas were confused and indiscernible, as one of relative darkness and chaos? Yet what would the Fathers, with their continual appeal to the tradition of the apostolic sees, have thought of such a contention?

[47]TSC p. 7.

What would St Paul, with his belief in a proximate advent, have thought of the view that his saving doctrine was but germinal and rudimentary, and that a fuller light was reserved for long ages to come?[48]

Thus the claim that, as a result of logical or dialectical development, we know more of revelation than apostles and fathers did, cannot be true because it is in effect denied in advance by those apostles and fathers themselves.

Tyrrell now turns to consider the *non-logical* or *Newmanian* theories of development. Again, he has two fundamental objections. The first resembles his second objection to the Scholastic theory. The non-logical theories maintain that we are not bound to the categories in which revelation and dogma were originally expressed, but only to belief in the realities and experiences that underlie those categories and which can be re-expressed in new categories today. But then such writers do not regard the primitive Creeds in the way in which the fathers did, namely, as the highest form of dogmatic truth. On the contrary, they must regard those creeds as the least perfect because the earliest attempt to formulate the mysteries of faith. Tyrrell's second objection is that these theologians:

assume what antiquity never dreamt of, that the realities and experiences which were the subject-matter of the apostolic revelation are still accessible to our investigation, and can serve as the criterion of our dogmatic re-statements, just as the abiding phenomena of Nature can be used to test our scientific re-statements.

And so Tyrrell rejects both major types of such theory found in the Church of his day:

If the conservative idea of merely dialectical development subjects the present to the past to the

[48]Ibid. pp. 8–9.

detriment of all scientific and historical liberty, this (the non-logical theory) subjects the past to the present, to the utter evacuation of the traditional appeal to Scripture and the apostolic age.[49]

Tyrrell reserves his sharpest criticism for the attempt to marry features of both famililes. This produces the worst of both worlds. The concept of an apostolic deposit makes it impossible to integrate faith with modern scholarship. The application of the idea of development to the Gospel reduces Christianity to an aspect of human nature and removes its eschatological character. The combination of the two engenders a conceptual monstrosity.[50]

But having seen off all such theories, at least to his own satisfaction, where is Tyrrell to turn? He wants to maintain two things. Firstly, the absolute, not merely relative, immutability of revelation. Secondly, a concept of dogma which will allow Catholic Christians total liberty as philosophers and historians. In his own words, he wants

> to reconcile perfect fidelity to the ancient principles of Catholic tradition with an equal fidelity to the fullest exigencies of scientific truth and moral truthfulness.[51]

How is this to be achieved? By re-thinking the very ideas of revelation and of dogma. Tyrrell's distinctive concept of *revelation*, comprises four elements. Firstly, revelation in itself contains neither propositions nor concepts but is a 'profound religious experience'. Secondly, the content of this experience is 'a prophetic vision of the Kingdom of God directed to the orientation of the spiritual life'. Thirdly, the language in which revelation is expressed simply 'illustrates' this visionary experience. It provides us with cues or aids with which to grasp it, but is not itself even partially constitutive of revelation. Fourthly, though the prophetic vision of God's Kingdom is non-theoretical, it constitutes a form of truth of

49Ibid. pp. 9–10.
50Ibid. pp. 139–54.
51Ibid. p. 10.

which Tyrrell can say only that it is a 'mysterious truth independent of those other truths used for its illustration'.[52]

But what, on such a view of revelation, could *dogma* be? Dogma simply protects and re-asserts revelation as described above, in no way adding to or developing it. In effect, dogma for Tyrrell is a unique kind of language whose purpose is to preserve the integral memory of the original revelation-experience. In itself dogma makes no truth-claims in the conceptual order, any more than does revelation itself. Truth is involved, but it is an utterly dark truth of which we can only say that it orientates the spiritual life towards the Kingdom of God. As such it is unchanging, not only substantially identical in each generation of the Church's life but absolutely and unconditionally identical. It is because revelation and dogma, thus re-interpreted, make no truth-claims that could possibly conflict with those of either philosophy or history that the denial of doctrinal development 'liberates' theology. Le Roy and Loisy, Blondel and Batiffol may go about their business in peace, without fear of intervention by the guardians of orthodoxy. Only historians of doctrine will suffer as a group within the Church. But their demise will be amply compensated by the emergence of historians of theology as a scientific discipline.

Conclusion

In his rejection of the multiple theories of doctrinal development which had proliferated since the mid-nineteenth century, Tyrrell returned, on one sense, to the view of revelation typified by Jacques-Bénigne Bossuet's affirmation that all innovation in matters of Christian faith is necessarily error. Yet in another sense, this was a *jeu d'esprit*; or, rather, Tyrrell had pared down the objective content of revelation to such a bare point that the assertion of its absolute unchangeability presented no problems in the historical order. The original vision, wherein event and interpretation were inextricably mingled, prompts a variety of interpretations, both as to what actually happened in the career of Jesus (history) and its meaning (philosophy). The rôle of doctrine

[52]Ibid. p. 11.

is to re-present the original vision as a call to *metanoia* while theology is the science that moderates the mutual relations of all these parties.

Tyrrell's denial of genuine doctrinal development belongs with his affirmation of the heterogeneity between theology on the one hand, and revelation and doctrine on the other. Both serve his insistence that Christian revelation is directed not to the mind, but only to the heart or will. At least until his last months, Tyrrell had a quite pellucid grasp of his aims and the means whereby they should be realised. The affective power of Catholic symbolism in texts and ritual must be placed at the service of the only deity likely to be recognised in the cultural space of Late Victorian and Edwardian England: Matthew Arnold's 'Power that makes for Righteousness'.[53] Catholicism thus redefined in the interests of a missionary and pastoral purpose will lose its intellectual scandal while retaining its emotional and thus moral potency. Tyrrell recognised the price that had to be paid: the surrender of the traditional homogeneity of revelation, theology and doctrine.

Yet Tyrrell did not think it especially likely that the Church authorities would accept his new-style defence of Catholicism. He compares the pope and his advisers to 'delirious patients (who) try to strangle those who would serve them'. One does not have to regard every jot and tittle of *Lamentabili* and *Pascendi* as well-chosen to wonder how beneficial such 'service' would prove. For Tyrrell had unravelled the characteristic pattern of Catholic belief. It is because insights gained on the basis of the Church's faith-experience may well be insights into the original revelation itself; can then be articulated theologically; and so find final sanction through the doctrinal authority of the Church's pastors, that the exact opposite of Tyrrell's contention is true. Revelation, theology and doctrine share the same content, though they refract that content in different media.[54] While Tyrrell's fundamental theology is far from making him, as is

[53]See N. Sagovsky, *Between Two Worlds. George Tyrrell's Relationship to the Thought of Matthew Arnold* (Cambridge 1983).

[54]Cf. A. Gardeil, *Le donné révélé et la théologie* (Paris 1909; 1932), p. 358.

sometimes alleged, a prophet of the Second Vatican Council, his account of a Gospel 'au risque de l'interprétation' is certainly reminiscent of the difficulties faced by 'hermeneutical theology' in the post-conciliar epoch.[55] Though I consider Tyrrell to be a poor guide in these realms, I accept that the questions he raised were those of a theological genius. English Catholicism has not produced so many that it can afford to forget this stormy petrel of the Edwardian age.

[55]C. Geffré, *Le Christianisme au risque de l'interprétation* (Paris 1983); for an instance of the difficulties which such an approach can involve, see the convolutions of the concluding section on doctrine in J.-F. Malherbe, *Le Langage théologique à l'âge de la science* (Paris 1985), pp. 246–56. I am grateful to the Editor of *New Blackfriars* for his permission to re-use material originally published in that journal.

5

Maurice Blondel

Blondel was born on 2 November 1861 at Dijon, the son of a notary; his family, on both sides, was long settled in Burgundy, to whose duke his ancestors had been equerries. They were solid Catholics, exemplary in the regular practice of their faith. The young Maurice studied first in the local *lycée*, where his philosophy teacher introduced him to the thought of Maine de Biran, and then at the University of Dijon where he made a special study of Leibniz. By way of complement, he was also a great observer of the countryside, where his family had a summer cottage at Saint-Seine-sur-Vingeanne: his particular interest was insects. In 1881, having passed out of University with flying colours, he was accepted at the prestigious Parisian *Ecole normale supérieure*.

His new situation presented him at once with the question, How could one be simultaneously Catholic and a philosopher? Indeed, it was from the shock of this initial encounter with the confident secularism of the *Ecole* that he drew his vocation to be a Christian philosopher. Hesitating for a moment as to whether he should not become a priest, he chose instead to be a teacher, so as to serve at once the Church and the University. After 'agrégation' in 1886, Blondel taught at various *lycées*, and then in the (Jesuit) Collège Stanislas, while preparing his theses for the doctorate, theses which he finally submitted in 1893. Besides the principal one, the controversial *L'Action*, he also offered a Latin dissertation on Leibniz' *Vinculum substantiae*, a work in whose pages he claimed to have found some of the conceptual nuclei of *L'Action* itself. The central question of *L'Action* was the burning question of traditional philosophy, 'Does life have a meaning, and man a destiny, yes or no?', but Blondel's answer, not a diplomatic one in the context of the time, was that the goal to which these questions led was the acceptance of Catholic practice. In 1894 he married Rose Royer, by whom he had three children. The next year, he was named *maître de conférences* at the faculty of letters in Lille, and some few months later *chargé de cours* at Aix-en-Provence where in 1896 he became professor. He would live at Aix for the rest of his life, though his increasing blindness obliged him to retire from teaching in 1927. He lived in the old Provençal house he had acquired at 15 rue Roux-Alphéran, until his death on 4 June 1949, which that year was the vigil of Pentecost.

After *L'Action*, Blondel felt the need to explain the method he had used in writing his master-work. This he did in the course of 1896, in a series of articles 'Sur les exigences de la pensée contemporaine en matière d'Apologétique'. Published in the *Annales de la philosophie chrétienne*, they are known currently, if not entirely correctly, as the 'Letter on Apologetics' ('Lettre sur l'apologétique'). These articles were somewhat better received by philosophers than by theologians, some of whom began to criticise Blondel in sharp terms. He dealt with some of the misunderstandings in further articles in the *Revue du clergé français*. The Modernist crisis was now in full preparation. Blondel remained cool, and loyal towards the Church. In *La Quinzaine*, in early 1904 he wrote three articles which proposed a solution to the difficulties created by historical scholarship and biblical exegesis: 'History and Dogma'.

Further articles followed, partly in elucidation of the latter, in the *Revue du clergé fran*çais and the *Bulletin de littérature ecclésiastique*, but also by way of developing his thinking on apologetics, something which he did between 1905 and 1907 in the *Annales de philosophie chrétienne*, taking as his lode-star the work of cardinal Deschamps of Malines, one of the fathers of the First Vatican Council. In the same review, an article of 1907 on the notion and rôle of miracles criticised the position of Édouard le Roy on that subject, while the journal also carried in 1908 to 1910 his defence of the 'social Catholics'. Meanwhile, he was taking further his ideas not only on faith (in the *Revue du clergé français* once again) but also his strictly philosophical interests. The latter produced articles on 'the Christianity of Descartes', the 'Idealist illusion' and a 'logic of the moral life', as well as on the 'departure point of philosophical research'. However, the placing on the Index, in 1913, of the issues of the *Annales de philosophie chrétienne* for the years 1905 to 1913, while it chiefly touched the review's secretary, the Oratorian Lucien Laberthonnière, deprived Blondel of one of his main organs of self-expression. Incidentally, pope Pius X had gone out of his way, at the heart of the Modernist crisis, in 1907, to assure Mgr Bonnefoy, the Archbishop of Aix, of his conviction of Blondel's orthodoxy.

In the years of the Great War and afterwards, Blondel took a further look at the philosophical tradition by which he had been nurtured, this in such articles as 'the anti-Cartesianism of Malebranche', 'the Jansenism and anti-Jansenism of Pascal' and, on the fifteenth centenary of the death of the bishop of Hippo, 'Saint Augustine; the original unity and permanent life of his teaching'. In 1923 he paid his debts to an old master in *Léon Ollé-Laprune: L'achèvement et l'avenir de son oeuvre*, as well as describing his own philosophical journey in 'L'itinéraire philosophique de Maurice Blondel', in the form of a conversation with Frédéric Lefèvre of *Nouvelles littéraires*. In the 1920s he interested himself in mysticism, via a debate with Maritain, wrote on the *Action française*, and addressed himself to the topic never far from his mind, the 'problem of Catholic philosophy'. In 1930 he published a French translation, with modifications, of his Latin thesis on Leibniz, and settled down to write his great trilogy. The two volumes of *La Pensée* appeared in 1934, *L'Être et les êtres* in 1935, and the two volumes of a new edition *L'Action* in 1936 and 1937. In 1944 and 1946 he brought out the two first parts of his final masterwork *La Philosophie et l'esprit chrétien*. He died without having completed the third and last section but two preparatory studies were made available posthumously under the title *Exigences philosophiques du Christianisme*, issued in 1950.

Blondel's life was a hard one, owing to the simultaneous but very differently motivated suspicion of philosophers and theologians in his regard; to the early death of his wife; and to the blindness which made his work depend on being read to and dictating. He evolved a routine almost monastic in character, attending Mass almost every day at 6 a.m. in the church of saint Jean-de-Malte at Aix – now the home of a fraternity of 'apostolic monks', an offshoot of the Dominican Province of Toulouse.

Blondel asked that his tomb should carry the words 'professeur de philosophie'. Pierre Gauthier, the student of his concept of tradition and doctrinal development, concluded his sketch of Blondel's life and work:

A fervent Catholic, he was, with equal faithfulness and equal happiness, the disciple of Socrates and of Jesus.[1]

Blondel on Tradition, and the Development of Doctrine

In mid November 1902, Loisy sent a copy of *L'Evangile et l'Eglise* to the young Catholic philosopher who had already made such a name for himself with *L'Action* (1893) and the 'Lettre sur les exigences contemporaines en matiére d'apologétique' (1896). On 5 December, Blondel's erstwhile contemporary at the *Ecole normale supérieure*, the Alsatian abbé Joannes Wehrlé (1865–1938) also wrote to him, precisely on the topic of Loisy's book. Loisy, so Wehrlé assured Blondel

traces with you the programme of the future. The plan of exegetical and theological renovation will be drawn up on the basis of both of your programmes. . . . You can do him much good, and the reading of his book can help you much with your own.[2]

The projected book of Blondel's to which Wehrlé referred

[1] P. Gauthier, *Newman et Blondel. Tradition et développement du dogme* (Paris 1988), p. 22.

[2] H. de Lubac, S.J. (ed.), *Blondel-Wehrlé. Correspondance* (Paris 1969), I., pp. 65–7 (=Letter 25).

was 'Esprit chrétien', a never-finished study for which Blondel
was accumulating materials but which he left aside in 1905.
As a matter of fact, a week or more earlier, Blondel had
already written to Loisy thanking him and giving him his
first impressions. On 10 December, he also wrote to Wehrlé,
confirming the latter's hunch that the two studies shared
points in common.

> Yes, the Church has been *in concreto* what it was
> necessary for her to be afterwards in order to subsist. . . .
> She has developed divinely, without becoming fixed in
> any form, without defining herself in any quintessence.

Blondel then added, however, a major reserve.

> There are moments when he (Loisy), as an historian
> exclusively preoccupied with the milieu and the time, as
> these are registered in the psychology of his personages,
> seems to subject the Christ himself to local and temporal
> contingencies; he declares that a given further
> development was 'foreign to his thought' when it
> sufficed to say that it remained 'foreign to his
> expressions', and such like; for what strikes me is that
> the Saviour, while speaking the language appropriate to
> his contemporaries, always reserves a part for obscurity
> and future suggestions; *non potestis portare modo*.[3]

And Blondel communicated to Wehrlé his anxiety that,
hidden beneath Loisy's work, there lay 'a Christology which
would leave Christ ignorant, as also the Church, of what he
is preparing and of what he will harvest'. Christ's person and
awareness are central to the dignity and greatness of his work;
Loisy, so Blondel already suspected, was in danger of making
Christ, in the words of Pierre Gauthier, 'an actor alien to his
rôle'.[4] For Blondel, by contrast, the Christian life itself was
an experience of the theandric action of the Word incarnate,

[3]Ibid., pp. 68–9 (= Letter 26).
[4]P. Gauthier, *Newman et Blondel*, op. cit., p. 214.

who had spoken by the prophets, was manifested in Christ, who continues his action, and will ever do so while time lasts, by his Spirit in the Church.[5]

Writing on 4 January 1903 to Henri Bremond, Blondel raised the same issue of Christ's awareness, but this time in terms of a philosophical presupposition concealed by a method of practising history.

> To separate systematically the historical viewpoint on the same matter from all that is metaphysical or theological . . . is to attribute a chimerical sufficiency to the *données de fait*, and to imagine that from the facts one may see arise, by an automatic process, the real explanation, the supernatural meaning, if there is one.[6]

Such a method, Blondel contended, could only lead to the suppression of the supernatural, 'the subjecting to the conditions of historical facts of what, by hypothesis, must be transcendent to the series of facts'. Replying to Wehrlé's protests of 6 January, Blondel confessed the legitimacy and importance of the problem Loisy had raised. We have not considered sufficiently the difficulties, both psychological and metaphysical, which the *Deus-homo* raises for minds formed by experimental psychology and scientific history. And in an important passage, which though professedly a discussion of Christology has vital consequences for Blondel's concept of tradition, and hence for his account of doctrinal development, Blondel continued:

> So far as the problem's solution is concerned, you will be in the right, I believe, to accept the idea not of growing perfection or of an *extensive* progress, but of an indefinite penetration and an intensive *accroissement* of the Divinity in the Humanity of Christ. In that,

[5]For a thoughtful account of Blondel's 'magnificent christological sketch', see X. Tilliette, 'Maurice Blondel et la controverse christoloqigue', in D. Dubarle (ed.), *Le Modernisme* (Paris 1980), pp. 129–60.

[6]A. Blanchet (ed.), *Henri Bremond – Maurice Blondel. Correspondance* (Paris 1970–1), I. pp. 451–2 (= Letter 257).

Christ is truly the image and exemplar of each of us,
and of the entire history of the Church. He expresses,
vis-à-vis his Father, the very relation of his mystical
Body *vis-à-vis* his own person, and of the Head in
relation to the members. And, what is much more, if
mobile time imitates immobile eternity, this indefinitely
deepened participation is the essential condition of the
hypostatic union of the finite with the Infinite.[7]

And Blondel proposed to Wehrlé that we should specify the
human characteristics of the knowledge of the Word
Incarnate not by minimising his awareness, but by
maximising it – by finding the 'reverberation' in Jesus' mind
and heart of all human sensibilities. For, through the
Incarnation a bond is forged, not only between the Word
and Jesus' individual humanity but, through him with all
human beings and, most especially, those who will form the
Church. In the service of his divine mission, Christ could,
and should, experience a unique solidarity with all men, and
also a universal 'affection' and awareness.[8] The importance of
this notion of the contents, and outreach, of Christ's
consciousness for the idea of doctrinal development will stand
out more plainly in a succession of later writers, beginning
with Blondel's Jesuit countryman, Pierre Rousselot, for
whom all later dogma is pre-contained in the mind of Christ.

   Writing directly to Loisy on 6 February 1903, Blondel
accepted the justice and fruitfulness of his central thesis – that
the Catholic Church is the legitimate product of the Gospel.[9]
Yet he criticised severely the manner in which that thesis was
put forth. To leave the New Testament witnesses'
understanding of Jesus at the mercy of an evolution whose
motive-force was change coming from without was bad enough
– since it made the original Christian idea of itself

---

[7]H. de Lubac, S.J. (ed.), *Blondel-Wehrlé. Correspondance*, op. cit., I. pp. 92–101 (=
Letter 32).

[8]P. Gauthier, *Newman et Blondel*, op. cit., p. 218.

[9]R. Marlé (ed.), *Au coeur de la Crise moderniste. Le dossier inédit d'une controverse.
Lettres de Maurice Blondel, Henri Bremond, Friedrich von Hügel, Alfred Loisy* (Paris
1960), pp. 72–80.

directionless. But even worse was to neglect the fact that Christ said and did more, and let more be gathered, than his first hearers themselves understood or reported – for this must be so if he is, in the truth, the Word Incarnate. Loisy's method must be, in a kind turn of phrase, 'perfected', since in its present state it leads to denial of Christ's divine consciousness and so to that of his Godhead itself. This correspondence was left suspended, on Loisy's side, but meanwhile Blondel has acquired another interlocutor in the person of von Hügel.

In a letter to von Hügel of 19 February 1903, Blondel offers a preliminary sketch of what will be his considered response to Loisy in the extended essay 'Histoire et dogme'. In the letter, Blondel distinguishes between three stages in the historian's work, stages which correspond to three degrees of understanding and explanation. First, the historical researcher constructs the 'exterior of the facts', by assembling, sorting and criticising materials from the past. This is a strictly sceintific labour, carried out in total independence of spirit. Next, the historian must make these facts live from within, and this resurrection he cannot bring about without allowing the testimonials he has gathered to yield 'an ensemble of life, a definite chain of ideas, a specific form of humanity'. But though the re-creation of this inner unity is much, even it will not suffice. In a third moment, the historian is bound to adopt some philosophical perspective on the unitary figure before him.

> The historian must will-he, nill-he, hang his work on the pegs of metaphysical and religious perspectives ('vues'), because human facts are full of metaphysics. If he does not so do explicitly, and with a critical sense, he will still do it all the same, and in that case he will take greater risks, and act partially, without a sense of measure.[10]

Such an historian will transgress both by separating out 'facts'

[10]Blondel's letter to von Hügel may be found in ibid., pp. 127–38.

from 'ideas', whereas in reality all human facts are soaked in ideas, and also, by, in effect, attempting to explain the facts before him through their empirical entailment by other preceding facts – in short, by opting for an historical determinism which Blondel roundly identifies with the positivist and evolutionistic metaphysic so favoured by the academic establishment of the Third French Republic of his day.[11]

What is needed, and what, in Blondel's eyes, Loisy had signally failed to provide are 'prolegomena to all sacred exegesis', of such a kind that the hypothesis of a special historical revelation is not eliminated in advance by the very manner in which the facts are examined. To Blondel, the very idea of such a special revelation – whose content must inevitably transcend common human perception, or it would not be worth revealing – implies that the earliest witnesses cannot be the only interpreters whose voice is to count. Such a revelation will be assimilated gradually, by an effort which both the 'springs of the intellectual and moral life' and 'the springs of the invisible Spirit' at once sustain. And this means that to interpret Jesus by the touchstone of the most primitive documents is necessarily insufficient, and gravely so.

> . . . Exegesis is nothing without tradition, that tradition which we err in regarding as simply conservative and limiting, since it must also be, and is, conquering, and developing.

To entrust oneself to the mercies of the historical method, as commonly practised, in order to arrive at the true Jesus is

> to fail to recognise the *hapax legomenon* (unique occurrence) of Christianity, and to reduce it to a movement of humanity's religious awareness – one such movement among many. It is to take away the medium for discerning corrupting aberration and lawful

---

[11]For the dominance of 'historicism' in France in this period, see R. Maritain, *Les grandes Amitiés* (Paris 1948), pp. 79–80.

transformations, by substituting the idea of evolution for that of development. Evolution is the result of external pressures; development is continuous creation beginning from a seed which trans-substantiates what it takes in.[12]

The sub-title of *Histoire et dogme* – 'The Philosophical Lacunae of Modern Exegesis' – gives us our cue for evaluating this *philosopher*'s contribution to our topic. Fundamentally, Blondel was concerned with the proper epistemology for a Christian investigation of Christian origins. But in carrying out this exploration of the inter-relation between the believing historian's researches and the Church's dogma, he put forward a concept of tradition which threw light not only on the genesis of dogma, but its subsequent development as well. The basic problem, as Blondel describes it, concerns the apparent, and ominous, gap between 'Christian facts' (history) and 'Christian beliefs' (dogma).[13] On the one hand: the historical data for the origins of the Gospel lie at the foundation of the Catholic faith, but of themselves can neither engender that faith, nor justify it completely. On the other hand: the Catholic faith, and the Church's authority which that faith implies, claim to extract from the facts by doctrinal interpretation an account of what really happened in history, though not one which the secular historian can even conceive, much less declare valid. If we are not to be trapped here within a vicious circle, there must be, in addition to brute facts and dogmatic ideas, 'a principle of explication and of movement' which renders possible this two-fold passage – from the historical data to the faith which exceeds those data, and from the Church's doctrine to an authentic, and wholly objective, Sacred History (the capital letters are Blondel's own), divinely introduced into 'banal history' at its heart.[14]

The first part of *Histoire et dogme* consists in the carefully argued laying aside of two inadequate solutions to this

[12]As above, note 9.

[13]*Histoire et dogme. Les Lacunes philosophiques de l'Exégèse moderne, Extrait de 'La Quinzaine' des 16 Janvier, 1 et 16 Février 1904* (La Chapelle-Montligéon 1904), p. 3.

[14]Ibid., p. 4.

problem. One, characteristic of the rationalising apologetics of the French Catholicism of his period, Blondel labels 'extrinsicism'. The other, which is Loisy's (and, in this period, but to a lesser degree, von Hügel's) he stigmatises as 'historicism'. The typical procedure of extrinsicism is to treat the peculiar historical facts of Christian origins as 'signs for the senses' (*les sens*), and 'proofs for common sense' (*le bon sens*). Here the apologist concentrates his attention on an extrinsic and general feature of the phenomena, namely, their miraculous or supernatural character. The intrinsic content of the facts, their relation to their milieu and to the doctrinal ideas which the Church will find incarnate in them – all of this falls into shadow.

> One fortifies one's position in the building to which history has, apparently, handed over the key. One thanks history for her provisional services. Henceforth, the house belongs to other people, and history is shown the door.[15]

And Blondel finds here a threefold extrinsicism: in the relation of the phenomenal sign to what it signifies; in the connexion of the facts with the dogmatic vision superimposed upon them; and in the link of human thinking, and human living, with the truths thus, apparently, proposed from without.

> The facts, without period, without local colour, disappear, by a kind of perpetual Docetism, into a light deprived of shadows. They are rubbed out by the weight of the Absolute which overwhelms them.[16]

Revelation ceases to be embodied in an authentic humanity, and its exponents must surrender all 'docility to experience' and 'suppleness of interpretation'.

Despite the harshness of his strictures on extrinsicism, Blondel leaves his readers in no doubt that his principal target

[15]Ibid., p. 6.
[16]Ibid., p. 10.

is historicism, 'le but principal de cette étude'. But because historicism is defined, in part, by its opposition to the 'old methods', we must come face to face with the image in order to understand its counter, or inversion. And here the question is:

> What attitude is the pure historian to take up in the presence of the Christian facts? Can he legitimately ignore the apologetic and dogmatic problems? And if he cannot, then what methods and what solutions, for these problems should he make his own?[17]

And, consonant with his attitude in the letter to von Hügel, Blondel insists from the outset that the 'critical spirit' can never be satisfied merely with the study of texts and testimonies. More than this, it must criticise knowledge itself, since the scholar is not the master of his domain except by full awareness of its boundaries, its openings on to other realms, and its indebtedness to other disciplines, and other realities. Blondel brings into play the philosophical acumen which he had already displayed at length in *L'Action*. Real history (that which historiography attempts to describe) is made up of human lives; and a human life is metaphysics in act. The historical phenomena (which provide whatever degree of reality historiography can effectively encapsulate) neither represent action in its wholeness, nor exhaust it. If, then, the historian should abstain in systematic fashion from opening up any dimension beyond that strictly his own, a paradox follows:

> This absolute reserve ends up, without his either wishing it or even knowing it, in a total usurpation: the only effective way of remaining legitimately on one's proper terrain, in such a matter, is to open doors and windows on other horizons than one's own.[18]

[17]Ibid., p. 13.
[18]Ibid., p. 19.

By exchanging scientific history for real history, on the spurious grounds that any account of the past derived in part from methods other than the critical is necessarily 'extra-historical', the historian of Christian origins misconceives three vital relationships: those between the historic Christ and his first witnesses (the main burden of Blondel's correspondence with Wehrlé, Loisy and von Hügel), between the Gospel and the Church (an unmistakable reference to the title of Loisy's first 'little red book'), and between revelation and tradition or (a continuation of the same thing) between the diverse moments of the Church's life. Under other names, Blondel refers here to dogma's genesis, and its subsequent development. Historicism can show the evolution of a series of events, but it can neither reach nor postulate 'an antecedent, concomitant and final cause of which the whole series would be nothing less than *the* organic development'.[19] This 'cause' is, as we shall see, Holy Tradition considered in its divine root, and divine enabling power.

For Blondel's ensuing discussion of how, in the portrayal of the Word Incarnate, Jesus Christ, history and dogma conspire, beyond the limitations both of extrinsicism and of historicism, will lead him on to consider the 'vital rôle and philosophical well-foundedness' of the idea of Tradition. To attain the 'real Christ', have we only the first, halting responses of witnesses, or, can we also draw on the resources provided by the 'total effort of believing generations, . . . all the floods of life and thought from nineteen evangelical centuries'?[20] If the Church at her birth was linked, only to the 'Christ of history' (the Christ who is commensurate with the immediate historical remains) and not to this 'real Christ', then, for Blondel, Christianity can still be described as founded *on* Christ – like a cathedral built on a geological stratum – but not as founded *by* him, for behind the historic facts we do not espy the permanent, substantial working – cosmic, redemptive, creative – of the Word Incarnate in the orders of nature and of grace. Yet

[19]Ibid., p. 22.
[20]Ibid., p. 26.

for us to be able to say that the Church is, not a simple chronological consequence, like many other possible or actual consequences, of the Gospel but its development, we have to confess that the voice which preached the Kingdom of God inserted into the determinism of history a *punctum movens* – a word whose repercussion was rather finely calculated to be the permanent echo of that voice, in a concert of a thousand players.[21]

Of course there is a *de facto* succession and continuity linking the Christian of the past with his co-religionist of the present. What Loisy thus presents as an answer to Harnack is merely an uninstructive truism. But is there also an *intelligible* continuity linking the various epochs of the Church's life, from genesis to contemporary maturity? And, more important still, are we dealing here with

the spiritual unity and organic continuity of one self-identical thought and life, which would make of the Church, as it were, one single immortal being?[22]

For this last to be the case, there must be, at the heart of the historic facts that which is itself not simply a fact but a *power* capable of directing the nascent Church, and mastering the elements of her environment on the Gospel's behalf, thus rendering the history of doctrine not merely an evolution, utterly beholden to external pressure and circumstance, but the development of what was originally given. And Blondel finds convincing evidence for the latter thesis in the way in which the doctrinal fragments of both New Testament and early patristic theologies so quickly constituted themselves into a 'speculative and practical system, vaster, more supple, more truly one than any system can be'.[23] Not only did the dogmatic teachings of the Church of the patristic golden age cohere, though drawn from diverse sources. They also coincided with the gospel narratives to the point of filling the

[21]Ibid., p. 33.
[22]Ibid., p. 38.
[23]Ibid., p. 35.

tiniest details of the life of Christ with a 'theology ever in act', as indeed they answered to the needs of the human condition, renewing man's interior being by the beneficent effect of the practices they suggested, such that, finally, dogmas, the story of Christ, and human living all formed one indivisible whole.

What we need, to lead us through the maze of problems wherein extrinsicism and historicism are but culs-de-sac, is an intermediary between history and dogma, a factor which can synthesise them and maintain their solidarity without, however, compromising the relative autonomy of each. Only a principle distinct at once from the historian's facts and the dogmatician's formulae can re-connect them, bring them into accord, fashion them into organic unity. And this is Tradition.

The idea of Tradition, for Blondel, is not simply the commonplace one of a transmission, chiefly oral, of facts, teachings, practices and customs. Should Tradition be considered as simply making good the deficiencies of the biblical texts, an oral supplement motivated, it may be, by 'a need for esotericism or some discipline of the secret', its authority and utility would be little enough today. And here Blondel mentions a number of factors that can only weaken our confidence in Tradition: the long interval that now distances us from Christian origins; the deceitfulness of folk memory, the growing effort of mankind to confide every informational detail and nuance of thought to paper, the *déracinement* of modern life which has undermined a sense for continuity, and so forth. It is true that, in theological discourse, 'Tradition' has a special sense – it is the oral revelation as echoed in the New Testament and the Fathers. Yet it seems that it can give us nothing which has not been consigned to written form, or could be so confided.

The Church, by contrast, testifies to a 'permanent and always equal confidence' in Tradition's power. The Tradition recognised by the Church preserves not only the past's intellectual aspect, but its 'vital reality'.[24] It finds its foundation not in texts alone but also in an ever actual

[24]Ibid., p. 50.

experience which allows it to be, in certain respects, the mistress of the texts rather than their servitor. And in each crisis of growth that punctuates Christian history, Tradition brings to the Church's awareness elements hitherto 'retained', simply, in the depths of faith and practice rather than expressed or reflected upon. And Blondel speaks of Tradition, accordingly, as

> this conserving power (which) is at the same time conquering, which discovers and formulates truths that the past has lived out without having being able to enunciate them or define them explicitly. (It) enriches the intellectual patrimony by converting the total deposit little by little into coin ('monnayant') and making it bring forth fruit.[25]

Turned 'lovingly' towards the past and its treasure Tradition moves forward into the future whence shines its 'light'. (Blondel's metaphor of the 'coining' of the deposit, and his suggestion – scarcely more than a hint thrown out *en passant* – that Tradition's understanding of its primordial Object includes, importantly, the element of 'amour', *love*, will re-appear, as we shall see, in both Rousselot and his younger confrère, Henri de Lubac.) Tradition, Blondel continues, not only preserves: it also initiates, yet does not, for all that, innovate. For even that which it discovers it is aware of re-finding in fidelity. Possessing 'its God and its all (*son tout*)' Tradition lacks nothing; yet it never ceases to teach us newly, by transforming what was lived implicitly into what is explicitly known. In this process, the labour involved is divided between the members of Christ's body. The saint perpetuates Jesus among us; the scholar has recourse to the sources; the philosopher acts as mid-wife to the 'Spirit of novelty', and anyone who lives and thinks in a Christian fashion makes some contribution of his or her own. But all this diffused effort is directed by the Head of the Body who, in his divinely assisted consciousness, harmonises and stimulates its progress.[26]

[25]Ibid.
[26]Ibid., p. 51.

Paradoxical as the statement may seem, Tradition, then, anticipates the future, illuminating it by the very effort it makes to be faithful to the past. Tradition is the guardian of the initial deposit, in so far as the latter has not been entirely formulated or expressly understood, though it is, to be sure, always 'fully possessed and employed'.[27]

From his concept of Tradition, Blondel draws the corollary that the Church 'is herself a proof', *index sui*. In her age-long experience and constant practice she carries with her through history a verification of what she believes and teaches. To move from the facts to the ideas, from history to dogma, the exact analysis of texts and the effort of individual thinking will not suffice. It is also necessary to have.

> the mediation of the collective life, and the slow, progressive labour, of Christian tradition ... the accumulated experiences of faithful action.[28]

Tradition, so understood, is not a 'let-out': when she appears before the bar of philosophical reason, she does not come empty-handed. Tradition, for Blondel, obeys reasonable, even rational, procedures, and her laws and logic can be established – at least, in terms of the philosophy of *L'Action*.[29] To guard the Word of God, the apostolic deposit, is, first and foremost, to *practise* it.

> Faithful action is the ark of the covenant where abide the confidences of God, the tabernacle where he perpetuates his presence and his teachings.[30]

Through Tradition, we ascend into the light of intelligibility

[27] Ibid.

[28] Ibid., pp. 52–3.

[29] 'He managed to exploit the occasion of the Modernist crisis, and to get beyond the obstacles it posed for him by the way in which he developed the inherent logic of the philosophy of *L'Action*': thus R. Virgoulay, *Blondel et le Modernisme* (Paris 1974), p. 15.

[30] *Histoire et dogme*, p. 57.

by way of a practical verification of speculative truths. And in this perspective, it is not the idea of development which is heterodox, but that of 'fixisme' which is, at any rate, a virtual heresy. To reach Christ and justify the dogmas (these two aims are, in Blondel's mind, inseparable), can only be done by

> throwing back on their source all the rays of light spread abroad in Christian awareness in the course of the centuries, (by) imitating through an indefinite progress the infinite richness of the God who is revealed and always hidden, hidden and ever revealed.[31]

The dogmatic definitions arise out of history *mediante praxi fidelium et traditione Ecclesiae* – 'through the mediation of the practice of the faithful and the Tradition of the Church'. That Church is not 'the guardian of a museum or an archive', 'the janissary of a seraglio'. Rather does she have the 'dignity and authority of a bride'.[32]

Tradition, then, for Blondel, is 'a particular and privileged case of action'.[33] The philosopher of Aix will remain faithful to the solution offered by *Histoire et dogme* for the rest of his life. In *Les Exigences philosophiques de christianisme*, he will describe the 'coincidence of historical reality and dogmatic truth' as the 'proper, and truly unique mark of Christianity'.[34] Inasmuch as they are singular, personal, and to all intents and purposes contingent, the facts on which Christianity is based belong to the positive order – humble events intermingled with the general texture of this passing world. Yet the selfsame facts serve also as the support for, or even the substance of, 'divine interventions', 'causes whose agency is supernatural and everlasting'.[35] Tradition is 'the voice of

[31]Ibid., p. 59.
[32]Ibid., p. 64.
[33]P. Gauthier, *Blondel et Newman*, op. cit., p. 301.
[34]In the long essay 'Le sens chrétien', which constitutes the first part of *Les Exigences philosophiques du christianisme* (Paris 1950), and here at p. 9.
[35]Ibid., pp. 9–10.

eternity in time';[36] it is the 'coining of eternity ... in expectation of being placed in possession of the treasure in its integrity'.[37]

In this apologia, however, Blondel had noted the anxieties of some that his theory of action was too *insouciant* towards the judgement, the proposition, the conceptual truth.[38] We must turn now to consider the contribution of those theologians working in the Scholastic tradition whom Blondel had in mind. We shall discover that Blondel's acute sense for tradition and its media, and for the Church's consciousness as itself a theological organ, will not prove alien to all the writers of the Neo-Scholastic revival – though it is only when we reach De Lubac, and the posthumous *oeuvre* of Rousselot, published under De Lubac's auspices, that the Blondelian stream, whose source was lay philosophy, enters at last the great river of theological culture, with life-giving consequences for the problem of dogmatic development.

[36]Ibid., p. 31.
[37]*La Philosophie et l'esprit chrétien* II (Paris 1946), p. 81.
[38]*Histoire et dogme*, op. cit., pp. 59–62.

6

Ambroise Gardeil

Ambroise Gardeil was born at Nancy in Lorraine in 1859. In one sense, he lived an uneventful life.[1] He entered the Dominican Order as a young man, in 1878, and remained in it, first as a student, then as a teacher, of Catholic philosophy and theology until his death in Paris in 1931. However, thanks to the anti-clericalism of successive French governments under the Third Republic, his life was a little less dull than it might have been otherwise. The French government suppressed the Dominican Order on French soil twice during Gardeil's lifetime. The first occasion when this happened, in 1880, led to his travelling half way round Europe, as the 'studium' (study-house) of the Dominican Province of France was transferred first to Spain, then to Austria and finally to Corsica. The second suppression took place in 1903 when the studium was moved to Belgium, to the famous Le Saulchoir de Kain where it would remain until 1938, after Gardeil's death. Yet his work shows no sign of these turbulent events, maintaining a serenity of tone throughout. He was evidently one of those people whose inner life flows on untroubled even with bombs dropping around them, like the English lady whose only concession to the Second World War was a daily prayer for 'that poor misguided Mr Hitler'.

Even when a student friar, as investigation of his extant letters shows, Gardeil's overriding concern was the

[1] For his life, a brief biography appears in the *Bulletin Thomiste* 1/3 (1931), pp. 5–10. A complete bibliography of his writings accompanied it, under the heading 'Notes et communications de la Bulletin Thomiste' at pp. 79*–92*. An interpretation of his theological work as a whole was offered by H.-D. Gardeil, O.P., *L'Oeuvre théologique du Père Ambroise Gardeil* (Etiolles-Paris 1956).

reconciliation, of *la science*, scientific scholarship, with *la religion*.[2] In 1893, he played a major part in the founding of the *Revue Thomiste* whose opening number gave as the journal's aim:

> to shed light on, most especially, the problems of the present moment though the teaching of St Thomas Aquinas . . . to use the doctrine, principles and method of the greatest of Catholic theologians in order to gain for, or preserve in, the faith and Church of Christ, the most brilliant spirits of our time.[3]

Gardeil's own interests were, to begin with, predominantly philosophical and within philosophy as a whole, found their focus in the theory of knowledge, epistemology. In his early articles, written just before and after 1900, Gardeil's aim was to defend, and re-pristinate, Thomism in relation, first and foremost, to Kant's critiques, but also with an eye on the voluntarist and pragmatist tendencies of the latest philosophy of the day. For these tendencies Gardeil coined the term 'Neo-Scotism'.[4] Like Scotus, these new philosophers – whose effect on Tyrrell we have already noted – stressed the rôle of the will, rather than the intellect, in encounter with reality. Gardeil did not, however, launch a crusade against Kant or the Neo-Scotists of whom Blondel was the most important Catholic representative. Instead, he tried to find out what exactly was both right and wrong with these philosophies.

What was right with Kant was his notion that the act of knowledge is immanent in the human mind, closer to us than is the world of objects. What was wrong with Kant was his failure to notice that on to the 'fundamental being', in Gardeil's words, of the immanent act of knowledge there is 'engrafted' a 'representative quality'. This quality follows from mind's tending towards the reality beyond itself, a tending of such a sort that every act of knowledge, no matter how immanent, how enclosed within us, bears a

[2]Ibid., pp. 22–3.
[3]'Notre Programme', *Revue Thomiste* 1 (1893), p. 7.
[4]A. Gardeil, 'Ce qu'il y a de vrai dans le néo-scotisme', *Revue Thomiste* 9 (1901).

representative value – as indeed human consciousness everywhere claims.[5]

What was right with the Neo-Scotists was their realisation that the dynamic structure of our will calls out for God as our ultimate end. What was wrong with the Neo-Scotists was their failure to grasp that mind is itself a living appetite destined to perceive being, to drink in reality. Our intellect has a 'vital ordering to being'.[6] These philosophical motifs will be taken up some years later in the course of Gardeil's response to the Modernist view of doctrinal development.

In 1904 Gardeil was already well aware of the challenge posed by Loisy. In an article in the *Revue Thomiste* for that year, he argued that there must be a middle way between Loisy's absolute relativism, where the content of the original revelation simply dissolves in the flux of history, leaving its trace only in the impressionistic shape of an ideal, spirit or hope, and the equally absolute dogmatism feared by Loisy, for which immutability attaches not just to the object of revealed knowledge but also to the form which that knowledge has taken in history.[7] In other words, in some manner yet to be identified, the formulae in which revelation is expressed must be both absolute and relative in character.

Gardeil was not really stirred to offer a full response to Modernism, however, until 1907 when the *Revue pratique d'apologétique* published Tyrrell's essay 'Théologisme'. Here Tyrrell proposed that theology must be re-defined as the 'fruit of a philosophical reflection on the realities of religious experience' – a religious experience of which the apostolic revelation is 'the centre and the norm'. For reasons we have already identified in relation to Tyrrell, the Jesuit writer insisted that theology must be unconditionally free to transform itself in the light of wider experience and broader reflection. Theology never reaches *permanently* valid conclusions. Gardeil reacted in the conclusion

[5]Idem., 'Devons nous traverser Kant?', *Revue Thomist* 5 (1897).

[6]Here Gardeil leaned heavily on Thomas Aquinas, *Summa Theologiae* Ia. IIae., q. I. A good summary of Gardeil's ideas on epistemology is found in H. D. Gardeil, *L'Oeuvre théologique du Père Ambroise Gardeil*, op. cit., pp. 55–9.

[7]A. Gardeil, 'La Relativité des formules dogmatiques', *Revue Thomiste* 12 (1904), pp. 48–76.

of a substantial article on the idea of a *locus theologicus*. Here, anticipating the argument of his later full-length treatment, *Le Donné révéle et la théologie*, Gardeil maintained that there is

> a conceptual homogenity which extends from the first inspired experience of revealed truth in the mind of the prophet to the revealed *donné* itself; and from the revealed *donné* to the dogma; then from the dogma to the immediate principles of theology, and from these immediate principles to theological conclusions.[8]

In the light of this homogeneity between the different stages of revelation and its prolongation in the Church in the form of dogma and theology, Gardeil regarded Scholastic theology as 'not a vain work, but a lawful promotion of revelation'. But he admitted that this claim was rather the programme for a book as yet unwritten than something self-evidently true in its own right. As he then just finishing the manuscript of his first major study, *La Credibilité et l'apologétique*, the time to expand this thesis had not yet come.

In 1908 Gardeil published that first book, *La Credibilité et l'apologétique*, a work which has some relevance to our theme.[9] Here Gardeil argued that, when assessing Christian origins, whereas in principle it should be possible to demonstate in rigorous fashion the divine origin of Christian revelation, in practice it may be that no more than a 'probable certitude' can be attained. That Jesus of Nazareth was truly God's legate or envoy, and that he founded a Church to teach in his name in a divinely guided way: these truths are sufficiently established if they can be shown to be probable. Basing this assertion on Aristotle's logical treatise the *Topics*, Gardeil insisted that *le vraisemblable*, 'the probable', is not *le douteux*, 'the doubtful' but that which is *semblable au vrai*, 'like the truth', since it resembles or approximates to truth. Furthermore, if a person who has carefully considered all the evidence for the divine origin of Christian revelation still has

[8]Idem., 'La Notion du lieu théologique', *Revue des Sciences Philosophiques et Théologiques* 2 (1908).

[9]Idem., *La Credibilité et l'apologétique* (Paris 1908).

difficulty in regarding that evidence as sufficiently convincing on the rational level, God will provide him or her with 'une suppléance morale ou mystique', an aid to discernment, which may be thought of as either moral or mystical in character: a purification, or illumination, of the mind's eye which will let the reason reach certitude enough to accept the fact of divine revelation. And yet, Gardeil continues, such a rational judgement of credibility, even when helped out by divine grace, remains just a natural judgement, a judgement of human prudence, like the many practical judgements we make about things or people before embarking on some course of action in their regard. For someone really to make the choice of divine faith, assenting to the content of revelation as the very word of God himself, he or she must make a *super*natural judgement. In such supernatural judgement, Gardeil explains, one gives credence to the claims of Christ and his Church on the ground of the Truth of God himself, who can neither deceive nor be deceived, and not on the ground of any natural arguments of a (predominantly) historical kind. Gardeil held that this second, supernatural, judgement of faith is quite independent of the natural prudential judgement about the rational credibility of the claims of revelation.[10] In this he announces what will be a major theme of his book on dogma and theology. The *content* of the revealed given which theology studies cannot be adequately *described* in a natural way – using, for example, the historical method – however much we may assert that the *fact* of a divine revelation can be *argued for* by such natural, and chiefly historical, means.

Some few months after the appearance of *La Credibilité et l'apologétique* the Institut Catholique invited Gardeil to give a lecture course in Paris on the nature of dogma. Held during

[10]Gardeil held, nevertheless, to the importance for the corporate faith of the Church of a speculative demonstration of credibility. Here his thought is at odds with that of P. Rousselot, in whose 'Les Yeux de la foi', *Recherches de Science religieuse* 1 (1910), pp. 241–59; 444–75, there is no truly distinct judgement of credibility: to perceive the credibility of revelation and to confess the faith are the same thing. Faith, on this account, is only reasonable when supernatural, and the preparatory phase of the *preambula fidei* is effectively suppressed.

the winter of 1908–9, the material was published in 1910 under the title *Le Donné révélé et la théologie*.[11] Despite its considerable merit, the book did not achieve a wide currency, but in 1932, the year after Gardeil's death, Père Marie-Dominique Chenu had it re-published as part of his own programme for theological renewal, adding a preface by himself. In his preface, Chenu remarks that Gardeil's work failed to make much impact since, at a time of polemics, he was not a polemicist. He belonged to the company of those who do not 'content themselves with unilateral replies and *simpliste* condemnations'. Hence his book has that 'spiritual equilibrium which is one of the assured signs of *la science*'. Chenu's comments echo Gardeil's own statement that he did not write so as to refute Modernism but so as to replace it.

The aim of the book is virtually identical with Tyrrell's in *Through Scylla and Charybdis*: to work out the inter-relations of revelation, dogma and theology. In the introduction, Gardeil states his programme. Theology is an intrinsically supernatural science whose conclusions are homogeneous with revelation, that is, with *le donné révélé*. The substance of revelation is to be found in the theological 'organism', but it exists there not in its original condition but transformed or, in his own term, 'transfused'.[12]

Owing to theology's homogeneity with revelation, it has two outstanding characteristics. First, it is transcendent, or autonomous, with respect to those human sciences that concern themselves with the revealed given from special viewpoints all their own – such human sciences as history, religious sociology, or the historical-critical method in textual analysis. Secondly, theology is internally related to the Christian life or existence which revelation has brought into being. Theology is capable, therefore, not only of nourishing and defending faith but also of engendering and enriching charity, and so is concerned with the whole of Christian living. It is, we may say, supernatural both in its subject-matter and in its effects.

[11] A. Gardeil, *Le Donné révélé et la théologie* (Paris 1910).

[12] Ibid., p. xx. Tyrrell's 'Théologisme', to which the book was, like the article of 1908 mentioned in note 8, above, a reply had appeared in the *Revue Pratique d'Apologétique* 4 (1907), pp. 499–526.

In order to commend this picture of theology we must, so Gardeil holds, reach a deeper understanding of the notion of dogma. Before showing how theology finds in the revealed given its specifying principle, we need to see how that given enjoys its own full value in the developed assertions of dogma which are theology's own immediate departure-point.

Gardeil's own starting-point in the body of his book is, however, a philosophical account of the nature of affirmation. *Prima facie* curious, the reason for this is really very simple. Though divine in its source, the revealed given takes the human form of affirmation. This it does when it is expressed in the thinking and language of those who receive revelation and pass it on to others. In this loving-kindness, God has 'condescended', stooped down to, us and our level. In revealing himself he has subjected his own action to the laws of our mental structure. But if revealed truth is to preserve its own identity in entering human minds, then its vehicle in those minds, namely, our capacity to affirm, must be adequate to the task in hand. We must be capable of what Gardeil calls 'absolute' affirmations: affirmations with an unconditional value as descriptions of reality. In his eyes, it was because the Modernists abandoned belief in the absolute character of human affirmation that they also lost their faith in the possibility that a substantially identical meaning might persist throughout the history of revealed truth from the apostles to ourselves.

How, then, can we show that absolute affirmation is possible? Gardeil claims to do so through reflection on two points. In the first place, all human beings make affirmations, yet this universal fact cannot be explained unless there is reality in some absolute sense, the reality of *being*. Here we see the influence, and can begin to chart the pertinence, of Gardeil's philosophical Thomism. Modern philosophy, he remarks, often caricatures the Scholastics by claiming that for them being was alien to thinking, a 'something' almost spatially distinct from the living thought of mind. (It is the Idealist tradition, stemming from the problems left to European philosophy by Kant, to which he is mainly addressing himself at this point.) Gardeil replies that, on the contrary, being is intimately present to thought as the condition of all affirmation. Being is 'something which is at home in us', *une chose qui a son chez soi chez nous*.[13] Being is objective reality become one body with spirit. It is reality itself, reflected in our idea of being. And the human activity of affirming manifests this intimate link. So Gardeil modifies Descartes' *cogito* which, at his hands, becomes rather different: *je pense, donc l'être est*, 'I think, so being is'. Now being as being includes all the possible modalities of existence for everything that is. But since the human mind is in possession of the crucial idea of being – an idea which successfully expresses the mind's own object, namely, reality, then in principle, the mind may discover being wherever it appears. Thus we find ourselves affirming: 'This flower is white'; 'man is a reasoning animal'; 'no effect is without its cause'.

Here Gardeil moves on to the second main philosophical consideration he wants us to attend to. In the concrete, our affirmations take the form of an attempt to re-constitute the objects of our sensuous intuitions in terms of that primordial reality which is being. To the extent that these affirmations succeed, we can speak of an absolute quality attaching to them, and to the truths which they set forth. But just how much success can we hope to have in conjoining the 'absolute' of being with the contingent data of our own limited and sense-bound understanding? Perhaps our particular affirmations only have a *portée relative*, a 'relevance' to us in terms of practical usefulness for our purposes in moving about the world, or by virtue of their ability to satisfy the needs of incarnate spirits such as men are. In other words, perhaps we must evaluate these affirmations in a Neo-Scotist sense which could, then, open the way to a Loisyesque or Tyrrellian relativism where religious truth is concerned.

Gardeil offers three reasons to back up his conviction that our concrete affirmations actually attain reality. First, he points to the human instinct not to rest until we have got hold of 'what is the case' in some matter. Secondly, there is the fact that our intuitive powers are only actualised through

---

[13]*Le Donné révélé et la théologie*, op. cit., p. 6.

being receptive to a reality other than themselves. It is only when we are affected that we go into action as knowing agents. We must be affected to become effective. Thirdly, Gardeil suggests that everywhere around us in the human world we find operating a *sens commun*, a 'common sense', whose spontaneous product is an almost identical series of affirmations uniting a tremendous variety of human beings on questions touching the objects of intuition, their definition, existence and chief properties. The existence of a general consensus about a vast number of objects of concrete intuition, ranging from ink-bottles through Italians to iguanas, is evidence supporting a positive or optimistic assessment of the validity of concrete intuition and the particular affirmations to which it leads.

Having thus established, at least to his own satisfaction, the possibility of absolutely valid affirmations, Gardeil turns to consider what the revealed given actually is. He offers us, that is, an account of revelation. Revelation happens when God, utilising a special charism, takes hold of the capacity for absolute affirmation possessed by the human being he has chosen as a privileged recipient of divine truth. The person so graced, whom Gardeil, following the mediaeval doctors, calls a 'prophet', by responsiveness to this charism, can express in human ideas, and so in language, the truths which God, at a given point in the process of salvation history, wishes to convey for man's salvation. The resultant revealed datum is itself 'absolute', that is, 'historical-change-defying', and that in two ways – as human affirmation and as divinely guaranteed truth. Therefore it can be transmitted without substantial change to all future generations of the Church.

In his account of revelation, Gardeil tries to avoid both the Modernist account of that subject, and what the Modernists took to be the traditional account which they were rejecting. The Modernists – and here Gardeil has Tyrrell especially in view – regarded revelation as an experience which arouses man's religious sensibility. In this experience, God becomes mysteriously known to men, but the primitive formulae in which the experience finds expression are not his work but theirs. In a confused fashion, those formulae articulate the orientation of the soul to God which follows on the revelatory experience, but they lack all absolute value as expressions of the divine reality. The Modernists defined their view over against the backdrop of what they considered to be the traditional position. In that position, revelation was understood anthropomorphically: God *speaks*, that is, he holds a conversation with men. Gardeil has little difficulty in showing that classical Latin theology, as found in St Thomas, was much more sophisticated than this. It saw revelation as, fundamentally, an interior prophetic inspiration – and so not a literal conversation at all.

But how does such inner prophetic inspiration differ from the Modernist definition of revelation in terms of religious experience? Gardeil agrees that there must surely be, in revelation, religious experience. What makes such experience truly revelation, however, is a factor neglected by the Modernists: namely, its 'guaranteed normative bearing'. By this he means that experience's divinely guaranteed value for all future ages of the Church. The purpose of the manifestation of God's Spirit in revelation is 'l'utilité générale', 'general usefulness', and this means that God must communicate here an object valid for everyone, and crystallised with sufficient clarity to allow of 'une participation socialisée', a 'sharing of a social kind'. And this in turn implies that God's revelatory action must come to light above all in our faculty for making absolute, universally valid, affirmations about the real. So revelation leaves mankind in possession of *a determinate truth which is indefinitely transmissible*. For this to happen, the charism of revelation must cover not only the genesis but also the articulation of revealed truth. The divine light continues to operate until such time as the receiver of revelation has found an appropriate form in which to communicate his judgement about divine things.

With these foundations laid, Gardeil can move on to consider the substantial homogeneity of revealed truth as its affirmations pass through a variety of historical forms. He turns first to the topic of *dogma*. The theologian – and here Gardeil has in mind the theologian in the Catholic schools of his own period – is not in immediate contact with the revealed given as this issues from God's revelatory action. Rather is he in immediate contact with dogma, that is, with the authorised public affirmation of the revealed given found in the Church's tradition. Unfortunately, there is a widespread feeling, reports Gardeil, that when revelation is thus formulated in a dogmatic shape, in a form that is sometimes technical and always indebted to the ideas of a particular age, it becomes no more than a poor substitute for the original word of God.

According to the Modernists – and here again Tyrrell's position is taken as typical – dogma, when traditionally conceived, is a monstrous hybrid, or, at any rate, a confused mixture, the result of an unhappy marriage between the idea of revelation with the idea of theology. For such writers, the attempt to define the revealed given presupposes that revelation is a series of propositions to whose terms systematic meanings can be assigned. But that is not revelation: it is theology. The union of the two chills the life of the soul and renders revelation itself the harder to defend in intellectual terms. Along with revelation, the would-be apologist must defend all the conceptual impedimenta which dogmatic definition draws in its train. The Modernist remedy is simple but drastic: it is to present Christian doctrine as the symbolic envelope of revelation, revelation's vehicle for moving across the sands of time – and so as no more substantially homogeneous with revelation's content than is an Arab with his camel, or a Rommel with his jeep.

To Gardeil's eyes, the customary orthodox response to the Modernist challenge was insufficient. Here he seems to have had in mind the restatement of the idea of Catholic theology found in Christian Scholasticism offered by his fellow–Dominican Réginald Garrigou-Lagrange in *Le Sens commun, la philosophie de l'être et les formules dogmatiques*, which had just appeared.[14] Garrigou-Lagrange held that, in between the

---

[14]R. Garrigou-Lagrange, O.P., *Le Sens commun, la philosophie de l'être et les formules dogmatiques* (Paris 1909). For an evaluation of this work see A. Lobato, O. P., 'Itinerario filosófico de R. Garrigou-Lagrange, O. P.', in *Reginaldi Garrigou-Lagrange, In Memoriam* [= *Angelicum* xvii, 1965, 1–2], p. 83. Garrigou, the outstanding Neo-

technical meaning attached to doctrinal terms by the Church and the purely symbolic interpretation of them by the Modernists there lay a *via media* which Neo-Scholasticism, with its philosophy of being and its realist epistemology, was well placed to explore. The intelligence of human beings at large finds expression, so Garrigou-Lagrange explained, in what a long-standing tradition, later to be charted by the father of German-language hermeneutical philosophy Hans-Georg Gadamer,[15] called the *sensus communis*. 'Common sense' can produce formulae which, whilst not bound to any single philosophy or theology, are instruments of settled truth, and not mere records of 'floating experiences or apocalyptic visions'. According to Garrigou-Lagrange, it is thanks to *le sens commun* that we may rest assured of the substantial homogeneity of dogmatic expressions when compared with the original revelatory moment. For, through his 'common sense', man's intellectual life forms a continuous sequence, such that anyone in any age may interpret dogmatic language aright and find the single revealed truth in its historically differentiated dogmatic forms.

Gardeil, though he shared much of Garrigou's approach, was by no means altogether convinced by this analysis. First, he points out that, historically, it cannot plausibly be denied that certain dogmatic definitions include terms not just in their *sensus communis* but precisely as technical terms adopted for their particular conceptual merits in some debate about doctrine. Only so may we explain the adoption of the term *homoousios* at Nicaea, or the teaching of Vienne on the soul as *per se forma corporis*. Secondly, Gardeil questioned whether the *sensus communis*, although a sufficient guide in those things required for human living at large, could be regarded as an adequate mentor in the understanding of doctrinal definitions. It stopped short, he believed, at a quite

---

Scholastic theologian of his generation, was interested in Modernism 'only in its metaphysical aspect': so M. R. Gagnebet, 'L'oeuvre du P. Garrigou-Lagrange', ibid., p. 15, and, accordingly, had little to contribute to our theme. For his characteristic approach, one might consult idem., 'L'immutabilité du dogme selon le Concile du Vatican, et le relativisme', *Angelicum* xxvi (1949), pp. 309–322; 'Le relativisme et l'immutabilité du dogme', ibid. xxvii (1950), pp. 219–246.

[15]H.-G. Gadamer, *Truth and Method* (ET London 1975, 1979²), pp. 19–28.

rudimentary level of understanding, suitable for *la catechèse des simples* but not for the questions posed by more mature or sophisticated minds.[16] Gardeil suggested a somewhat different scheme. Appealing to a musical metaphor, that of the Church organ, he proposed that human affirmation, including dogmatic affirmation, has three 'manuals' on which to play.

The first of these manuals consists of the deliverances, *données*, of experiential common sense. The second is constituted by general notions arising spontaneously out of these original deliverances. The third is made up of general concepts – the shift of terminology is meant to indicate the more elaborated character of the ideas belonging to this manual – produced by reflecting on and analysing the general notions generated by the *sensus communis*. All three manuals, so Gardeil held, can be used by the mind in its affirmations about the real. And furthermore, those Spirit-assisted men who make up the teaching Church from age to age did in point of fact use them all so as to define what is given to us by revelation concerning the divine reality.

This plan allows Gardeil to agree that dogmatic definitions do at times contain strictly technical terms, and require greater virtuosity of understanding than the *sensus communis* by itself permits. But at the same time, he can also assert that, nonetheless, all the terms used in dogmatic definition derive from 'common sense'. Gardeil offers examples of 'play' on each manual. When the Apostles' Creed declares that Christ 'suffered under Pontius Pilate' it is using the first manual: it is registering a fact in the pure language of the common sense. Again, when that Creed says that Christ 'descended into hell', we are dealing with what is evidently a general notion expressed through a metaphor: the general notion being that of the *universality* of Christ's redeeming work, which extends even to the dead. Finally, and this is the most difficult case, when the Church, in her dogmatic definitions, uses such terms as 'person', 'substance', 'nature', 'consubstantiality', 'transubstantiation', these are, for Gardeil, general concepts produced by reflective analysis of the notions spontaneously

---

[16]*Le Donné révélé et la théologie*, op. cit., p. 93.

arising from the *sensus communis*. In other words, here, on this third manual, we are dealing with ideas so well-founded on the universal *sensus communis* of the human race that, despite the mediateness of their derivation from that sense, they may be recognised as categories expressive of differentiations in being itself. Whilst some particular historic philosophy, such as Aristoteleanism, may, as a matter of fact, be responsible for the clear and argued articulation of these terms, they do not in themselves depend on any such philosophy. They are, rather, terms which any ontological analysis, in whatever idiom, could be expected to come up with. Thus a philosophical idea is only embodied in a dogma in so far as it can serve to identify the divine reality intended by the definition. We do not invite people to a double conversion: first to Scholasticism, and then to Catholicism. The technical philosophical element in dogma can be shown to be simply a reflective expression of the intellectual *sensus communis*.

Gardeil goes on to look at two problems which are highly pertinent to any discussion of the concept of authoritative Christian doctrine. The first, which need not long detain us here, is the idea of analogy. How can human language be applied to God? Holding fast the formulae of the revealed given, we relate them to the naturally intelligible meanings found in the world around us, thus operating with terms which can only be highly imperfect as an expression of God's self-communication yet, by being used, extend our understanding of him. The concept of analogy, which Gardeil takes as the key to unlock this problem, is a familiar feature of the theological universe. More germane to our purposes is the second difficulty Gardeil identifies. For this is, quite explicitly, the problem of doctrinal development itself.

Gardeil opens by conceding to the radicals that doctrinal development is not just a matter of evolution in terminology. In some sense – just *which* sense remains to be established – the content, not simply the expression, is new. Now theology, by treating dogmatic developments as an honoured part of its own primary materials, presupposes their homogeneity with revealed truth. But this is precisely what some people are questioning. Gardeil formulates the problem in the following way. Divine revelation, in the later history of the Church, appears in the guise of doctrinal statements whose form differs markedly from that of the originating moment of Christianity. This being so, how may we explain the fact that these later doctrinal affirmations are not only sanctioned by the Church but even imposed by her on Christ's faithful as the authentic – that is, authoritative – expression of revelation?

What we should look for is a theory which allows for genuine development in doctrine yet respects the substantial homogeneity of revealed truth. Gardeil considers that the various theories on offer can be grouped into three classes which he labels: first, transformistic theories; secondly, organic growth theories, and thirdly, theories of a *sui generis* development – unique, but grasped in analogical fashion by comparison with the development of ideas in the human and especially, as we shall see, the *scientific*, community.

In the first group, Gardeil lumps together the Modernists and the nineteenth century German school known as 'Semi-rationalism' and associated above all with the figure of Anton Günther (1783–1863).[17] For the Modernists, all development in the understanding of the Gospel after the original revelatory experience can only be a matter of theology. It bears no authority beyond that of the force of it own arguments. For Günther, doctrinal developments, when defined by the Church, are the divinely authenticated substitution of rational teaching in harmony with secular knowledge for the original doctrines of Christian antiquity. In each case, it is accepted that the meaning of the dogma later defined is no longer the meaning of the primitive deposit. This is what justifies bringing both under the title 'Transformism'. Gardeil lays them aside, since, in denying the substantial homogeneity of later doctrine with revealed

[17]See P. Wenzel, *Das wissenschaftliche Anliegen des Güntherianismus* (Essen 1961); the canon of the First Vatican Council insisting the doctrinal progress is always consonant with the Church's primitive understanding of her own dogmas was elicited by Güntherianism. See on this L. Orbán, *Theologia Güntheriana et Concilium Vaticanum* (Rome 1942–9; = *Analecta Gregoriana* XXVIII and I).

truth, neither is a theory that a Catholic could legitimately accept.

Next, Gardeil treats of the organic development theory, described by him as an 'expressive comparison' with a horticulturalist's seed, for the latter grows continually, yet without changing its nature. In the case of doctrine the 'seed' is the (understanding of the) primitive deposit. One major difference, however, separating the case of growth in doctrine from all purely natural developments is the rôle taken in the former by the Spirit of God. The Spirit, in a fashion uncompromisingly non-Deistic, does not abandon the seed it once sowed, but watches in secret to protect, by a special Providence, its development. On this theory, the Church too has a distinctive task.

> The Church, assisted by God, intervenes as a divine gardener by external initiatives – sometimes to cut back a harmful growth, a wild branch which threatens to use up sap to no purpose, sometimes to redress developments that are not in the line of the Spirit's intimate impulse, sometimes to sanction the normal results, legitimately harvested fruits of a growth that has at last reached its maturity.[18]

In Gardeil's judgement, this biological analogy has two incontestable merits. First, it does justice to the (preponderant) rôle of divine influence – itself both interior, the Spirit-given impulse, and exterior, the Spirit-guided apostolic ministry – in the developing life of a 'seed' that is itself essentially supernatural. Secondly, it splendidly illuminates what he calls the interplay of fundamental identity with creative innovation which characterises Church tradition.

Thus there are good reasons for accepting the organic growth theory. Yet Gardeil does not in fact accept it. He believed that, in the wake of the Modernist crisis, two weaknesses in the theory had become plain. On the one hand, the organic growth theory had proved all too malleable in

[18]*Le Donné révélé et la théologie*, op. cit., p. 155.

the hands of the Modernists, anxious as these were to commend a new view of Christianity, for which there never was an objective revelation with a determinate intellectual content of the sort presupposed by the existence of historic doctrine. For them, the original seed could simply be the good news of the Kingdom of God, declared to the soul, or, again, the in-breaking (in general terms) of the *eschaton*, the 'final age'. On the other hand, the Modernists themselves rightly pointed out that organic growth theories suffer from a regrettable tendency to elide the distinction between the life of a vegetable and the life of a mind.

For Gardeil, these two objections point to corresponding deficiencies in the organic model. An ambiguity in that model allowed the Modernists to make it their instrument. In biological organisms, growth is owed to an incessant circulation of materials. Materials are absorbed, but are eliminated later. The organism takes in food, is nourished by it, and then evacuates it from its system. In dogmatic development, by contrast, the external materials become fully integrated. The developed form of the dogma cannot be separated from the ideas used to develop it, even though those ideas were at first other than the dogma. And secondly, when we compare the growth of a seed with the growth of a dogma, we come upon a striking lack of correspondence which concerns the 'mode of deployment' in the two cases. The seed develops itself from within by a quasi-automatic dis-engagement of the parts that compose it. It develops from itself, by itself. But doctrine does not behave in that fashion. Every development in dogma is the result of some human mind, albeit some mind under the influence of God's Spirit. The deposit, in so far as it is acted upon by the power of human intelligence, is affected by a factor exterior to itself. Newman's seven 'notes' of doctrinal development may be the tests of whether that development has proceeded in a legitimate way but, says Gardeil (who assumes that Newman's own theory is a pure example of the organic growth model) they cannot serve to identify dogmatic development's moving force.

And so he moves on to a third and final theory which he

will make his own. Gardeil, taking up an occasional hint in such contemporary theologians as Léonce de Grandmaison and Jean-Vincent Bainvel,[19] proposed to compare dogmatic development with the life of a scientific community. Such a science as physics or chemistry, he points out, presupposes its own object. The object of science does not change merely because the science in question makes progress. What that progress involves is rather, a better grasp of the internal relation of the elements found within the object, and the object's external relations with other things. Such advances in scientific understanding take place, Gardeil reminds us, as a result of collaboration. A large number of people, over space and time, stimulate each other's efforts, correct each other, and, finally, unite in approving a result which, even if it be not the last word, represents nonetheless a permanent acquisition of knowledge.

Admittedly, not everything about this process resembles what happens in dogmatic development. First, the theological object, the revealed given, is itself a derivative object whose purpose it is to illumine the ultimate object of Christian faith: God himself. Secondly, the corporate co-operation of believers reflecting on the theological object is not a purely human affair, for it is Spirit-aided. Thirdly, and similarly, the definitive acceptance of a development in the faith-community is not a matter of a general perception in the Church of the self-evident correlation between some development and the original deposit. Instead, definitiveness of that kind attaches to the verdict of the episcopal magisterium, the bearers of the apostolic ministry, a specialised group, then, within the community of faith. For it is the bishops alone, with the Pope at their head, who are invited to promulgate in an authoritative way 'the solidarity of a human affirmation with the divine reality'.

And yet, so Gardeil insists, the similarities are even more

---

[19]L. de Grandmaison, 'Le développement du dogme chrétien', in *Revue pratique de l'apologétique* for 15 September 1908, p. 90; = *Le Dogme chrétien. Sa nature, ses formules, son développement* (Paris 1928), p. 266; cf. J. V. Bainvel, *De magisterio vivo et traditione* (Paris 1905), p. 145. See below, chapter 7, for these writers.

striking. Take the idea of a primordial *donné*, not wholly understood on account of its fullness or richness, but grasped by a fundamental intuition. With this we can compare, in the case of the scientific community, a fundamental awareness of the cosmos as a structured unity – a *universe* – a perception, this, underlying all science. Next, we note that, in both cases, under the influence of this intuition, a 'fermentation' begins in the human mind. All kinds of theses, hypotheses, proliferate, aiming to throw light on the primordial object. Finally, in both science and doctrine, there arises a clear perception of the correspondence between the 'given' and its 'developments', and this perception sanctions the developments in question in a definitive way. In other words: in both spheres the human mind grasps reality primitively *en bloc* – all it can do at first because of reality's 'force de plénitude débordante', its 'full to overflowing force' – and then, subsequently, determines the real more exactly through the careful re-formulation of the original intuition.[20]

There seem, then, to be three essential stages in the development of doctrine:

1. Global intuition by faith. A new and important *donné* capable of arousing intellectual disturbance enters our awareness.
2. Mental fermentation, produced by the diffusion of this *donné* in lively minds.

---

[20]This 'model' for what is involved in dogmatic development has recently been revived by Hugo Meynell. In his essay 'Newman on Revelation and Doctrinal Development', *Journal of Theological Studies* NS XXXI (April 1979), pp. 138–52 he espouses, without, it seems, awareness of the fact, a Gardeil-like solution. Pointing out that, for contemporary students of scientific method, three factors are stressed – the need for the corroboration of theory by observation and experiment (Karl Popper), the rôle of the scientific community in determining which theory is to be preferred (Thomas Kuhn), and the imperative that no limitation should be imposed on the theoretical fertility of scientists (Paul Feyerabend), Meynell proposes that to these there correspond, in the development of doctrine, respectively: the rôle of Scripture; the function of the magisterium of the Church, and the creative activity of the speculative theologian.

3. An effort to confront the results of the second stage with the first stage, and to sanction, where appropriate, what that second stage represents as an acquisition of genuine understanding of the first.

What rôle did Gardeil see in all this for the theological enterprise? Theology finds its given, which is at one and the same time its starting-point and its subject-matter, in revelation and dogma. Theological science aims to 'prolong' the given it has received by developing what is 'virtual' within it. In this task, it uses a variety of instruments: logical reasoning, self-evident rational principles, truths of common sense, and perspectives or viewpoints capable of presenting in a synthetic way the various elements of the given. Examples of the latter might be the theme of grace of Augustine's theology, or the concept of causality in that of Thomas. For Gardeil, when theological science has told us everything that is demonstrably certain in theology – for instance, that, in our salvation, God's grace is prevenient, or that, in Christology, Christ's humanity is the conjoined instrument of the Logos – large areas still remain in shadow. It is these shadow realms which the various theological systems attempt to illuminate. If such a system succeeds in bringing out the maximal homogeneity of its own ideas on some point with the revealed given itself, then what it has to say about some aspect of revelation changes its formal status. It passes over from the somewhat hypothetical status which it has endured in being part and parcel of an individual system, and takes on the more exalted, since assured, status of an intergrated feature of theological science as such.

To Gardeil, as a spokesman of the Thomist renaissance, Thomism was naturally the most fruitful of hypotheses in this sense. But he recognised that earlier attempts at synthesis, each with precious insights to offer, had entered into the making of Thomism, and notably the theologies of John Damascene and of Augustine. He speaks of Thomism as like a giant tree which could not overshadow the rest of the forest unless other growths had nourished it with their humus.

Gardeil's contribution to the understanding of the development of doctrine lies in his sane and generous view of propositional truth – its importance and its dignity. For, whatever else doctrines are, they are propositions, and no account of revelation which would exclude propositions wholly from its purview could do justice to the rôle of doctrines in Catholic Christianity. It seems worth citing in this connexion some words on this subject from a very different debate, this time on the relation not so much of Catholic teaching to history as of that teaching to culture, as envisaged by a contemporary American writer, Professor David Schindler, who writes:

> The intention of propositionalism, at its deepest thrust, is merely to insists that the features of intelligence and truth, of reasonableness, of nature (cosmos), and of universality be seen, not as exclusive of or extrinsic to, but on the contrary as intrinsic to the Christian vision – . . . however much that vision is shaped (as of course it is) simultaneously and fundamentally by decision, faith, grace . . . and particularity.[21]

But secondly, and not perhaps of any lesser importance, if the rôle of dogma in the Church, and in Christian theology, is to be secured, then the origins of the dogmatic impulse must be traced back – as Gardeil tried to trace it – to the apostles themselves. Although Gardeil did not have the exegetical sophistication to undertake a thoroughly persuasive account of the origins of dogma in the apostolic preaching, later writers in the Catholic tradition would point to the significant rôle there of confessional formulae as *praesymbola*, 'Creeds before the Creed', produced by the apostolic witnesses. Such embryonic *dogmata* were not the mere *parti pris* of individual human beings, though they were arrived at by utilising the resources of heart and mind, imagination and reasoning. More than this, however, they were offered in fulfilment of the mandate received from the Son, to testify to

[21]D. L. Schindler, 'Once Again: George Weigel, Catholicism and American Culture' *Communio* XV. I (Spring 1988), pp. 92–120, and here at p. 116.

the self-revelation of God in Christ; they were proclaimed in the assurance, too, of the guidance of his Holy Spirit.[22]

[22]See H. Schlier, 'Kerygma und Sophia. Zur neutestamentlichen Grundlegung des Dogmas', in *Evangelische Theologie* 11 (1950–1), re-printed after Schlier's conversion to Catholicism in idem., *Die Zeit der Kirche* (Freiburg 1966), pp. 206–32. Schlier's work suggests the origin of dogma at a point chronologically prior to the completion of Scripture – as was pointed out by H. Diem, in 'Dogmatische und Biblische Theologie' in idem., *Dogmatik* II (Munich 1955), pp. 40–9, where this author writes, 'Dogma is nothing other' (for Schlier) 'than the kerygma in later form', p. 45. On this whole aspect, a good discussion will be found in P. Schrodt, *The Problem of the Beginning of Dogma in Recent Theology* (Frankfurt 1978).

7

Other Neo-Scholastic Figures

How were Gardeil's views received by other figures in the Scholastic Revival which was such a marked feature of the Catholic theological scene from the pontificate of Leo XIII onwards? Not only were his colleagues undecided as to the entire satisfactoriness of his treatment of the issue of doctrinal development. He himself was less than wholly convinced by his own solution. His difficulties concerned two related issues: the logical connection of the original revelation with subsequent dogma, and the factors involved in generating the process of dogmatic development. Of the two, it was the first that seemed the more problematic. For, under the influence of his Scholastic sources, Gardeil believed that, once a new doctrinal understanding had, by mental fermentation, arisen, it should be possible to show the virtual or implicit presence of that new understanding in the original revelation – new truths being logically implied by old. If, on the other hand, the process of mental fermentation had the effect of eliciting new propositions that were not so implied, then the later Church, in sanctioning them, would – *per impossible* – have destroyed that essential homogeneity which should unite both revelation and dogma in one seamless garment. Either a belief is part of the apostolic deposit, to be accepted with divine faith, or it is not. And when we say that it is 'part' of the apostolic deposit, we mean, in the case of doctrine developed only in the course of history, that a given belief is *logically* part of the deposit. And yet in some cases, such as the Marian doctrine of the Immaculate Conception, it was hard to see that such logical entailment was present. Or, if it

were, it had certainly escaped the attention of most
Dominican theologians from Thomas until the solemn
definition of 1854.[1] To overcome the difficulty he himself
had raised, Gardeil had recourse to what he called 'the charism
of the social *sensus Ecclesiae*'. Although candidates for
acceptance as genuine Christian doctrine may lack full
homogeneity with the primordial revealed datum, they can
acquire it later as a result of the approval they meet through
the outworking of this charism in the community. But
Gardeil soon realised that this would not do. The *sensus
Ecclesiae* is the Church's instinct for discerning what was
always there – what was, in fact, implicit or virtual – in the
original apostolic revelation. It is a corporate gift of
discernment, given for the registration of something which
exists both antecedently and independently, in its own biblical
and traditional right. Thus, if a later dogma lacked
homogeneity with the primordial revelation, the charism of
the social *sensus Ecclesiae* could not supply it.[2]

At this point, Gardeil was helped out by the emergence of
a second Neo-Thomist Dominican author, Francisco Marín-
Sola. Born in Navarre in 1873, he entered the Dominican
missionary Province of the Philippines (now known as the
Province of Our Lady of the Rosary) as a mere thirteen year
old. Being thus below the canonical age, he did not receive
the habit, but was allowed the commence his philosophical
studies. In 1897 he arrived in the Philippines just in time for
the outbreak of the Filipono revolution, whereupon he was
arrested and imprisoned by the revolutionary authorities,
intent as these were on the creation of a Filipino National

---

[1]Some Dominicans, notably in Spain, had maintained the doctrine: see W. R.
Bonniwell, O.P., *A History of the Dominican Liturgy, 1215–1945* (New York 1945),[2]
p. 258.

[2]For Marín-Sola's criticism of Gardeil on this point, see *L'Evolution homogène du
dogme chrétien* (Fribourg 1924), I pp. 10–12. These reservations had already been
voiced by the Spanish theologian in the Neo-Thomistic journal *La Ciencia tomista*.
Gardeil wrote in response in the *Revue des Sciences Philosophiques et Théologiques* for
October 1912 that he believed Marín-Sola's articles to be on the right lines. The
social sense of the Church, directed by the Holy Spirit, can be a criterion or external
proof of the homogeneity of a development, but it cannot diagnose it where it does
not exist.

Catholic Church independent not only of Spain but also of Rome. In 1904 he was given the chair of philosophy at the University of Santo Tomas, Manila, where his fame as a pedagogue was such that many Spaniards made the journey to the Far East to study under him. In 1906 he was brought back to Spain to teach theology at the Province's study-house in Avila. It was there that, in the immediate aftermath of the Modernist crisis, he conceived his *La Evolución Homogénea del Dogma católico.* He spent the rest of his life teaching – at Notre Dame, Indiana; at Fribourg in Switzerland; (briefly) at the Roman Collegio Angelico, where his attempt to reconcile the Dominican and Jesuit positions on grace encountered the fierce resistance of the formidable Garrigou-Lagrange; and finally at Manila once again. He died there in 1932 at the age of 59.[3]

Since Marín-Sola accepted Gardeil's solution to the problem of dogmatic development in its general lines, he was obliged to confront the issue just mentioned, which Gardeil had come to believe was the Achilles' heel of his theory. In *La Evolución Homogénea del Dogma católico,* and as a result of delvings into the Scholastic background to the idea of the logical entailment of later doctrine in earlier, Marín-Sola came up with a partial, at least, solution to the problem.[4] He showed that Scholastic theology after the seventeenth century had misread the earlier Thomists (and, especially, Thomas himself and his namesake, Thomas of Vio, cardinal Cajetan) on the crucial idea of the explicitation of revelation. The stream, so Marín-Sola showed, had first been muddied by the Spanish Jesuit cardinal Francis Suarez, followed by de Lugo, the *Salmanticenses* or Carmelite doctors of the College of Saint Elias at Salamanca, and their fellow-countryman the Dominican John of Saint-Thomas. The confusion which Marín-Sola, as an historian of theology, managed to identify turns on the Scholastic concept of the 'virtually revealed'.

[3]For his life, see E. Sauras, 'Introducción General', *La Evolución Homogénea del Dogma Católico (por F. Marín-Sola)* (Madrid 1952), pp. 11–26.

[4]The Spanish original appeared in Valencia in 1923, but consisted in the amalgamation of articles published not only in *La Ciencia tomista* but also in its French counterpart, the *Revue Thomiste.* For the French translation, here cited, Marín-Sola revised the book, adding at least one entirely new section.

For St Thomas, as for later Thomists, the apostles had possessed the fullness of divine revelation. This was owing to their position as *capita*, 'heads' or 'leaders' of the New Testament Church. By an infused divine light, they enjoyed an explicit knowledge of divine revelation greater than that of all later theologians or even of the whole later Church.[5] Through God's grace, all the potentialities of the revealed idea were actualised in the apostles' minds. But, in this case, in what sense is dogmatic progress possible for Thomas, or Thomists?

Such progress is possible in relation to the mind not of the apostles, but of the primitive Church. For, as Marín-Sola puts it, the apostles did not communicate to the Church a perfect explication of the whole implicit meaning which they knew explicitly. They did, however, give the Church a permanent doctrinal magisterium which would allow believers to explicate, or further disengage, what was implicit in the revealed deposit they left behind – as the needs of each age might require. This magisterium works on the human formulae bequeathed by the apostles, formulae which are, according to Marín-Sola, 'full of virtuality', jam-packed with latent meaning just waiting to be expressed.

And here we come to the crux of the matter as the Spanish Thomist saw it. All theologians are agreed that the formal content of the formulae of the apostolic faith – their directly stated content – is divinely revealed. But what of their virtual content, their latent further meaning? Is this too genuinely a revealed meaning? If the answer to this question be in the negative, then there can be no such things as doctrinal development. Marín-Sola pointed out that most contemporary Scholastics either denied that there had been dogmatic development or despaired of reconciling the Scholastic tradition on this point with the facts of history. Marín-Sola deplored these attitudes as wholly unnecessary – the fruits of following an unfortunate aberration in Suárez' treatise *De Fide*.[6]

Suárez, in the course of his discission of the nature of faith,

---

[5]Thomas, *Summa Theologiae* IIa IIae. q. 106, a. 4.
[6]F de Suárez, *De Fide*, disp. 3, ii.

had decided to bracket together two kinds of inference from the apostolic deposit, namely:

1. Theological conclusions which consist simply in explaining terms used in the original language of revelation.
2. Theological conclusions that are distinct from their own revealed premises only in a conceptual way – in other words, through explaining in a different idiom ideas used in the original revelation.

These Suárez had brought together under the umbrella term 'the confusedly-formally revealed'. Something may be said to be, in this unlovely jargon, 'confusedly-formally revealed' if it is simply a paraphrase, in a changed linguistic or conceptual idiom, of what is already found in an explicit state in the apostolic deposit. We can think of it as something revealed by God in a somewhat less than pellucid way, owing to the lack of suitable philosophical lights among the Jewish people in ancient times. Had the prophets or apostles been familiar with Aristotle or thinkers of a similar ilk then the language and ideas of Scripture and the oral tradition stemming from the New Testament period would not be in the state that they are. Had the history of ancient Near Eastern culture been different, there would have been no 'confusedly-formally revealed', only the 'formally revealed' *tout court*.

What room, then, did Suárez leave for the more traditional partner of the 'formally revealed', namely the 'virtually revealed'? By the 'virtually revealed', Suárez understood a theological conclusion which was not just a translation of something given in the apostolic age, but a quite new truth, achieved through the interposition of constructive processes of thought. For instance, when we hear Jesus say, 'I and the Father are one', we can recognise a confused expression of a formally revealed truth, the consubstantiality of the Son with the Father. The only rational mediation needed here – and provided at the First Ecumenical Council, Nicaea I – is that of supplying the linguistic or conceptual deficiencies of a Semitic writer or speaker. By contrast, in order to reach the teachings of the Sixth Ecumenical Council, Constantinople III, that in Christ there are two wills, one human, the other divine, we need to interpose a piece of constructive metaphysics, namely, the assertion that the structure of spirit is of such a kind that no spiritual nature, such as human and divine nature (in an infinite diversity of modes) must be, can lack its own will. Here we are in firmly in the realm of the 'virtually revealed' – which is, in fact, for Suárez, not the revealed at all. Since it does not form part of the original apostolic deposit, it cannot be assented to by divine faith, though it may for all that be imposed by the Church's teaching office as a truth sufficiently bound up with the integrity of the deposit to require the adhesion of all the faithful.

For Suárez, therefore, the only sort of dogmatic explication or development we may legitimately recognise is one which consists in a bare re-formulation of the original Gospel, not a true elucidation of its further implications. But, Marín-Sola asked, granted that Suarez' approach makes life so much more difficult for a Scholastic divine who feels obliged by the sheer weight of historical evidence to posit a true development of doctrine from virtuality into actuality, and not simply from confusion into clarity, why follow it? Suárez, after all, was not St Thomas: no Thomist need feel obliged by a sense of intellectual consistency to defend Suarezian positions. Gardeil gratefully accepted Marín-Sola's conclusion that, for someone who wishes to be faithful to Thomas, it should be possible to accept a more generous view of what is involved in unfolding the virtualities of the deposit. Marín-Sola insisted that there must be, certainly, a rational homogeneity between later doctrine and the apostolic deposit, but argued that this rational homogeneity could be understood in a wider sense than recent Scholasticism had allowed it. It could survive the intervention of a constructive metaphysic, as in the doctrine of the two wills of the Redeemer; it need not be restricted to mere linguistic or logical analysis.

Marín-Sola's approach was, for some critics, still too rationalist; for others, not rational enough. He expected a theologian to be able to show the rational coherence of all later doctrine with the deposit, rejecting appeal to some purely theological coherence of the two that might not be fully expressible in terms of pure reason: hence the accusation of excessive rationalism. Again, though holding that the ultimate outcome of a process of doctrine development must be a rationally demonstrable connexion, he did not believe that the concrete factors operating in Church history to push that process forward need themselves always be rational: hence the accusation of insufficient rationality.

Perhaps his most important contribution to the subject lay in his discrimination between two inter-related yet distinct issues: on the one hand, the logical connexion of later dogmas with the deposit; on the other, the motive-forces impelling development. To Marín-Sola, to illustrate the distinction by an example, it seemed entirely possible that, in the case of some particular doctrine, let us say the Immaculate Conception, the factors of development were largely devotional,[7] but even in this case it must be possible for theology to show that the doctrine generated by devotion to Mary in her radical holiness is connected in a rationally comprehensible manner to other earlier doctrines, such as that of Mary's divine motherhood. It is easy to see why some regarded this as an inherently unstable position. *Prima facie*, it seemed more plausible to say one of two things: either that both the connexion of the later doctrine with an earlier, and the factors which impelled the making of that later doctrine, were logical or rational, or that neither the connexion of a later doctrine with an earlier nor the factors which impelled the making of the later doctrine need necessarily be logical or rational.

Those who held to the position that *both* the connexion of subsequent doctrine with the apostolic deposit *and* the historical genesis of such doctrine must be thought of as essentially logical in character may be termed – in a word coined by Père (now Cardinal) Henri de Lubac – 'Logicists'. The two most important Logicists were the Louvain Dominican Marcolinus Maria Tuyaerts, and the Roman Jesuit Charles Boyer, the one writing soon after the First World

[7]For the rôle of affectivity in dogmatic development, see F. Marín-Sola, O.P., *L'Evolution homogène du dogme catholique*, op. cit., pp. 353–92. Dogmatic understanding can progress in either a logical or a 'vital' or 'affective' manner, 'une voie vitale. . . affective'. The Church is tied neither to the reasoning of theologians nor to the feelings of the faithful, but uses now one, now the other, as she thinks fit.

War, the other during the Second. Tuyaerts, was born at Everberg, in the Belgian province of Brabant, in 1878, and died in Louvain in 1948. He wrote on a variety of characteristically Neo-Thomist topics, from the distinctive causality of the sacraments in the order of grace to a defence of the notion of 'supernaturalised' virtues. In his 1919 study *L'Evolution du dogme*, he managed to attack not only Newman, the Modernists and Blondel but Gardeil too.[8] He argued that the development of dogma consisted purely and simply in working out the logical implications of the formulae of the apostolic deposit, or of the doctrines deduced from those formulae in the age of the great Councils and Creeds.[8a] Tuyaerts explained that, in practice, this meant two things. First, any theological conclusion drawn by a logical process from established doctrine can be made into a dogma by the Church. Thus Tuyaerts believed that almost all the articles of Thomas' *Summa Theologiae* could be erected into dogmas. Whether they were or not so defined should turn solely on whether the pope and bishops considered that, in given circumstances, it would be for the *bene esse*, the general welfare, of the Church to do so. Secondly, Tuyaerts considered that *only* theological conclusions drawn from ancient doctrine by such a logical process could be turned into dogmas. Any attempt by pope and bishops to erect as dogma a putative doctrine whose logical connexion with the earlier doctrines had not been established would constitute a grave abuse of their office.

In the early years of the pontificate of Pius XII, Tuyaerts' view showed signs of extending its influence. The Logicist revival, as we may call it, was fuelled by the feeling that Catholic theology was becoming a prey to irrationalism, or to a vague mysticism, as a result of the adoption of non-Scholastic philosophies as handmaids to the understanding of divine revelation. This feeling would soon explode with full force in the attack on the so-called *Nouvellé Théologie* associated with, above all, the Jesuits of Lyon-Fourvières and

[8] M. M. Tuyaerts, O.P., *L'Evolution du dogme. Etude dogmatique* (Louvain 1919).

[8a] 'The nature both of dogma and of our spirit makes possible only one procedure in dogmatic evaluation: that of dialectic or reasoning', ibid. p. 236.

notably Henri de Lubac and Jean Daniélou. The wider implications of the Logicist revival may be seen from the title of an influential Gregorianum article of 1940 in which Boyer set forth his view of doctrinal development: 'Qu'est-ce que la théologie? (What is *Theology*?) Réflexions sur une controverse'.[9] Boyer, who was born in 1884 in the Haute-Loire, and died at the ripe age of ninety-five, combined an informed enthusiasm for St Augustine with a passionate commitment to St Thomas, seen in the light of the Neo-Thomist revival.[10] His rôle in the last generation of that revival's story proved a central one: to his professorship at the Gregorian University he joined the *cattedra San Tommaso* of the Lateran University (both in Rome) and the post of general secretary of the influential *Accademia Romana di S. Tommaso d'Aquino*. He also edited the Thomistic periodical *Doctor communis*.[11] Boyer could write about the nature of doctrinal development by setting forth his account of what theology is since for him, the Church's magisterium, in defining doctrine, simply consecrates rationally valid theological speculation. At the moment of definition – whether in ecumenical Council, or in the preparing of a papal *ex cathedra* definition, the Holy Spirit enables the bearers of the teaching office to place their authority on that side of a theological discussion which represents sound logic. Granted that neither episcopal consecration nor papal election make one an expert in philosophical logic, or even increase the reasoning capacities of the human mind, there is need for a special supernatural gift of divine guidance which will enable the Church's pastors, when need arises, to identify precisely those theological conclusions which follow in a logically sound manner from earlier doctrine.[12] Boyer's

---

[9]C. Boyer, S. J., 'Qu'est-ce que la théologie? Réflexions sur une controverse', *Gregorianum* XXI (1946).

[10]For his voluminous output, see A. Rizzo, *Bibliografia di P. Charles Boyer* (Rome 170).

[11]For a characteristic statement of his Neo-Thomist vision, see 'St Thomas et certaines tendances de la pensée moderne', *Doctor Communis* 12 (1952), pp. 1–10.

[12]Other relevant essays of Boyer's are: 'Relazione tra il progresso filosofico, teologico, dogmatico', *Gregorianum* 33 (1952), pp. 168–182; 'Lo sviluppo del dogma', in (Auctores varii) *Problemi e orientamenti di teologia dommatica* (Milan 1957), pp. 359–380.

position represents the acme of Logicism, presented in so stark a fashion that, as we shall see, it prompted the young Henri de Lubac to offer an alternative view of the whole matter.[13]

It should not be thought, however, that the Logicists completely dominated the field before De Lubac stepped onto it. On the contrary, Tuyaerts' manifesto of Logicism had met with immediate criticism back in 1919, not least from Gardeil. In his comments on it in the *Revue des Sciences Philosophiques et Théologiques* for 1920, Gardeil had this to say of Tuyaerts' approach:

> Too limited, too inclined to measure the divine word, given us after all to guide us to heaven, by the exclusive demands of a reasoning given us for our instruction on earth. Too generous to logic and not generous enough to the freedom of God's initiatives and the unknown ways and means that God's providence uses in the history of dogma as in the world at large.[14]

In these words, Gardeil distanced himself from the somewhat exclusive stress he had earlier laid on the intellectual factors in the process of dogmatic genesis. The model of the scientific community at work would not, apparently, suffice. There must also be, as Marín-Sola had insisted, an 'affective way'.

And in any case, as early as *Le Donné révélé et la théologie* itself, Gardeil had made the point that many first-rate theological conclusions – such as the affirmation that the persons of the Trinity are subsistent relationships – are not dogmas, whilst other inferences from the deposit scarcely more than rationally probable (such as Mary's Immaculate Conception) have been solemnly defined by the Church.[15] From this it must follow, he thought, that the ground on which dogmatic definitions are prepared cannot be 'the ground of dialectic alone'. It must be, rather, that of the

---

[13]For Boyer's reaction to de Lubac, we have his 'Notes sur Le *Mystère du Surnaturel* du P. Henri de Lubac', in *Gregorianum* 48 (1967), pp. 130–2.

[14]A. Gardeil, O. P., 'Bulletin de théologie speculative', in *Revue des Sciences philosophiques et théologiques* IX (1920).

[15]Idem., *Le Donné révélé et la théologie*, op. cit., pp. 171–182.

'living, social faith of the Church, of the whole Church, teaching and taught': that is, of both episcopate and laity, the entire people of God. The difference between correct theological conclusions and definable truths must lie in what Gardeil terms 'the social order of the Church', her corporate living out of the Christian faith, where it will depend on fundamentally supernatural factors, the Holy Spirit prompting the development of doctrinal understanding in a given direction as the needs of the Church, in faith, hope, and charity, may require.

Much the same line was taken by Gardeil's contemporary the French Jesuit Léonce de Grandmaison whose articles in response to Loisy were published posthumously in book form as *Le Dogme chrétien. Sa nature, ses formules, son développement.*[16] This work made a major contribution to rendering the Scholastic tradition more historically aware. His 'Histoire de la question' contains, in astonishingly brief compass, a reliable *exposé* of the chief approaches in the patristic, mediaeval and early modern 'pre-history' of the notion of doctrinal development before Newman. He recognises, clearly enough, the latter's crucial place in his story:

> Among the Catholics who, since Newman, have raised the question of dogmatic development, and treated it with any thoroughness, there is scarcely one who does not refer to the analyses, and accept at least some of the principles of the master of Oriel.[17]

De Grandmaison accepted that Newman's subtle sinuosities were impossible to combine with the austere theo-logic of a Scholastic manual. The presence of the first in the pages of the second would be as 'surprising as a Corot sky in a landscape by Nicolas Poussin'.[18] Yet his own programme amounted to little less than such a collage of styles, not merely

---

[16]L. de Grandmaison, S.J., *Le Développement du dogme chrétien, sa nature, ses formules, son développement* (Paris 1928).

[17]Ibid., p. 111.

[18]Ibid., p. 115.

of writing but also of thought. The sense for the concrete texture of history in all its contingency, as exemplified in Newman, must take as its partner the feeling for general principles of intelligibility characteristic of Scholasticism.

De Grandmaison blends together an account of the definitive giveness of revealed truth with a confession of the 'elasticity' of its formulae. The apostolic preaching clothed divine revelation in forms that were not always the 'best possible' – bound up as they are with images and ways of speaking familiar to one epoch, culture, mind-set, but not to another.[19] And yet, its efforts sufficed to enshrine and transmit to posterity the 'first judgement' of those human minds wherein, as the inspired witness of revelation, the word of God took up its dwelling. There is, therefore, a deposit of faith, as both the Pastoral Epistles and the universal consent of the Fathers testify. This sets limits to development, which cannot, then, be an-archic, unprincipled, open in all possible directions. Yet development there certainly is: a true *progressus fidelium in fide*, 'progress of the faithful in the faith', if not a *progressus fidei in fidelibus*, 'progress of the faith in the faithful'. The relative indeterminacy of the early formulae, itself exceeded by that of the gestures of the liturgies and the faith-attitudes transmitted by the primitive generations, left scope enough for inadequate interpretations, whether the perpetrators of these sinned by defect, by exaggeration or by perversity. But in each case

> the enigmas thus posed, slowly matured thanks to controversy, the Church's practise, and the precisions of the doctors, ended by yielding up, as of their own volition, their divine word, under the efficacious action – itself profound, and respectful of human activities – of the Holy Spirit.[20]

If De Grandmaison makes use of the biological analogy for dogmatic development, he does so on the grounds that

[19]Ibid., p. 179.
[20]Ibid., p. 242.

organic growth, unlike the formation of crystals, is supple, and includes the element of the unexpected. The movement from implicit to explicit, from the original, immediate, personal, 'real' moment of the apostles' understanding to our own later, reflective, didactic one, with its mingled loss and gain, takes place in just such a non-geometric fashion, in a history which ranges from 'errors vanquished' to 'fecund appeals to the piety of the faithful'.[21]

In the latter respect, the circumstances surrounding the definition of the doctrine of the Immaculate Conception were especially eloquent. One of De Grandmaison's own sources, Jean-Vincent Bainvel, himself writing in the heart of the Modernist crisis, had drawn attention, in his study of the evolution of belief in Mary's original righteousness, to the 'great independence' which the Roman see had shown in regard to the Church's divines. He spoke of the 1854 doctrine as a case of Christian piety:

> I do not say triumphing over theological science, but rather advancing it, stimulating it, enlightening it, and finally leading it to ratify the intuitions of love and devotion.[22]

De Grandmaison too speaks of the Church's 'occasional' power to go beyond the natural force of historical and logical discourse that prepares the way for a definition. Here the word 'intuition' recurs, for he describes this power as, precisely.

> a higher gift of intuition, which leads the Church to enjoy a clear awareness of truth that no demonstrative argument has shown to be self-evidently present in the revealed deposit.[23]

Such statements needed some kind of further backing in

[21]Ibid., pp. 267–8.

[22]J.-V. Bainvel, 'L'Histoire d'un dogme', *Etudes* 101 (1904), pp. 623–4.

[23]L. de Grandmaison, S. J., *Le Développement du dogme chrétien, sa nature, ses formules, son développement*, op. cit. pp. 262–3.

terms of an account of how Christian piety can itself be truth-discerning. How can the 'intuitions of love and devotion' actually produce insight into what does or does not belong to the apostolic deposit? Further light was thrown here by the work of another Gregorian Jesuit Edgar Dhanis. A Fleming, born in Ghent in 1902 and dying in 1978, Dhanis published little, but produced a number of Latin and Italian syntheses of his teaching in fundamental theology, especially on the apologetic aspects of Christology – Jesus' 'religious personality', his 'self-witness', miracles and Resurrection – for the benefit of students in the Theology Faculty of the Gregorian University. The point of departure for Dhanis' contribution to the problem of doctrinal development was the description of the 'light of faith', *lumen fidei*, offered by Augustine and Thomas.[24] Both the Latin father and the great Scholastic speak of the light of faith as expressing itself in the form of an *attractio* or *inclinatio*, whereby the intellect and will direct themselves towards God, and adhere to the message he communicates in revealing himself. The resultant illumination of our minds is certainly not a private revelation, nor is it, even, a highly conscious state as in the life-stories of the mystics. Rather is it, in Dhanis' chosen terms, lived and experienced rather than reflective and conscious. Nevertheless, it is pertinent to the making of Christian doctrine, since it comes into play as a power of judgement about divine truth at the moment when we commit ourselves to God's concrete self-revelation in history. It gives us what Dhanis calls a 'connaturality' or 'complicity' in the transcendent realities which the formulations of the apostolic deposit set before us.

This *inclinatio fidei* is, Dhanis suggests, a true principle of doctrinal development. More, it is that development's essential principle – the logical principle having, by contrast, a merely secondary force. Human rationality works on the materials of the apostolic deposit, and draws forth certain inferences. But without the *inclinatio fidei*, these inferences are purely a work of natural reason. They lack a properly supernatural credibility, and thus the attestation, the

[24]E. Dhanis, 'Révélation explicite et implicite', *Gregorianum* XXXIV (1935).

testimony, of the self-revealing God. Thought they may be true theological conclusions, we cannot say of them that God has willed these truths to be an intrinsic part of his self-revelation, to be used in the appropriating by human beings of their own salvation. And that is as much as to say: without the contribution of the *inclinatio fidei*, inferences from the deposit could not become dogmas.

However, Dhanis adds a nuance which is by way of being something of a concession to the Logicist position. He distinguishes between candidates for dogmatic definition which are logically certain inferences from the deposit, and those that are only probable. In the first case, we can reach a natural certainty that a doctrine is part of the deposit; here the *inclinatio fidei* simply confers a supernatural character on our certitude, enabling our assent to rest not just in our grasp of the logical connexion involved, but on the truth of God revealing. In the second case, where the link of the putative doctrine with the teachings of revelation is only probable in logical character, the *inclinatio fidei* does more. It makes the credibility of the new doctrine pass over from a state of mere probability to one of full certitude. Here the *inclinatio fidei* really comes into its own: the light of faith not only grants to a rationally inferred conclusion God's seal of approval but also, using such inference as one would an instrument, is itself the real power which discerns the coherence of the new doctrine with the old deposit. The eyes of faith are looking, and, whilst gratefully accepting the help that rationality gives, their vision is their own.

What total picture of the process of doctrinal development emerges from Dhanis' work? Since the beginning, the Christian community has adhered to the one divine self-revelation, made in the fullness of time, when the Father, by the Spirit, sent the only Son into the world. Through the light of faith, the Church has ever held to the content of that revelation, receiving it as the very Word of God. Yet the content of that revelation – to which the *inclinatio fidei* directed the thought of the believing Church – was not an object wholly explicitated, fully articulated in doctrinal propositions. Though in part it was so explicitated, and articulated, there were other aspects of the content of revelation, and these too the Word of God covered with its authority. These other points of doctrine, the divine Word retained for the time being enveloped in the deposit, by a pedagogy of mercy – a reference to the saying of Jesus in John 16, 'I have many other things to tell you, but you cannot bear them now'. Of these other, implicit aspects of doctrine, we can say that the Church experienced a mysterious inclination to believe them, and – yet more – that she already believed them by an indistinct, undetermined faith, awaiting their presentation to her common mind in the eloquence of propositions. In due course, the natural gifts of rationality enjoyed by members of the Church, working through inference on the deposit, render persuasive various propositions – entailing, say, the two wills of the Word Incarnate, or the all-pure conception of Mary. At the moment when this is done, the *inclinatio fidei* dispersed throughout the people of God is incapable of *not* responding positively to these propositions. It seizes on these truths as truths of faith itself, truths from the treasury of the apostolic witness.

So far in this scheme nothing has been said about the rôle of the Church's teaching office. In fact, Dhanis left it a due place in the ratifying of the intuitions of love and devotion which the inclination of faith brings forth. But how does he expound this special role for episcopate and papacy?

Since faith can only be entertained by individual persons, any account of the *inclinatio fidei*, in its contribution to dogmatic development, must needs begin at the level of the individual. For that individual person – let us say an Anglo-Norman monk of the twelfth century reading for the first time Eadmer of Canterbury's argument for the Immaculate Conception, the inclination of faith, in Dhanis' words, 'insinuates into the spirit a secret assurance conspiring with the suggestion of the persuasive inference', the inference he has just met in Eadmer's treatise. The conjuncture of this super-natural light with the rational arguments intensifies the credibility of the doctrine proposed but does not confer certitude upon it. However, as more and more believers replicate the experience of the Anglo-Norman monk reading

Eadmer in being not only rationally impressed by the coherence of the new doctrine with old revelation but feeling supernaturally drawn to its truth the personal *inclinatio fidei* comes to have a wider repercussion in the social body of the Church. As this happens, the new doctrine begins to manifest its own truth in a social fashion, for instance in producing positive benefits for the Christian life. Gradually, its harmony with the rest of Christian life and practice becomes clear. Little by little, the body of the faithful becomes generally persuaded of the doctrine's truth. The bearers of the Church's teaching office may well consider that general persuasion as a reliable index of divine attestation for the theologoumenon concerned. Bishops and pope are then justified in taking the final step of proposing the new doctrinal 'precision' as a dogma – that is, an integral part of the apostolic faith.

Dhanis' approach received confirmation in the same year, 1935, from the Angelicum Thomist Henri-Dominique Simonin.[25] Born in 1900, Simonin was affected by the greater awareness of historical theology gradually seeping into the Neo-Scholastic tradition. Although he was concerned with a variety of issues bequeathed by mediaeval epistemology, such as the Angels' power of self knowledge, and their knowledge of created being at large, as well as the views of the Franciscan masters on the human understanding of individual material things, and – perhaps aroused by the work of Pierre Rousselot, to whom we shall turn in a moment, St Thomas' reflections on the nature of love,[25a] and wrote, too, on the typically Neo-Scholastic topic of the 'theological conclusion', Simonin was also absorbed in the wider 'argument from Tradition' in theology. Irenaeus of Lyons was his model theologian: no doubt partly for reasons of Gallic loyalty.[25b] Writing in the journal *Angelicum*, he argued that, whilst Thomas has no theory of doctrinal development, and hardly even envisages it as a problem 'dans son ensemble', nevertheless, in his account of the nature of faith in the

---

[25]H. D. Simonin, O.P., 'La théologie thomiste de la foi et le développement du dogma', *Revue Thomiste* 18 (1935), pp. 537–556.

[25a] *Autour de la solution thomiste du problème de l'Amour* (Paris 1931)

[25b] 'Sanctus Irenaeus Lugdunensis Theologus', *Angelicum* xi (1934), pp. 3–22.

opening question of the *Secunda Secundae* he laid down the principles necessary for its resolution. In effect, what this comes down to is the statement that the object of faith which in itself simple, is materially complex in the apprehension of the believer. It is found in the mind of the believer only according to the kind of knowledge connatural to the human mind: that is, by way of multiple articulations. And Simonin concluded, in a generous statement of the essential historicity of dogma, that

> the explication, more or less perfect, of the faith depends at each moment on the subjective conditions of believers. Similarly, it will also vary in the course of history by reference to such factors as the state of civilisation and of the psychological, intellectual and social aptitudes of humanity.[26]

Thus, where Dhanis had seen only two factors – rational theological inference and the *inclinatio fidei,* Simonin added a most important third: the state of human culture in any given time and place, its qualities and its interests. These at any rate condition the making of fresh doctrine, even if they do not positively stimulate it. One can detect, then, in these two contributions from Roman theologians the growing influence of a more historically minded Scholasticism, associated with De Lubac among the Jesuits and Marie-Dominique Chenu among the Dominicans. The stage is thus set for the attempt of the first of these to administer the *coup de grâce* to any exclusively Logicist theory of development of a body of doctrine supernatural in its origin, its mode of communication and its end.

[26]Ibid., p. 548; cf. idem., ' "Implicite" et "explicite" dans le développement du dogme', *Angelicum* 14 (1931), pp. 126–145.

8

Henri de Lubac and Pierre Rousselot

Henri de Lubac was born in Cambrai, in northern France, in 1896, the son of a banker.[1] When his father's work took him to Lyons, the family moved with him. There it was that the young Henri discovered the Jesuits, since he was sent for his schooling to the nearby Jesuit college of Mongré where, until shortly before, Teilhard de Chardin had been a pupil, and whose teaching staff had included the illustrious historian of the 'religious sentiment in France', Henri Bremond. It was Bremond who, under the pseudonym of 'Sylvain Leblanc', had authored a semi-apologetic life of Loisy and who, after his own departure from the Society of Jesus for the diocesan clergy, had presided at the burial of Tyrrell.

After finishing one year of a law course at the University of Lyons, De Lubac entered the Jesuit noviciate, which, as a result of the anti-clerical policies of the Third French Republic, had been removed to England, and now found itself among the chintz and cheeriness of a small Sussex seaside town, St Leonard's-on-Sea. The next year, 1914, he moved no great distance to the Jesuit scholasticate at Hastings. There he was befriended by a certain Père Auguste Valensin of the Society, a man whom the German Jesuit Herbert Vorgrimler, in his short study of De Lubac, describes as 'philosopher, Dante scholar and spiritual writer'.[2] Valensin put De Lubac

[1]For a general overview of De Lubac's life and work, see H. U. von Balthasar – G. Chantraine, *Le cardinal Henri de Lubac, l'homme et son oeuvre. Avec une lettre de Paul VI* (Paris 1983).

[2]H. Vorgrimler, 'Henri de Lubac', in R. van der Gucht –H. Vorgrimler (eds.), *Bilan de la théologie du XXe siècle* (Paris 1970), II., pp. 806–20, De Lubac wrote two essays in Valensin's memory, 'Le Père Auguste Valensin. Philosophe et apôtre' and

in touch with the lay philosopher who had done so much for a sane Catholic response to Modernism, Maurice Blondel. He also suggested that De Lubac should study the manuscripts left behind by a brilliant confrère, Pierre Rousselot, who had just died, tragically young, in the Battle of the Somme.[3] Later, De Lubac would publish considerable quantities of Blondel's correspondence with both Valensin and Teilhard.[4] More important for our purposes he would also publish, on the fiftieth anniversary of Rousselot's death, an essay by the latter entitled 'Petite Théorie du développement du dogme'.[5] Not only did De Lubac remain throughout his life a fervent admirer of Rousselot, whom he thought of as someone who wished to put back into Thomism the contemplative and mystical dimension present in the thought of St Thomas, but neglected by somewhat rationalising theologians in the Thomistic Revival. More than this, De Lubac's own contribution to our subject, the substantial article 'Bulletin de Théologie fondamentale: le Problème du développement du dogme' of 1948, carries unmistakable echoes of Rousselot's thought and language.[6]

It is impossible to make sense of De Lubac's views without

'L'Amour de Jésus-Christ. Présence actuelle du Christ. Témoignage du Père Valensin', both republished in idem., *Théologies d'occasion* (Paris 1984), pp. 437–52. Relevant to Valensin's commending of Rousselot (and Blondel) to the young De Lubac, is a fragment of the first mentioned of these two essays:

> Pascal had helped him – he who was so rational – to see that thought does not wholly rest 'on the surface, where the dialectic of *la raison raisonnante* flourishes'. . . It was to the service of a profoundly Pascalian thinking that he set what he called his idealism', op. cit., pp. 440–1.

[3]For Rousselot's life and work, see J. Lebreton, 'Rousselot, Pierre', in *Dictionnaire de Théologie Catholique* XIV. cols. 134–8; also E. Marty, *Le Témoignage de Pierre Rousselot, S.J., 1878–195* (Paris 1946).

[4]H. de Lubac (ed.), *Maurice Blondel et Auguste Valensin. Correspondence* (Paris 1957–65); idem., (ed.) *P. Teilhard de Chardin et Maurice Blondel. Correspondence* (Paris 1967). See also P. Teilhard de Chardin, *Lettres intimes à Auguste Valensin, Bruno de Solage, Henri de Lubac, André Ravier 1919–1955. Introduction et notes par Henri de Lubac* (Paris 1974).

[5]P. Rousselot, S.J., 'Petite théorie du développement du dogme', *Recherches de Science Religieuse* 53 (1965), pp. 355–90.

[6]H. de Lubac, 'Bulletin de théologie fondamentale: le problème du développement du dogme', in *Recherches de Science religieuse* XXXV (1948), pp. 130–60.

considering those of Rousselot: and hence a brief remark on *his* background may not be out of place. Born at Nantes in 1878, he was christened the day after his birth – a testimony to the intensity of the Breton Catholicism of his family, constant, to the point of martyrdom, during the upheavals of the Great Revolution. At the age of sixteen Rousselot became a Jesuit. Initiated into philosophy, he became discontented with the standard Neo-Thomisms of his day, and 'returned to the sources' of Aquinas' texts. There he discovered that

> Grace was not such much an additional storey built upon the already completed house of nature as an inner, nourishing sap that drove the seeds of nature from the dark earth through the obstacles of sin upward to the vivifying light of God.[7]

This find would be turned to theological use in the dogmatics of De Lubac, and notably his *Mystère du surnaturel*,[8] as also in the transcendental aesthetics of Hans Urs von Balthasar.[9] Before his thirtieth birthday, Rousselot defended two philosophical theses at the Sorbonne – without taking out any time from the ordinary cycle of Jesuit training. These were *L'Intellectualisme de saint Thomas*, which drew attention to the continuing vitality, in Thomas' synthesis, of Christian Platonism, and *Le Problème de l'amour au moyen âge*, a study which proved a fertile source of themes for later students of mediaeval philosophy and theology. Appointed professor at the Institut Catholique, his first lecture course concerned 'The Eyes of Faith', an attempt to rescue the theology of the act of faith from the pit into which an over-rationalistic apologetics had cast it.[10] With the outbreak of the Great War, Rousselot

[7]J. M. McDermott, S.J., *Love and Understanding. The Relation of Will and Intellect in Pierre Rousselot's Christological Vision* (Rome 1983), pp. 1–2. The account of Rousselot's life, work and influence given here is taken from this study.

[8]H. de Lubac, S.J., *Le Mystère du surnaturel* (Paris 1965²), pp. 29; 48; 51; 235 ff.; 268.

[9]H. U. von Balthasar, *Herrlichkeit* I (Einsiedeln 1961), pp. 168–70.

[10]For Newman's influence on 'Les Yeux de la foi', art. cit., see M. Nédoncelle, 'L'influence de Newman sur les "Yeux de la foi" de Rousselot', *Revue des Sciences religieuses* 27 (1953), pp. 321–32.

became a military chaplain, and it was in that capacity that he died, on 25 April 1915, on the battlefield of Eparges.

Rousselot's essay on doctrinal development considers two questions. First, how is it possible that dogma, at whatever period of its development, can be described as substantially one body with what the holy apostles knew – and even as adding nothing to their knowledge? Secondly, how does the Church come to that clear awareness which allows her to define a dogma – once again, without adding anything to what she possessed before?

Rousselot suggests that these problems are not insoluble if we bear in mind two inter-connected principles which are foundational truths of all thought. These two principles consist in the affirmation that what is truly intelligible is 'l'esprit vivant', 'the living mind', and that the fullest knowledge of that mind is 'la connaissance amoureuse', 'loving knowledge'.[11] The spirit or mind, Rousselot explained, is what is *primo et per se intelligibilis*, the physical world only having meaning for God and thus intrinsic (because created) intelligibility as a means to the perfection of the minds embodied within it. The *loving* knowledge of such a spirit or mind is that knowledge which bears primarily on the substance or essential being of another reality. In Rousselot's words, loving knowledge 'instals' itself at the very centre of that other being, and, in so doing, it puts itself in a position where it can grasp the other being's inner law of harmony – whatever it is that explains how all its manifestations cohere with each other.

These two principles: what is intelligible is mind, and mind's knowledge at its highest is sympathetic knowledge – will readily be found at work in Rousselot's interpretation of Aquinas, *L'intellectualisme de Saint Thomas*, a book attacked by the Dominicans of the Collegio Angelico for turning Thomas into an Idealist on the German model.[12] In the 'Petite

[11]'Petite théorie', art cit.

[12]P. Rousselot, *L'Intellectualisme de saint Thomas* (Paris 1908; 1934²; 1936³). The third edition contains a notice on the author, with bibliography of his work by the Jesuit student of doctrinal development Léonce de Grandmaison, whose work was touched on in the last chapter.

Théorie', Rousselot conceded that his two principles are by no means a pure distillation of the thought of Thomas. In formulating them he had tried to combine an approach based fundamentally on the latter with two other elements. The first of these was an attempt to salvage the nugget of truth in Idealism. Suitably purified and corrected, what is true in Idealism is the claim that the world's finality is intellectual. It is not just that, as a result of the world's being here, we who have minds know the world. Rather, the world is here so that we who have minds may know it, and in knowing it bring the world to its goal. The second non-Thomist element Rousselot took, with acknowledgement, from Blondel, and other contemporary French writers who shared an emphasis on instinct, feeling, will. And this is the notion that our knowledge of realities other than ourselves takes the form of sympathy or love-knowledge.[13]

But what light can this throw on the idea of the development of doctrine? According to Rousselot, what is problematic about that idea is the reconciliation of 'a certain unity' with 'a certain plurality'. The *unity* is affirmed *a priori* by the Church when she maintains that her faith is at all times substantially one and the same with the faith of the apostles. The *plurality* is discovered *a posteriori* by historians looking at the evidence of history. For Rousselot these two terms – unity, plurality – do not describe the same order of knowledge, and therefore the way to a reconciliation between the claims of faith and those of history may lie open. Since the self-revelation of God, found in the deposit of faith, must be absolutely one, that deposit cannot be conceived as

> a sum-total of distinct truths, limited in number, presented under the form of logical propositions like the *Augsburg Confession* or even the *Apostles' Creed*.[14]

Should the deposit consist essentially in such a collection of

[13]For the inter-relation of these two in his work, see J. M. MacDermott, S. J., *Love and Understanding. The Relation of Will and Intellect in Pierre Rousselot's Christological Vision* op. cit., *passim*.

[14]'Petite théorie', 23, p. 359.

propositions, it would be a set of judgements, assertions or acts of knowledge (*connaissances*) external to each other – like a row of bottles on a wall. Much the same follows if we think of the deposit as a complex of ideas, rather than a set of propositions: 'the Lordship of Jesus' rather than 'Jesus is Lord', 'the holiness of Mary' rather than 'Mary is holy'. What we must seek, then, is a kind of knowledge which is indefinitely cashable (*monnayable*) in distinct ideas and propositions, but where the coin of such ideas and propositions explicitate a unitary knowing without being able to exhaust it, and without in any way claiming to supplement it.

For guidance Rousselot turns, as his erstwhile critics among the Roman Dominicans would not have been surprised to hear, to Hegel's *Logic*. In that work, Hegel asks at one point which is the more truly infinite: the indefinite decimal fraction which is equal to two-sevenths, namely 0.285714 etc., or two-sevenths itself. The true infinite, Hegel maintains, is two-sevenths and not its rival, since, in that rival, digits can be added endlessly without ever reaching their term, which is to equal two-sevenths. In the latter, we meet a true infinite since there

> the interior principle of impulsion which is the cause of all this movement in the decimal fraction finds itself once again . . . and coincides with itself in a transparent duality, where impulse, labour, potentiality, pain are transformed into possession, peace, enjoyment and repose.[15]

For those of us who, unlike Hegel, find it hard to wax lyrical over a fraction, Rousselot adds a second comparison, drawn this time from Thomas' angelology. According to Thomas, since the Angels are pure minds, they are 'interiorly infinite', knowing themselves continuously by intuition of their own essence. Humans, by contrast, lack such inner infinitude, since they must continually look for themselves, travel in mental search of their own identity, without ever reaching the pure

[15]Cited in ibid. 27–8, pp. 363–4

self-knowledge which characterises the Cherubim. These are, Rousselot warns, only metaphors to help us with our problem. But they are vital metaphors, for they set us out on the right road. The many dogmas defined by the Church, and the complex ideas through whose instrumentality they develop, stand in relation to the initial, personal, concrete knowledge possessed by the apostles in something of the way that Hegel's imperfect decimal fraction relates to the complete fraction which its digits cash, or express in greater detail, yet never manage to equal, even in their sum. Similar, too, is the manner wherein human beings, in their autobiographical confessions, though they have the psychological acumen of Augustine or Proust, do no more than stammer when their efforts are compared with the self-understanding of the Angels.

And here the related notions of sympathetic understanding and the immanent intelligibility of the living mind begin to come into their own. For, as Rousselot puts it:

> The whole dogmatics of the Church, even in its most abstract concepts and judgments, is nothing other than the explicitation of the concrete personal knowledge which the apostles had of the man Jesus, and which they transmitted, as they were able, to their disciples.[16]

By thus placing Jesus Christ, sympathetically grasped by the living mind of the apostles, at the centre of his solution to the problem of development, Rousselot achieves what De Lubac would later imitate, namely, in a phrase of Karl Barth's which De Lubac made his own: a 'Christological concentration' of the issues involved. In Rousselot's words:

> The whole of Tradition issues in a catechesis about Jesus Christ, because all the saving truths were in Jesus Christ. His person is not an object of doctrine. His person is the source, goal, reality, truth, of all doctrine. Why? Because he is God made sensuous, God manifested, God manifesting himself.[17]

[16]Ibid., 29, p. 365.
[17]Ibid., 37–8, pp. 373–4.

And here Rousselot is able to cite some words of St Thomas in the *Summa Theologiae* to the effect that the Word Incarnate is 'in a certain sense one single thing with the truth', *unum quodammodo cum ipsa veritate*.[18] And as Rousselot justly remarks, it is the adverb *quodammodo* which his theory seeks to explain. All the treasures of divine truth lie hidden in the Word Incarnate, who contains its *pleroma* or plenitude. No one has seen God, but the only Son has made him known; whoever sees him, sees the Father.

All dogmatic development, then, is an attempt to *monnayer Jésus*, to commute the incarnate Word into convenient coin. He is the 'privileged object which contains in itself all the rest'. Or again, in more technical language:

> Just as one's own self-definition or, better, one's own intelligible self-possession, is the desired moving force, the ideal goal, the regulative idea of all natural intellectual life, and just as the intelligible possession of God in the beatific Vision is the counterpart of those terms in all supernatural life, so the definition of Jesus, the intelligible possession of Jesus, is the moving force and regulative idea of the whole life of faith.[19]

Rousselot stresses, however, that even the apostles could not have had a full 'synthetic possession' of the person of Christ; they could not have grasped his intelligibility totally. For Christ is God, and such an exhaustive understanding of God is impossible, even in the beatific Vision.

Rousselot has thus answered, at least to his own satisfaction, his first question: How can the faith of the Church be substantially identical with that of the apostles? His answer, it turns out, concentrates on the mode in which the many dogmas are precontained in the single changeless knowledge which is the apostolic deposit. That mode is not, as the Baroque and later Scholastics thought, logical; it is Christological.

[18]*Cf. Summa Theologiae.* IIIa., q. 59, a. 2, ad i; q. 3, a. 8: 'Verbum est conceptus aeternae sapientiae a qua omnis sapientia hominum derivatur.'
[19]'Petite théorie', 39, cf. p. 375.

He must now deal, then, with his second problem: the mechanism whereby these various dogmas are explicated. Rousselot sees this process as taking place through the transformation of sympathetic knowledge into conceptual. One can know chastity by attending a course on moral theology in which the concept of chastity is explained; one can also know chastity by being chaste, by developing an affinity with that virtue, by growing in its *habitus* and thus exhibiting that which the concept defines. Following St Thomas, Rousselot insists that this second, connatural or sympathetic way of knowing is no less intellectual than abstractive, conceptual knowing. It is, rather, intellectual in a different way. Whilst these two types of knowledge are not mutually inclusive but genuinely distinct, they may support and supplement each other. For Rousselot, the sympathetic knowledge of the christologically concentrated New Testament revelation is lodged in the Church as a whole. Yet, in addition, the Church has, in the historic episcopate, a 'magisterium' whose function, exercised on behalf of all, is to *prendre conscience*, to become aware of the revelation thus sympathetically grasped when it takes appropriate conceptual form. The propositional definition of dogma by this magisterium is not new cognition. It is *recognition*, 'reconnaissance'.

In recognition, at least as Rousselot uses that term, one looks at oneself acting and, having acted, expresses the meaning of one's action either in reply to a question lodged by some other person, or in internal dramatic monologue, to answer a question one has thought of oneself. True, vital knowledge exists undivided, remarks Rousselot in evident dependence upon the key idea of Blondel, 'dans l'action même', in action itself. And this explains, he concludes, how the Church has only to watch herself believing or doing in order to be able to give her response in interpreting, in 'cashing' the deposit. This she can do, Rousselot insists, not only without using syllogisms worked out by her theologians (*pace* the later Scholastics) but even (pace, surely, Newman) without recourse to historic tradition. The passage from lived knowledge, that is, the possession of the changeless deposit, to conceptual knowledge, namely, the detailed articulation of dogma, may be achieved in a twinkling. It can be long and laborious, but it need not be. Of course, historians can show the remote origins and gradual, protracted development of the background to an act of doctrinal definition. But for Rousselot, what they are describing is not, strictly speaking, the development of the doctrine, but the emergence of the explicit question to which the doctrine is an answer. Certainly, that process of emergence may take centuries, during which an 'infinitely complex and at first incoherent concourse of circumstances' finally issues in a clear question, such as: Was, or was not, Mary preserved from all stain of original sin on the grounds of the foreseen redemptive value of her Son's atoning work? The trouble, the travail, lies not so much in thinking of the answer, but in formulating the question. By contrast, we could conceive a crisis in the passing on of Tradition so violent and acute, an attack of a sudden kind on so crucial a point of faith, that the Church would quasi-instantaneously become aware of both the danger and the dogma, and 'utter her response like a cry'. It is, perhaps, more to the credit of the environment of Hastings than to that of his theological sources that Rousselot goes on to compare the Church to a competent tennis-player who may yet be unable to state the rules by which he plays, until one day his partner in the men's doubles hesitates on a point, or the boy who picks up the used balls asks him after the match.

De Lubac, having had the privilege of access as a very young man to this remarkable paper, amassed a store of Christian erudition during his studies both in Sussex, and, after the return of the French Jesuits from exile in 1926, at Lyon-Fourvières, soon to be almost synonymous with the 'New Theology'. His chosen materials were the Fathers, the great Mediaevals, and two philosophers, the Christian Platonist Maine de Biran and Blondel.[20] In his own literary restrospect, *Mémoires sur l'occasion de mes écrits*, De Lubac would define his own theological purpose in these terms:

[20]For De Lubac as a practitioner of *ressourcement*, see H. U. von Balthasar, *Henri de Lubac. Sein organisches Lebenswerk* (Einsiedeln 1976); instructive is the title of the Italian version of this study, *Il padre Henri de Lubac. La tradizione fonte di rinnovamento* (Milan 1978).

Without claiming to open up new avenues of thought, I have sought rather, without any antiquarianism, to make known some of the great common areas of Catholic tradition. I wanted to make it loved, to show its ever-present fruitfulness.

For this reason, he would continue, he rejected any view of *ressourcement* that scorned later developments as a history of decadence:

The Latins have not pushed aside the Greeks for me, nor has St Augustine diverted me from St Anselm or St Thomas Aquinas; nor has the latter ever seemed to me either to make the twelve centuries that preceded him useless or to condemn his disciples to a failure to see and understand fully what has followed him.[21]

The first fruits of his prodigiously retentive mind would be *Catholicisme. Les aspects sociaux du dogme* (1938), an attempt to think through the main teachings of the Church as aspects of a single whole, what Newman would have called the 'Christian Idea'.[22] According to De Lubac, this 'Idea' is the mystery of Christ, seen as the basis for the unity of the Church, itself regarded as the means whereby the human race is eschatologically united in the Vision of God. The first chapter, despite its title, 'Dogme', has nothing directly to our purposes, save in so far as De Lubac is clearly picking up Rousselot's 'Christological concentration': presenting revelation in terms of Christ's re-creation of the unity of man.

After *Catholicisme* came the Second World War. Between spells in a German detention centre, De Lubac began to produce that swift-flowing stream of books which has never

[21]H. de Lubac, S. J., *Mémoires sur l'occasion de mes écrits* (Namur, 1989), pp. 147–148.

[22]H. de Lubac, *Catholicisme. Les aspects sociaux du dogme* (Paris 1938, and subsequent editions up to 1983[7]). On the thematic of this study, see E. Maier, *Einigung der Welt in Gott. Das Katholische bei Henri de Lubac* (Einsiedeln 1983).

since dried up.[23] At the same, he became the target of criticism from the representatives of the Neo-Scholastic party. Whether it was his approach to the existence of God (deemed irrational), or his Eucharistic theology (regarded as downplaying trans-substantiation), or his work on grace (considered as threatening the gratuity of the supernatural and its distinctness from the purely natural order), the accusations, by, say, 1946, were flying thick and fast. The quarrel with Catholic divinity over 'la Nouvelle Théologie' came to its head in 1950, the year of publication of Pope Pius XII's encyclical *Humani generis*, widely interpreted as an attack on that movement, and of De Lubac's own removal from teaching by the Jesuit General. But these were also the years when De Lubac turned to the topic of doctrinal development in his own right.[24]

De Lubac's chief *ex professo* contribution to the subject was a 'bulletin' in which he expounded his own views by describing and criticising those of other people, and notably the Neo-Thomist writers from Gardeil to Boyer.[25] De Lubac was especially concerned to define his own position over against 'Logicist' approaches of whatever kind, and especially by distinguishing it from that of his confrère Boyer. His positive remarks are hardly more than a re-statement of Rousselot's case, the latter being, of course, unknown since unpublished. Providence having ways that are not ours, De Lubac's *Bulletin* would bear fruit not only in Karl Rahner's more massive exploration of its central theme but also in the making of *Dei Verbum*, the Dogmatic Constitution of the Second Vatican Council on divine revelation.

De Lubac's forthright rejection of logicism was based on three arguments. First, Boyer's view did not fit the known facts. Where Boyer saw only a linear development of theological logic, history shows what De Lubac called

---

[23]See, up to 1974, K. H. Neufeld – M. Sales, *Bibliographie Henri de Lubac, S. J. 1925–1974* (Einsiedeln 1974²).

[24]Cf. A. Hammans, *Die neueren katholischen Erklärungen der Dogmenentwicklung* (Essen 1965), p. 4: 'Many of the ideas which would be put forward in the "theological" explanations of dogmatic development have their sources in the "New Theology".'

[25]'Bulletin de théologie fondamentale: le problème du développement du dogme', art. cit.: referred to henceforth as 'Bulletin'.

a perpetual reaction to the surrounding environment, by way of defence, elimination, sorting out, transformation, assimilation.[26]

In other words, no historian could write an account of how a doctrine has developed, without speaking about the wider history of culture and ideas in which the growth of that doctrine was situated. Whether by acceptance or rejection, the development of doctrine is certainly indebted to non-logical factors. Secondly, Boyer's thesis reduced dogmatic development, in De Lubac's view, to the same ordinary level as the natural processes of the human mind. True, St Thomas, in the opening question of his *Summa Theologiae* speaks of how *sacra doctrina* argues from the articles of the Creed to other truths. But this article is not about doctrinal development: *doctrina* in this context is for Thomas simply theology. Moreover, even where the task of theology is concerned, Thomas does not describe its mission as the deducing of new conclusions from revealed truths, but as a relating of some one group of revealed truths to another, in order to highlight the coherence which unites the fundamental revealed principles of the Gospel to the rest of Christianity's detailed teaching.[27] Thirdly, Boyer's position does not really take into account how the Catholic Church actually behaves. In making a solemn doctrinal judgment, the Church does not pronounce on the strictly rational worth of the reasonings put forward in favour of the point of view she sanctions.

What she looks for is not whether a given proposition is or is not correctly deduced, but whether it is or is not contained in her faith.[28]

De Lubac concludes, then, from his survey of Logicist writing on the topic of doctrinal development that we must speak

[26]Ibid., p. 139.
[27]Here De Lubac was indebted to M.-R. Gagnebet, 'La Nature de la théologie speculative', *Revue Thomiste* XXXIV (1938).
[28]'Bulletin', art. cit., p. 145.

not simply of natural logic but, more profoundly, of 'une certaine logique du sens chrétien', 'a logic proper to the meaning of Christianity'.[29] Since human reasoning did not originate divine revelation, it cannot master it either. In this connexion, De Lubac highlights two respects in which theologians excessively impressed by their chosen philosophical handmaids may fail to allow the self-revealing God his freedom to disclose his truth in the way which pleases him, rather than them. First, the divine mystery may express itself concretely, in images, and these require imaginative sensibility, rather than reasoning skills, for their interpretation. Although De Lubac seems to have in mind here chiefly the linguistic images embedded in the scriptural witness to revelation, the point might well be extended to include the enacted images of the divine Glory and the divine Drama, (an engaged observer of the *Nouvelle Théologie*, the Swiss theologian Hans Urs von Balthasar *would* so extend it in years to come.)[30] But secondly, De Lubac insisted that, even where revelation in Christ yields such 'abstract' doctrine as that subjacent to the Fifth Ecumenical Council, Constantinople II, for whose 'Neo-Chalcedonian' majority there is (thanks to the intervention of the hypostasis of the Word of God), no metaphysical personality in the human Jesus, it would be a mistake to see such Christological dogma as the issue of pure intellectualising of a somewhat glacial kind. It was, he maintains, a strictly religious 'exigence' that pressed the Christian intellect towards discoveries in the philosophical order – concerning, above all, the clear distinctness of the ideas of personality and nature – which it then used in the elaboration of the dogma. That 'exigence' was the religious perception of Christ's unity, *quod unus sit Christus*, 'That Christ is One', as Cyril of Alexandria entitled a treatise highly influential in the rise of his own Christology to conciliar fame and fortune.

But if, in these ways, we allow the imagination, and the religious spirit, to act as channels for the development of

---

[29]Ibid., p. 147.

[30]H. U. von Balthasar, *Herrlichkeit* (Einsiedeln 1961–9); *Theodramatik* (Einsiedeln 1973–6).

doctrine from out of the apostolic deposit, how shall we answer the charge that the result of such activities is innovation – new truths which earlier Christian generations never dreamed of? And what, in particular, of the Logicist contention that, were we to abandon the claim that later dogmas were logically pre-contained in earlier, as conclusions concealed in their own premises, we should be forced to admit that the development of dogma provides the Church with nothing less than new revelation? De Lubac deals with this problem on two levels. At one level, the more superficial of the two, he offers some debating points, which are limited though not without value. Thus, he points out that there may be more than one way to extract a truth from another truth held earlier. Logical pre-containment may not be the only kind of pre-containment. Evidently, he was thinking of the Christological pre-containment suggested to him by Rousselot's essay: there, our understanding of aspects of the Church's dogmatic faith through a conceptual mode of knowing is said to be pre-contained in the grasp of Jesus enjoyed by the minds of the apostles in loving sympathy. Or again, De Lubac insists, against Boyer, that even a logically-contained doctrine, once extracted, is in a sense new. To deny this one would have to show how a truth could be at one and the same time revealed in itself, and yet not perceived by any actual human mind. And this would involve postulating that dogma can exist independently of the minds to which it is meant to be communicated. That, for example, the dogma of papal infallibility as defined at Vatican I already existed as a dogma in the second century, even though no actual second century person was aware of the fact.

De Lubac's response to Boyer on this level is barely more than agreement with him that, in the matter of the novelty of post-apostolic doctrine, we face a difficulty – but the difficulty, adds De Lubac, attaches to Logicism too. To underline the seriousness of the problem, he reminds us that Marín-Sola had gone so far along the path of concession to the idea of the post-apostolic revelation as to speak of a 'mediate revelation' taking place whenever doctrine moved out of a latent, virtual condition into its manifest and

actualised state. So as to guard himself against the charge of
denying that revelation is completed with the death of the
last apostle, Marín-Sola had revived the ancient Thomist idea
that the apostles and they alone of all early Christians, knew
all doctrine in an explicit fashion. But, remarks de Lubac,
what a price is being paid here in terms of historical
verisimilitude! How could the apostles have expressed to
themselves truths whose formulation presupposes later habits
of thought? How can we explain their refusing or neglecting
to pass on these truths to their successors? Or, if they did pass
them on, how are we to explain *ce déluge d'oubli*, this 'flood
of forgetfulness', which must have overwhelmed the Church
in the second Christian generation?[31]

Our problem admits no resolution until such time as we
re-formulate – so De Lubac contends – our very idea of
revelation itself. Here too we may discern the hand of
Rousselot, who had suggested exactly the same thing. To call
the original content of revelation a 'series of propositions' is
not, De Lubac complains, to designate it 'exactly or
sufficiently'. The content of revelation is that divine
redemptive *action* which is summed up in God's gift of his
Son. The mystery of Christ, is the 'Objet globale' of
revelation. The mystery of Christ is 'le Tout du dogme',
dogma in its unified entirety. But this is not to say, De Lubac
hastens to add, that propositional truth is alien to revelation.
It is simply that such propositions are arrived at on the basis
of revelation only by a process of abstraction. This process
has two stages. In the first stage, we distinguish
between the redemptive act itself, and our knowledge of it.
Our response to the redemptive act, and this holds true for
the apostles as well, is not itself a matter of reflective
understanding. It is a lived knowledge, what Rousselot would
term a vital knowledge immanent in our action, in our
activity of responding to the mystery of Christ, wherein all
our powers, and not just mind but will and sensibility also
are engaged. De Lubac prefers to say that it is only through
an abstraction that we thus distinguish, first, between the

[31]'Bulletin', p. 153.

mystery in act and the mystery proposed to our faith, and, subsequently, in a second stage of abstractive thinking, between, on the one hand, certain propositional truths concerning, it may be, the Trinity, Christology, grace, and, on the other, the totality of the global revelation. Such abstractive processes are legitimate, even necessary, since the human mind can only preserve the total truth by reflecting on it according to its own mental laws. And yet, De Lubac warns, an essential condition for the integrity of such processes has it that we must not lose our hold on the mystery of Christ, 'le Tout du dogme' in all its concreteness.[32]

By getting this abstractive process into clear perspective, therefore, we can simultaneously accept the testimony of history that Christian doctrine has undergone massive development *and* preserve the truth that in Jesus Christ the whole of revelation was presented to man at one moment and one moment alone. All the doctrinal explications that follow the apostolic age are simply *le monnayage*, the conversion into small coin, of a treasure already possessed in its entirety by the primitive Church. *Monnayage* was, of course, Rousselot's term: 'cashing' Jesus. All the Church has done, De Lubac concludes, is to convert an original arithmetical unit into 'more distinct fractions'; once again, an echo of Rousselot's metaphor drawn from Hegel's *Logic*.[33]

What both the logical and the organic school have forgotten, then, is that revealed truth is a unique case. It cannot be identified with a body of logic or the being of an embryo. Revelation and doctrinal development must be rethought in terms proper to the mystery of Christ who gave Christianity its distinctive truth–content and its specific manner of arriving at truth.[34]

---

[32]De Lubac's explicit references in this context are, however, to the Jesuit exegete Joseph Huby's 'La Connaissance de la foi dans s. Jean', in idem., *Le Discours après la Cène* (Paris 1932), p. 153, and Augustine, *Epistolae* 187, 34 (PL 38, 845): 'Non est enim aliud Dei mysterium nisi Christus'.

[33]'Bulletin', pp. 157–8.

[34]*Dei Verbum* I. 2.

When in 1960 de Lubac found himself rehabilitated and taken into the warmth of papal favour, being appointed by Pope John XXIII to the pre-conciliar theological commission in preparation for Vatican II, he had the chance to offer this Christological view of revelation and development to the wider Church. And sure enough, if we turn to *Dei Verbum* chapter I, there we find it in the very first paragraph.

There we read that, through divine revelation, the most profound truth about God as well as about human salvation shines out for us *in Christo . . . qui mediator simul et plenitudo totius revelationis existit*: 'Christ . . . who is at one and the same time the mediator and the plenitude of the whole of revelation'. And in his 1968 commentary on *Dei Verbum*, *La Revelation divine*, de Lubac remarks, with surely a degree of personal satisfaction, 'The Council could say no better than this'. Yet while pointing out that the Council made a significant breakthrough in calling Christ not only *le révélateur* but also *le révélé*, not just the revealer but the revealed, de Lubac is able to cite among the texts of Tradition that back this up certain words in the German language:

In Jesus Christus, dem Menschgewordenen Gottesohn, ist die Fülle der göttlichen Offenbarung erschienen.
In Jesus Christ the Son of God become man, the fullness of divine revelation has appeared.[35]

Words written in 1937, at the end of Karl Rahner's first year of teaching in the theological faculty of Innsbruck University which, through the *Anschluss*, the forcible annexation of Austria to Germany, had just become part of Hitler's Third Reich. But the author of these words was not Karl Rahner, though it is unthinkable that he did not read them at the time. The author was Pius XI, and the occasion was the anti-Nazi encyclical *Mit brennender Sorge*. This is, then, a suitable point at which to divert our

---

[35]H. de Lubac, *La Révélation divine* (*Commentaire du préamble et du chapitre 1 de la Constitution 'Dei Verbum' du Concile Vatican II*, Paris 1983³), p. 44.

attention from England to France, where it has hitherto been focused, and to look at what was happening in the German-speaking world, and notably in its greatest, if maverick, Scholastic theologian, Rahner himself.[36]

[36]Cited from *Acta Apostolicae Sedis* 29 (1937), p. 150.

9

Karl Rahner

Life and work
Karl Rahner was born on 5 March 1904 at Freiburg-im-Breisgau.[1] His father, like his grandfather before him, was a school master. The family, which included six siblings of Rahner, one of whom, Hugo, would also become a Jesuit theologian and scholar, was practising and devout. Rahner appears to have had a particular devotion of his own to his mother, who lived to the age of one hundred and eight. When he was eighteen, he entered the noviciate of the society of Jesus at Feldkirch in the Austrian Voralberg, and subsequently studied philosophy at the Jesuit scholasticate of Pullach, near Munich, and theology at its equivalent at Valkenburg, in the Netherlands. Since he was destined by his superiors to teach the history of philosophy, he was sent to his home town, Freiburg, whose University was celebrated for this discipline, thanks to such figures as the Neo-Thomist Martin Honecker (1888–1941), and his near-namesake, the highly original re-interpreter of the history of Western 'thinking of being', Martin Heidegger (1889–1982). Although Honecker was Rahner's official mentor, his participation in Heidegger's celebrated seminars meant more to him personally, and accounts for his membership of what his fellow-Jesuit, Erich Przywara, called the 'Catholic Heideggerian school', whose other members included J. B.

---

[1]For Rahner's life, see H. Vorgrimler, *Understanding Karl Rahner. An Introduction to his life and thought* (Et London 1986[2]).

Lotz, G. Siewerth, M. Müller and B. Welte.[2] Honecker, indeed, found Rahner's doctoral dissertation on Thomas' epistemology, later published under the title *Geist in Welt*,[3] far too Heideggerian, and rejected it accordingly as an essay in *eisegesis*.[4] Rahner went on to qualify in theology at the Jesuit faculty of Innsbrück, where he produced a more acceptable lucubration this time on a very different theme, the origin of the Church from the side of the crucified, according to patristic exegesis of John 19, 34.[5] Much of the intrinsic interest, as also the problematic quality, of Rahner's work lies in the interplay between these two very different sides of his inheritance – the philosophical element, itself not only Scholastic and, to a degree, as with all 'Transcendental Thomists', Kantian, but also Heideggerian, and the mystical-contemplative element, which was not only patristic but also Ignatian.[6] As to the former, it is worth recalling that Heidegger himself considered any philosophical reflection worthy of the name to issue from *alêtheia*, the 'unveiling' of the truth of being – the self-same metaphor, of course, that the term 'revelation' also contains.

Rahner remained at Innsbrück, engaged in teaching work, until 1939, when the National Socialist government suppressed

[2]For this school, see K. Lehmann, 'Karl Rahner', in H. Vorgrimler-R. van der Gucht (eds.), *Bilan de la théologie du XXe siècle* (Tournai 1970), pp. 836ff.

[3]*Geist in Welt* (Innsbruck 1937).

[4]Rahner's rejection of the noble but doomed enterprise of Neo-Thomism (as he saw it) is obvious: see G. McCool, S. J., 'Karl Rahner and the Christian Philosophy of St. Thomas Aquinas', in W. J. Kelly, S. J. (ed.), *Theology and Discovery. Essays in Honour of Karl Rahner, S. J.* (Milwaukee 1980), pp. 63–93. The Neo-Thomist background to Rahner's Scholastic inheritance is helpfully described in idem., *Catholic Theology in the Nineteenth Century. The Quest for a Unitary Method* (New York 1977). To what extent Rahner remained in the wider Thomist tradition is a matter of dispute. A negative, but fully argued verdict, is offered by C. Fabro, *La svolta antropologica di Karl Rahner* (Milan 1974).

[5]*'E latere Christi*: Der Ursprung der Kirche als zweite Eva aus der Seite Christi des zweiten Adams. Eine Untersuchung über den typologischen Sinn von Jo. 19, 34', Diss., Innsbruck University 1936.

[6]This interplay is well brought out, in the context of Rahner's Christology, in particular, by J. H. P. Wong, in his *Logos-Symbol in the Christology of Karl Rahner* (Rome 1984). In his foreword, however, Rahner confesses that too often he left the insights deriving from these two inheritances unconnected.

the Jesuit faculty, and paid Rahner the special compliment of expelling him from the Tyrol under a 'district prohibition' order. After the War, he again taught at Innsbrück: from 1948 to 1964, when he succeeded Romano Guardini in the Chair of Christianity and the Philosophy of Religion at Munich. Soon enough, however, and much to Guardini's disappointment, Rahner abandoned Munich for Münster in northern Germany, where the faculty would allow him advanced students in theology proper. These were also the years of his considerable involvement in the Second Vatican Council, where he assisted the German bishops as a *peritus*. In 1971 he retired back to Munich, where he lived in a house set aside for Jesuit writers, a *domus scriptorum*. He died at Innsbrück on 30 March 1984.

Rahner's works are forbidding in extent – over four thousand titles, ranging over the whole gamut of theological themes, and drawing on not only the Scriptures, the Fathers, the mediaeval divines, and those of the Baroque and modern periods, but also on selected theologians belonging to traditions other than his own. They can also be forbidding in style - thanks not only to his philosophical transcendentalism, but also to his desire to use all the possibilities of syntax (and notably the German participles) to help him express his theological meaning.

The 'Pre-Conciliar' Essays on development
Rahner's first contribution to our subject, the essay 'Zur Frage der Dogmenentwicklung', was written in 1954, and cites de Lubac's 'Bulletin' as one of its own sources.[7] Rahner opens with the warning that this is a subject which cannot be treated in an *a priori* manner. A sound theory of development:

> cannot be deduced with the necessary exactness and precision from general theological considerations alone, but must be arrived at inductively from the actual facts of such a development.[8]

[7]'Zur Frage der Dogmenentwicklung', *Schriften zur Theologie* I (Einsiedeln 1954); Et: 'The Development of Dogma', *Theological Investigations* I (London 1961; 1964).
[8]Ibid., pp. 39–41.

We need, in other words, the fullest historical research into just how development took place. Here we may note Rahner's concern, in the theological enterprise at large, to integrate positive theology into systematic: a concern evidenced by his own doctoral thesis on the origin of the Church in the riven side of Christ, according to the Fathers; by his study of the history of penance in the early Church, and by his editorial work on the historically comprehensive *Lexikon für Theologie und Kirche.*

But can Church history, by itself, supply us with the theoretical understanding we seek? Rahner gives three reasons why it cannot. First, growth in historical understanding depends on making illuminating comparisons between different historical processes. For instance: by comparing what we call the French Revolution with the American Revolution which preceded it we come to a better grasp of what revolutionary transformation may be. But in the case of Christian doctrine, we have only one example of this process, that which is given in the history of the apostolic Church. We might, however, Rahner concedes, profitably compare *segments* of this single total process. Secondly, the process of development in doctrine will not come to an end until the Parousia. But a complete law of dogmatic development cannot be stated until that total process is complete – and for all we know this may take millenia. Thirdly, the process of doctrinal development involves two freedoms or spontaneities: the freedom of man in history, and the transcendent freedom of the Holy Spirit. So we can never expect there to be an iron law of development.

This being so – there being no possibility of stating full or adequate laws of doctrinal development – must we regard the total process as simply anarchic, at any rate *quoad nos*? As Rahner puts it

Are we not leaving the field open to the rankest proliferations of pseudo-theological speculation and callow visionary enthusiasm?[9]

[9]Ibid., p. 42.

One thinks, perhaps, of the more extravagant Mariological and Josephological theses that some bishops are said to have wished defined as dogmas when they left the Iberian peninsula for the Second Vatican Council.

Rahner assures his readers, however, that we are not reduced to regarding doctrinal development as, to all intents and purposes, an anarchy. First, although we can state no perfect laws of development, we may well be able to state imperfect ones.

> There are, of course, certain laws of dogmatic development which, because they are known *a priori* ... may be applied to 'developments' in an obvious way – though certainly with prudence – in order to determine whether they are genuine developments of the faith of the Church ...[10]

What these incomplete *a priori* 'laws' may be he will describe later. As a second reason for thinking that we are not simply here floating on a boundless sea, Rahner points out that, of its nature, dogmatic development becomes slower and slower as time goes on. As he explains:

> The fuller and clearer truth becomes, the more strict it becomes, and the more thoroughly it excludes possibilities of error.[11]

Thus, for instance, in Christology, once we have travelled as far as Nicaea it is a comparatively short journey to Chalcedon, whilst beyond Chacedon, Constantinople III, the anti-Monothelite council, is scarcely more than round the corner.

Thirdly, and here we have what Rahner regards as the decisive factor, the process of development might, through human weakness, get out of control, but in fact we have the promise of the Holy Spirit, who will guide the Church, and thus the Church's consciousness, the Church's dogma.

[10]Ibid.
[11]Ibid.

At this juncture, Rahner turns back to consider the incomplete *a priori* 'laws' of development he mentioned earlier. They turn out to be a number of general principles – three in all – bearing on the idea of dogmatic evolution. The first states that a development can never overthrow a revealed truth. Any revealed truth, no matter how primitively expressed, remains permanently valid. The second reminds us that, despite what has just been said, the statements in which faith expresses God's saving truth are, like all human statements, finite. Rahner highlights the implications of this for our subject when he writes:

> Our statements about the infinite divine realities are finite, and hence in this sense inadequate. That is, while actually corresponding to reality, they do not simply cover it in its entirety. So, every formula in which the faith is expressed can in principle be surpassed while still retaining its truth. That is to say, in principle at least, it can be replaced by another formula which states the same thing, and what is more states it . . . by . . . opening up more extensive – more delicately nuanced – prospects (*Ausblicke*), on to facts, realities, truths: things which had not been seen explicitly in the earlier formulation and which make it possible to see the same reality from a new point of view, in a fresh perspective.[12]

And this leads Rahner to the making of his third 'law'. He insists that such evolution in dogmatic formulae is not just a matter of an intellectual advance, only of interest to theologians or philosophers. It may have direct relevance to human salvation. This is because men always receive salvation in the way appropriate to their historical conditions, and so their historical mind-set.

> For it is not just man's unchangeable metaphysical essence (*Wesen*) which he has to insert into the economy of God's message, but his concrete, historical contingent reality, his existence (*Dasein*), with all it includes.

[12]Ibid., p. 44.

And under this heading Rahner places

> the spirit of the times, the possibilities of his epoch, his
> concepts, which, granting all the fixity (*Stetigkeit*) of
> metaphysical truth, are none the less historically
> conditioned.[13]

Where, then, do these three considerations (the word 'law' is
hardly appropriate for such affirmations) finally leave us?
They present us, Rahner remarks, with a pre-conception of
development as change *within* identity – not change *of*
identity. The decisive feature, in other words, is not progress,
nor does the Church become cleverer as time proceeds. In
this context change takes place within a self-identical reality
and truth. The change in question is change appropriate to a
given age of the Church's history, but it does not imply the
abandonment of an earlier perspective. The Church possesses
a memory, and this memory integrates all that she has ever
known, and preserves it safe and sound.

At this juncture, Rahner raises a major point which had
occurred to Tyrrell also. All this business about improved
formulae and changing perspectives – is it not really the
history of *theology* that we are talking about, rather than the
history of faith itself? Is not the subject of this discussion
something which, in Rahner's words:

> could never become the authentic and plenary revealed
> Word which grasps revelation itself?[14]

Rahner deals with this objection in two ways. First, he appeals
to the fact of the Church's practice. The Church understands
her doctrinal decisions not just as theology but as
Glaubenswort, the 'Word of faith' – not indeed as new
revelation, but nevertheless as the Word uttering revelation
itself, truly and with binding force. Secondly, Rahner argues
that a certain development of dogma, and not just of

[13]Ibid., p. 45.
[14]Ibid., p. 46.

theology, can be shown to be necessary. God's revealing Word is directed through the medium of the historical process at the *total* history of humanity. In any given age, the real understanding of what has been revealed, and its existential appropriation by human beings, depends on the transformation of the original propositions of faith into propositions which relate the original revelation to the people in the new historical situation. Indeed, Rahner goes so far as to say:

> It is only thus that they become propositions of faith, emerging into the real, historically conditioned human world of human decision and action.[15]

(This stress on the hard, historical necessity of dogma is Newmanesque, but Rahner's account of why dogma is thus necessary is reminiscent of Blondel.) If these transformed propositions, Rahner continues, were merely private interpretations – the *theologoumena* proposed by particular subjects, and in that sense subjective theologising – then there could be no guarantee that they correspond to the original revelation. And in that case, we should not have, in any post-apostolic generation of the Church's life, *eine Aneignung des Glaubens, die selber Glaube ist*, 'an appropriation of the faith which is itself faith'.

To grasp this more deeply, Rahner turns, as had Rousselot and De Lubac, to the idea of revelation itself, and, more especially, to what is implied in saying that revelation is closed with the last apostle's death. Does this mean, Rahner asks, that apostolic revelation is a kind of 'definitive catechism'? Such a view would do justice neither to the nature of human understanding nor the divine gift. And he writes, in a manner which throws back the mind to De Lubac's work:

> Revelation is not the communication of a definite number of propositions . . . to which additions may conceivably be made at will, or which can suddenly and

[15]Ibid. p. 47.

arbitrarily be limited. Rather is revelation an historical dialogue between God and man in which something happens, and in which the communication (*Mitteilung*), is related to the happening, the divine action (*das Geschehen, das Handeln Gottes*) . . . Revelation is a saving happening, and only then and in relation to this a communication of truths.[16]

Rahner goes on to explain that in Christ God has communicated himself definitively to the world in such a way that his saving plan is fully visible. As Rahner puts it

everything has been said and given in the Son of love, in whom God and the world have become one forever without confusion, but for ever undivided.[17]

Here we have Rousselot's, and De Lubac's, christological 'concentration', but now given a clearer rationale in terms of the Chalcedonian definition. Everything we say about the God-world relationship now turns on the Incarnation. And so the statement that revelation has been closed turns out to be, in fact, a positive statement: it tells us that in Christ the divine fullness is already given and received. We cannot conceive of revelation without thinking of a receiver as well as a giver – a revelation which no one accepted would not be a revelation. Rahner stresses that this 'closed' revelation is made *to the Church* which, as a result, truly possesses the revealed Reality. Whereas, and *pace* the Modernists, knowledge of the revealed reality comes from obedient faith, from the divine Word, and not from 'religious experience' in the Church, nevertheless, in that divine Word, the divine reality itself is truly given to the Church. As Rahner writes:

The believing Church possesses what she believes – Christ, his Spirit, the earnest of eternal life and its quickening power. The Church cannot leave the Word

[16]Ibid., p. 48.
[17]Ibid., p. 49.

behind in order to grasp this reality. But neither does she possess a word *about* the reality rather than the reality itself.[18]

This is an important passage in which Rahner – in effect – defends against Tyrrell the idea that the Church enjoys here and now a contemplative possession of the saving reality, whilst agreeing with Tyrrell that it is also true that, in traditional theology, the later Church's knowledge of God comes entirely from hearing – *fides ex auditu*, from the sovereign Word of God (as Karl Barth would say) and not from any experience. Rahner integrates these two at first sight incompatible ideas by saying that what is given through faith in the Word is the divine reality itself, even though this reality cannot be apprehended or described except through the Word. This position enables Rahner to go on:

> Consequently, the Church's hearing of the Word and her reflexion upon the Word heard are not *merely* a logical activity, an attempt gradually to squeeze out all the logical virtualities and consequences of the Word heard as though it were a numerical sum of propositions.[19]

Instead, the Church's reflection on the Word takes place 'in living contact with the reality itself'. But how are we to understand this more-than-logical reflection on revelation? For Rahner, the light of faith and the assistance of the Holy Spirit, given us to help in our grasp of revelation, are far from simply being 'a sort of supervision given by a teacher'. They are not just what Boyer, for instance, conceived as negative assistance preventing the Church from making false logical deductions from revealed propositions. Rather, remarks Rahner, the hidden but present and posited Reality takes part in its own understanding.[20]

To appreciate the depths of this remark we may need to

[18]Ibid.
[19]Ibid.
[20]Ibid., p. 50.

bear in mind that much of Rahner's early work was in the history and theology of mysticism, while in the years between the Second World War and the writing of this essay on doctrinal development he produced a considerable output of spiritual theology.[21] Mystically, the light of faith provides us with a kind of structure of intuition – what Rahner calls a subjective *a priori* under grace, comparing such a gracious enabling of understanding with Kant's idea that only the mind's pre-possession of certained structured operations allows it to find pattern in the world about it. This is, clearly enough, Dhanis, *inclinatio fidei*, and Rahner makes here the important point that we cannot expect to observe that inclination of faith in some quasi-empirical way, any more than we can expect to observe in such a fashion the object itself which the light of faith illumines.

> The light of faith, the impulse of the Spirit, do not permit of being isolated for inspection in a reflexive process in which attention is turned back upon itself and withdrawn from the object of faith. They are the brightness which illuminates the object of faith, the horizon within which it is contained, the mysterious sympathy with which it is understood . . . .[22]

And so the object of faith is not something merely passive which we could examine in a detached spirit to see whether or not we might develop its content. The object of faith is, at one and the same time, a true object – something independent of ourselves – and also that very principle by which it is itself grasped.

Rahner now turns to the rôle in dogmatic development of human reasoning activity, as that sets to work on what he calls the 'original propositions', given to us in and with the object of faith, the self-revealing God, in Christ and by his Spirit. Rahner, it should be noted, has no intention of simply de-bunking this approach, as found in the Baroque and Neo-

[21]Especially in *Schriften zur Theologie* III (Einsiedeln 1956); Et *Theological Investigations* III (London 1967).
[22]The Development of Dogma', art. cit., p. 51.

Scholastics up to Gardeil and Marín-Sola. Rather does he make his own the terminology of 'implicit' and 'explicit' common in the Thomist tradition to which, in a distinctly oblique and tortuous way, he belonged. The Church discovers what is *implicitly contained in* these propositions. But Rahner denies that this is just a matter of logic. Other forms of theological reasoning are also strictly relevant here, such as arguments from *convenientia*, 'fittingness', of the kind beloved by Thomas, or the 'probable' arguments from Scripture and Tradition espoused by such later divines as the Jesuit Würzburg theologians of the eighteenth century. As Rahner says:

> It may occur that a more particular or more exact statement appears to fit in harmoniously with a more general, less determined combination of statements or ideas. In this way, each throws light on and supports the other without its being possible to see that the more particular statement can be inferred with logical stringency from the more general one as its only possible consequence.[23]

Thus, for instance, the fact of Mary's assumption is not a strict deduction from the hope for the general resurrection of the redeemed, yet the more particular statement illuminates the more general, and vice versa. The grounds on which Rahner welcomes such non-logical forms of argumentation here derive from his basic position on revelation and faith as we have already charted it. The Church:

> through the luminous power of the Spirit is in contact with the *res* [reality] itself. This power makes use of logical processes but its influence does not cease there, because it possesses the very *res* in question as a present principle of knowledge, of it, and not just propositions about a remote reality.

[23]Ibid., p. 52.

Rahner at once adds, however:

> always remembering that the present knowledge cannot
> be had without a basic minimum of such propositions[24]

– one of the numerous qualifications in Rahner which show
that he did not, as is sometimes alleged, reject the
propositional element in revelation. Furthermore, Rahner
stresses that it is not for the individual to say whether assured
progress in doctrinal development has been achieved by way
of such arguments. All that he or she can judge is their
natural probative force. The decision rests with the faith of
the Church, a Church who finds herself in possession of a
definitive knowledge of faith by means of such arguments
(or, Rahner adds, sometimes *despite* them), and a Church,
too, who sees that the development in her understanding has
taken place in the light of the Spirit. And so Rahner accepts
that it may be impossible for theologians *hic et nunc* to
demonstrate that a now explicit knowledge in faith was truly
contained in a less explicit earlier knowledge.

However, Rahner firmly insists that, despite what has just
been said, we must maintain that, objectively speaking, new
formulations of dogma were indeed 'contained' in an earlier
form of faith-consciousness. Should we fail to assert this,
either we shall have to concede that a later proposition is new
revelation, or we must agree that there can be an
apprehension of the revealed object quite independent of the
earlier divine pronouncements about that object. And neither
course is acceptable. How, then, does Rahner see this 'pre-
containment' which is such an important feature of our
subject?

Rahner's account is divided into two parts. First, he
considers the deduction of new propositions from old, from
out of the 'original propositions' given in revelation. In
Marín-Sola's terms this is the problem of the virtually revealed.
And the reader will recall that the Spanish Thomist, accepting
that the deduced truths are genuinely fresh truths, felt obliged

[24]Ibid., pp. 52–3.

to call the Church's definition of such truths 'mediate revelation': in other words, a *sort* of new revelation. Rahner has a different viewpoint.

> It is not particularly hard (he writes) in the case of God's utterances, to answer the question why a proposition of this kind – the result of an explicitation of what is virtually implicit – should be conceived of as stated by God and hence credible on God's personal authority.[25]

He explains why by drawing a contrast with a human speaker, who 'never can survey all that necessary consequences which in fact follow from his statements'. Let us take a real historical example: say, the foreign policy speeches of the Weimar Republic's foreign minister, Gustav Stresemann, which according to the English historian of twentieth century German politics A. J. P. Taylor committed liberal democratic policy to precisely the same foreign policy goals as those of Hitler. We who study such human words cannot be sure whether all the consequences drawn by Taylor were really intended as a communication of the speaker's own mind. But, so Rahner maintains:

> when God speaks, the case is different. He is necessarily conscious of the actual vitality and dynamism of his immediate communication, and aware of all its virtualities and consequences. Moreover, he has from the very beginning the intention and the will to bring about its explicitation and to guide it with his Spirit. Thus virtual explicitation, looked at from the point of view of God as speaker, is simply explicitation and nothing more, even if it requires real deduction by us looked at from our point of view as hearers.[26]

The second part of Rahner's response to the question, How

[25]Ibid., p. 60.
[26]Ibid., p. 61.

are later dogmas objectively precontained in revelation? begins from the observation that the starting-point of a dogmatic development need not always be a proposition. In the natural order, we certainly come across a kind of knowledge which is not itself articulated in propositions, yet forms the point of departure for an intellectual process that can generate propositions. Rahner takes the example of awareness that one loves another.

> The lover knows of his love. This knowledge of himself forms an essential element in the very love itself. The knowledge is infinitely richer, simpler and denser than any body of propositions about the love could be. Yet it never lacks a certain measure of reflexive articulateness.[27]

The example would surely have delighted Rousselot with his concept of the apostles' *connaissance aimante* of Christ. And Rahner goes on to describe how this reflexive articulateness might develop itself more fully, leading the lover to comprehend the nature of his love more clearly. What happens if we apply this notion to the development of dogma? Rahner suggests that the apostles would have enjoyed a global experience of this kind, lying behind propositions and forming what he calls

> an inexhaustible source for the articulation and explication of the faith in propositions.

Even in those cases where Christ's spoken word as such was the necessary starting-point of the apostles' faith – since the actual content of revelation could have been available in no other way, as with Christ's *logia* about the Father – the words embodying those assertions were always heard in the context of a vivid experience of the Lord himself. Thus such words

> require the complete experience, which in turn becomes

[27]Ibid., p. 65.

continually more explicit and reflexively intelligible as the content of these sayings is unfolded.[28]

This is what we are observing in the theology of the New Testament. By handing on not simply Christ's words but his living presence in the Spirit to those who came after them, the apostles ensured that this same process of development would continue in the later Church. We have to distinguish, therefore, between *ein formell Gesagtes*, 'something directly stated', and *ein formell Mitgeteiltes*, 'something directly communicated'. Much in historical revelation may have been directly communicated that was not directly stated. Thus when, for instance, someone says that 'Christ died for us', everyone understands what is meant by dying, or by death, in that statement. The whole human experience of death can be really communicated and heard, even though neither speaker nor hearer has ever translated the idea of death into adequate propositions.

Rahner was nothing if not continually conscious of his own enterprise as a theologian. Not surprisingly, then, he finishes his account of dogmatic development in *Schriften zur Theologie* I by drawing some conclusions about theological method. Investigation of the nature of doctrinal development provides us with the context in which theology must set to work. The inferences he draws, at this early period in his work, are conservative in character. An account of the nature of doctrinal development will encourage theology to persevere with its time-honoured tools. First, it must retain its concern for the exact meaning of revelation using all available instruments that lie to hand for this task. Secondly, it must continue to practise the 'analogy of faith': comparing and correlating the propositions it hears nd understands through scanning the original revelation in its records. Thirdly, theology must take the form of an enquiry into the logical consequences of these correlations – but with the new confidence, offered by Rahner's essay, that, however complex and protracted its explorations here may be, they

[28]Ibid., p. 66.

need not necessarily go outside the sphere of what the revealing God has actually communicated.

The bridge to Rahner's second attempt to investigate the subject is provided by his own paragraph of 'signing off' in *Schriften zur Theologie* I, which is a reasoned affirmation of how judgement about dogmatic development can only be made in the Church a such.

> It was only to the Church as a whole that the promise was made that she should possess the original faith entire and unclouded. She alone and not any isolated individual has the organs which, without fear of error, can bring this reflexion to completion with universally binding authority. In the last resort, this is why it is only in the Church that there is a secure guarantee of a permanent connexion between the original faith (in part global and implicit) in contact with the reality itself by grace and the light of faith, and the 'new' explicitation by theological means. The individual recognises the faith as binding and certain only as he grasps it in the Church and with her.[29]

Rahner's second contribution to the topic, much less full, detailed and bibliographically informative than the first, was an Innsbrück lecture of 1957, later reproduced in *Schriften zur Theologie* IV.[30] In Überlegungen zur Dogmenentwicklung', Rahner refines a number of points made in the earlier easy. But, to begin with, he places our subject – the idea of doctrinal development from the Victorians to the mid-twentieth century Church – in the illuminating context of controversial theology.

> In the nineteenth century, Protestant liberal theology reproached the Catholic Church with an unreal and fatal petrifaction of ancient dogma. Now neo-Protestant orthodoxy, with a renovated doctrine of *sola Scriptura*,

[29]Ibid., p. 76.
[30]Überlegungen zur Dogmenentwicklung', *Schriften zur Theologie* IV (Einsiedeln 1960; Et *Theological Investigations* IV (London 1966).

charges the Catholic magisterium with an arbitrary search for novelty, which creates new dogmas without any foundation in Scripture. Hence while we formerly had to defend our maintenance of ancient Christian dogma, in fact and on principle, and our right to understand it today as it has been understood for fifteen hundred years, now on the contrary we have to uphold positively the right of dogma to undergo development.[31]

The central question, therefore, controverted from the two sides, concerns the reconciliation of 'authentic identity' with 'really genuine development'. Its intrinsic difficulty, Rahner remarks, is compounded by the fact that it raises ultimate questions about the relationship of being and becoming, of identity in change, and raises those questions not only in the register of ontology but also in that of the philosophy of mind, where they appear in a somewhat different guise – as questions about the self-identity of truth, and yet truth's genuine involvement in history. In the face of these formidable issues it is, from the viewpoint of Catholic apologetics, consoling to reflect that the very same process of development may already be detected within the inspired Scriptures of the New Testament itself.

What, then, does Rahner's second, and last, 'pre-conciliar' contribution to the subject add substantively to his first, and more major essay? The principal novelty is a fuller account of the respective rôles of theologians and the magisterium. Speaking of the crucial rôle of the teaching office here, Rahner writes:

The Word of God is always the Word delivered by the authorised bearer of doctrine and tradition in the hierarchically constituted Church. The element of being officially delivered, the reference back to an authorised teacher, the hearing of the Word *from* the authoritative teaching person, belongs to the constitutive moments of

[31]Ibid., p. 5.

dogma, and hence also of dogmatic development. This is because dogma as such must be proclaimed by the magisterium, the teaching authority, in order that it can be believed *fide ecclesiastica* along with the Church. Thus dogmatic development does not depend merely on the office *in facto esse*. It also depends on the magisterium in its *fieri*.[32]

But Rahner goes on to insist that, nonetheless, the 'unofficial' element of development – the *charismata* or gifts of the Holy Spirit, and the work of theology – always 'anticipate the thought of the (teaching) office' in the sense that, as history suggests, the magisterium only promotes doctrinal development after the momentum of such development has already been launched by other forces.

Thus the decision to canonise a doctrinal development must be 'preceded and justified' by an insight into the meaning and place of such a development within the Christian faith as a whole. And yet the decision itself, once made

possesses its own evidence, which is intrinsic to it and is only attainable in the decision.[33]

And in an important passage, Rahner explains in what sense the Roman pope, in defining *ex cathedra* a teaching which has matured under the guidance of the ordinary magisterium, may be said to codify the faith of the whole Church.

We do not maintain that the faith of the Church prior to a papal definition has no connexion with the ordinary magisterium. On the contrary, it is precisely when this faith grows and ripens under the guidance of the ordinary magisterium, even when this does not make itself heard clearly by exercising its supreme authority, that the importance of the magisterium, working in harmony with the faith of the listening Church, is all

[32]Ibid., p. 15.
[33]Ibid., p. 31.

the clearer and greater. The ordinary magisterium, in papal encyclicals, addresses, etc., makes a decisive contribution to the ripening of the self-awareness of the believing consciousness of the whole Church. But the process of ripening, as history shows, is more manifold, multi-storied, organic and harmonious than it would be if reduced, as some imagine, to what survives in a methodical, juridical formalising of the process: namely, the authoritative decree and its obedient acceptance.

And Rahner adds that, furthermore,

the faith of the whole Church, existing prior to the definition, does not by any means imply that every individual member already explicitly believes the proposition in question as something revealed by God. It only means that this faith exists in the Church as an attribute of this moral person which is the whole Church. The function of the papal decision is precisely to ascertain this faith and so to impart this general faith of the whole Church to those who do not yet believe. The pope is the point at which the collective consciousness of the whole Church attains effective self-awareness, in a manner which is authoritative for the individual members of the Church.[34]

In 'Überlegungen', Rahner was also wrote interestingly of the dialectic not between office on the one hand, and devotion and theology on the other – what Newman would have termed the regal office, *vis-à-vis* the pastoral and prophetic functions in the Church – but also between what he termed an 'expansive' and an 'intensive' or 'concentrative' moment in the various phases that doctrinal development exhibits. For on the one hand, there is in the history of tradition a

constantly increasing articulateness in the unfolding of the objects comprised within (faith's) horizon . . .

[34]Ibid., pp. 32–3.

and so an *expansive* moment, whilst, on the other, we can also observe a

> dynamism of compression and simplification, tending towards the blessed darkness of the one mystery of God.[35]

For faith in the triune God in his self-communication tends at once to display the multifaceted significance of that special history in which Father, Son and Holy Spirit have showed themselves in the world, and yet also to draw all those many facets, expressed in the many tenets of the Church's belief, into a surer and deeper unity. Faith, in other words, tends both to proliferate in its assertions, thanks to the richness of the Gospel revelation, but also to distinguish ever more clearly those themes that are really ultimate in that multiplicity. This tension between expansion and concentration was, however, as we shall see, collapsed by Rahner in his later, post-conciliar writings in favour of the second, intensive moment.

Rahner's account, as found in these writings of pre-1962, is a masterly response to the problem which this book has considered. Particularly attractive is the eirenic but lucid way in which he integrates elements drawn from different, and apparently opposed, schools: especially, the combination of Neo-Scholastic elements with those taken from 'la nouvelle théologie'. It is, however, Newman who stands behind the whole.[36] During the years of Rahner's writing, the

[35]Ibid., pp. 25–16.

[36]Newman's name stands first in the bibliography offered at the opening of 'Zur Frage der Dogmentwicklung'. The absence of reference to the work of Möhler and the Tübingen school at large is noteworthy. At least among the German Jesuits, Möhler's discovery of the notion (and reality) of doctrinal development seems to have been still born. For Möhler's work, see H. R. Nienaltowski, O. F. M. Cap., *Johann Adam Möhler's Theory of Doctrinal Development. Its Genesis and Formulation*, op. cit; for the previous forty years Möhler's relevant writings had aroused the interest of theological historians, but their influence on the doctrinal theologians whom this study treats was not pronounced – until, that is, the emergence of Congar. Earlier studies of Möhler include: A. Lösch, 'J. A. Möhler und die Lehre von der Entwicklung des Dogmas', *Theologische Quartalschrift* 99 (1917–18), pp. 28–59; 129–52; A. Minon, 'L'Attitude de Jean Adam Möhler dans la question du

appreciation of Newman had greatly advanced in Germany, thanks not least to the *Newman-Studien*, collaboratively edited by Rahner's friend and Jesuit colleague, Heinrich Fries.[37] In Rahner's early work, the ravenous beast, called up from the depths by the Modernists, as heirs, after a fashion, of Newman's idea of development, in their attempt to justify the heterogenerous transformation of Catholicism, is domesticated, and becomes, if not quite a lamb, then at least a house-dog with which one could live in relative comfort. It will remain for the two Dominicans, Edward Schillebeeckx and Yves Congar, to place the various writers who contributed involuntarily to Rahner's synthesis, into some kind of theological order. Unfortunately, as we shall see, the serenity and equilibrium which this subject had reached by the opening of the Second Vatican Council in 1962, was not to last. The differing subsequent careers of Rahner, Schillebeeckx and Congar, to be considered briefly in the concluding 'Retrospect and Prospect', will suggest why.

développement du dogma', *Ephemerides Lovaniesnes* 16 (1939), pp. 328–84; G. Voss, 'Johann Adam Möhler and the Development of Dogma', *Theological Studies* 4 (1943), pp. 420–44.

[37]The *Internationale Cardinal-Newman-Studien*, edited by G. Biemer and H. Fries, and published at Sigmaringendorf, achieved their twelfth volume in 1988.

10

Edward Schillebeeckx

Edward Schillebeeckx was born Cornelis Florentius Alfons on 12 November 1914 in Antwerp, Belgium, the sixth of fourteen children.[1] His father was a chartered accountant. Both his parents were distinctly devout: there were a great many household prayers, and the family attended Mass each morning at 6.30. This did not prevent his father from being somewhat anti-clerical. Schillebeeckx was educated by the Jesuits at Turnhout: they gave him an excellent grounding in the classical languages, and also awakened his interest in philosophy, as in the 'social problem'. However, he found the Jesuit atmosphere, as then existing, too formal and rigid. As a result of his gleanings in Church history, he decided, when the idea of a vocation to the priesthood and religious life arose, to opt for the Dominicans instead. After a noviciate with the Flemish Dominicans at Ghent, Schillebeeckx moved to Louvain for three years of philosophy. The Dominican prior in that University city was also, as it happened, president of the School of Social Studies there: his influence served to heighten Schillebeeckx's own social concern. At least equal in importance was the rôle of his student master, Dominicus de Petter, a philosopher whose epistemology and metaphysics (Thomistic, yet influenced by both Kant and Hegel) would remain with the young friar.[2] De Petter also introduced

[1]Biographical materials about Schillebeeckx here come from J. Bowden, *Edward Schillebeeckx. Portrait of a Theologian* (London 1983).

[2]P. Bourgy, 'Edward Schillebeeckx', in R. van der Gucht and H. Vorgrimler, *Bilan de la théologie du XXe siècle* (Tournai 1970), II., pp. 883 ff., offers a useful summary of De Petter's thought. See too on this P. Kennedy, O.P., 'Continuity underlying Discontinuity: Schillebeeckx's Philosophical Background', *New Blackfriars*

Schillebeeckx to the Catholic Tübingen theologian Karl Adam whose books *Das Wesen des Katholizismus* and *Christus unser Bruder* were enjoying a particular vogue at that time.[3] Adam's discussion of the psychology of Jesus as the Word Incarnate stimulated in Schillebeeckx, according to the latter's English biographer, John Bowden, an 'overriding interest in experience'.[4] After military service, which appears to have been a complete formality, except for instruction in First Aid – he devoted most of his time to reading the fathers of phenomenology, Heidegger, Edmund Husserl and Maurice Merleau-Ponty, as well as Karl Marx – Schillebeeckx returned to Louvain for his theological studies, which he regarded as distinctly *vieux-jeu*.

In 1941 he was ordained priest. About the same time, de Petter was removed from his teaching position by an intervention of the Order's Roman mother-house, Santa Sabina. Schillebeeckx's doctorate, which he gained in 1943, concerned the concept of *sarx* in Paul – an exegetical subject, then, which he chose, it seems, out of frustration with the state of systematic or dogmatic theology at Louvain. Nevertheless, he accepted a post as lecturer in dogmatics there, and retained it for the remaining months of the Second World War. That War seems to have made remarkably little impression upon him, something which Bowden ascribes, curiously, to the circumstance that the German military governor of his country had a Belgian wife! After the War, Schillebeeckx was sent for post-doctoral study to Le Saulchoir, where he made the acquaintance of Marie-Dominique Chenu, the historian of mediaeval theology and enthusiastic promoter of the social mission of the Church. Schillebeeckx came to regard Chenu as the twentieth

---

70. 828 (June 1989), pp. 264–77, which brings out the (probably excessive) depreciation of the cognitive capacity of the concept in De Petter's version of Thomism.

[3]*Das Wesen des Katholizismus* (Düsseldorf 1925); Et *The Spirit of Catholicism* (London 1929); *Christus unser Bruder* (Regensburg 1929) Et *Christ our Brother* (London 1931). For a complete bibliography, see M. Reding (ed.), *Abhandlungen über Theologie und Kirche. Festgabe für Karl Adam* (Düsseldorf 1952), pp. 319–20.

[4]J. Bowden, *Edward Schillebeeckx*, op. cit., pp. 26–7.

century's greatest theologian, basing this admiration on Chenu's combination of historical exploration of the Church's tradition with advocacy of her involvement in the world.[5] The former aspect of this enthusiasm throws light on Schillebeeckx's desire to document his work as fully as possible with reference to texts of all periods; in the latter respect, he regarded Chenu as a political theologian before the term 'political theology' was ever minted. Chenu had indeed spoken of the Church as, theologically, the 'Church of the poor and humble', the messianic community of the poor.

In 1947 he was called back to Louvain in order to write a second thesis, the *Habilitationsschrift* of the Germanic academic system, seen as a necessary qualification for higher level teaching. For this he wished to take as his subject the relation of nature and super-nature, the world and religion, but his colleagues actually needed a sacramental theologian. So Schillebeeckx produced his great and still untranslated *De sacramentele heilseconomie*,[6] lavishly and even hyperbolically praised by Père Albert Patfoort (later to be one of his examiners at the Congregation for the Doctrine of the Faith under Pope John Paul II):

> There is (Patfoort wrote) perhaps no other example of a treatise or, if one may say so, of a *summa* or encyclopaedia, that comprises such a lively and harmonious application of the whole range of aspects, both positive and speculative, that the understanding of a theological subject requires.[7]

Apart from this work, Schillebeeckx spent the lion's share of the period between 1947 and 1963 in the composition of articles, especially dictionary articles, some of which, however, reach to more than a hundred columns. In 1958 he was made professor of dogmatics and the history of theology

[5]On Chenu, see O. de la Brosse, *Le Père Chenu. La liberté dans la foi* (Paris 1969).

[6]*De sacramentele heilseconomie: Theologische bezinning op St Thomas' sacramentenleer in het licht van de traditie en van de hedendaagse sacramentsproblematiek* (Antwerp 1952).

[7]Père Patfoort was noting Schillebeeckx's great study in the *Bulletin Thomiste*.

at Nijmegen in the Netherlands, and remained in that post until his retirement in 1983.

Schillebeeckx's approach to dogmatic theology and the idea of development of doctrine.
In the background to Schillebeeckx's early dogmatic writings, the principal figure is that of the historic Thomas – by way of distinction from the re-constructed Aquinas of the neo-Scholastics. Rightly, he was not content simply to repeat the words of his theological masters – Thomas, and behind the latter, other mediaeval *magistri*, with, further back again, the Fathers of the Church. He wished to re-express the content of their teaching, drawing on what he regarded as the best philosophical thought of his time, and notably the Christian Existentialism of Gabriel Marcel, and the phenomenology of Maurice Merleau-Ponty, leading French philosophers of the decades immediately following the Second World War. Yet while the idiom of both Existentialism and phenomenology is discernable in for instance, *Christ, the Sacrament of Encounter with God*, it is not intrusive.[8] The theology, and the idea of theology, remain cast in a firmly traditional mould. The language of 'encounter' gives an attractive modern sound to what Schillebeeckx has to say, but what he has to say is in itself determined by traditional theological loci or sources.

Thus, for example, in *The Eucharist*, Schillebeeckx criticised what he perceived as a basic methodological fault in some contemporary Catholic approaches to the Eucharist which started out from a phenomenological point of departure without first clarifying what the Church's doctrine 'demands of one as a believing Catholic'.[9] In contrast to such positions. Schillebeeckx asserts that the first question to be asked is, 'What does God's word of revelation, in the Church's authoritative interpretation, tell me about the Eucharistic event?' It is easy to see in the light of such citations, how one recent student of Schillebeeckx's work can write, 'prior to

---

[8]*De Christusontmoeting als sacrament van de Godsontmoeting* (Antwerp 1958; 1959); Et *Christ, the Sacrament of the Encounter with God* (London 1963).

[9]*Christus' tegenwoordigheid in de eucharistie* (Bilthoven 1967); Et *The Eucharist* (New York and London 1968), p. 19.

the mid-1960s the starting-point for Schillebeeckx's theological reflection was the dogma of the Church'.[10] In the essay collection translated into English as *Revelation and Theology*, he insists that God's revelation grounds the human response of faith.[11] He accepted Thomas' position that revelation necessarily includes both an objective dimension – the action of God in creation and history as recorded and handed on in the 'articles of faith', and a subjective dimension – the inner illumination of the mind by which the Holy Spirit enables the believer to assent to what the intellect could never fully grasp as intelligible. He also held with Thomas that, while assent to the articles provides the necessary mediation of faith, faith's ultimate term is a spiritual union between the believer and God.

Transforming Thomas' understanding of revelation and faith into the phenomenological key of encounter between God and humanity, Schillebeeckx emphasised the dialogical character of the revelatory process. Divine initiative and human response make up the two sides of a relationship of mutual self-disclosure – what Schillebeeckx called 'revelation-in-reality'. Because the human partner in this dialogue is a body-spirit unity who comes to self-awareness through the concrete mediation both of the material world and of the 'other', the offer of encounter with a God who is, by contrast, pure Spirit must necessarily be made by way of a concrete, visible human history if human beings are to be able to hear and respond to that offer. Whereas all of creation and human history may be thought of as in some fashion revelatory of God for humanity, that general state of affairs only reaches truly lucid expression in the particularity of the Judaeo-Christian history of salvation culminating as it does in God's very self-expression in Jesus Christ.

However, Schillebeeckx stresses that all history – including even salvation history – remains ambiguous as such an offer of relationship until such time as it is explicitly identified for

[10]M. C. Hilkert, O.P., 'Hermeneutics of History in the Theology of Edward Schillebeeckx', *The Thomist* 51, 1 (1987), p. 99.

[11]*Openbaring en Theologie. Theologische Peilingen* I (Bilthoven 1964), ET *Revelation and Theology* (London 1967).

what it is through *naming* in the words of the prophets of Jesus Christ and his Church. To human beings, words and concepts are needful for genuine personal encounter to take place. While the body and bodily actions reveal a great deal about the inner person – the face, as Wittgenstein remarks, is the best picture of the soul – only the free choice to unveil one's deepest level of identity through words truly 'reveals' the person and allows authentic communication between dialogue partners as centres of freedom. For words clarify one's intentions, and disclose the true meaning in and behind the external manifestation. And so Schillebeeckx concluded that there are two inseparable aspects of the single offer of encounter with God: 'revelation-in-reality' (the mystery of actual encounter with God) is necessarily mediated through 'revelation-in-word'; and yet revelation-in-word never captures or exhausts the fullness of revelation-in-reality.[12]

Though maintaining that revelation, as encounter between God and humanity, is offered in some way to all, Schillebeeckx did not hesitate to grant the claim of Catholic doctrine that revelation is 'closed' with the ending of the apostolic generation. Writing in (originally) 1952, he declared that, while not solemnly defined as dogma, this claim was universally accepted by the ordinary teaching authority of the Church.[13] With the 'Christ-event', the 'constitutive' phase of revelation reached completion. God's self-revelation was finalised in that event, which Schillebeeckx describe as incorporating the preparation for Christ's coming recorded in the Old Testament, together with the saving mysteries of Christ's life, death and resurrection and the account of the mystery of human redemption found in the New Testament. Since the apostles were at once those who had known the earthly Jesus and the immediate witnesses of the risen Christ, their testimony established the essential continuity expressed in the Christian confession that Jesus of Nazareth is the world's exalted Lord. Once again, revelation-in-reality requires revelation-in-word. Schillebeeckx stressed that,

[12]Ibid., pp. 36–54.
[13]Ibid., p. 63

although the post-apostolic Church continues to live in the power of the Spirit of the risen Christ, the personal experience and testimony of the apostles bears a unique and non-recurrent character. The living tradition of the Church finds its *norma non normata* of authenticity in the apostolic Church and the latter's written tradition, the Scriptures. As revelation-in-word, the Scriptures function as a necessary but incomplete mediation of the faith-awareness of the apostolic body.

> The living reality is always richer than the written expression of this reality, at least as far as its literal and explicit meaning is concerned. But this written expression in itself contains a dynamism which embraces an inner reference to the fullness of saving truth.[14]

It is this objective dynamism, inherent in the mystery of revelation-in-reality as ever surpassing its own expression in the revelation-in-word, which governs Schillebeeckx's account of the development of doctrine.

Schillebeeckx's principal essay on doctrinal development takes the form of an article, 'Dogma-ontwikkeling', written for a Dutch encyclopaedia, the *Theologisch Woordenboek*.[15] He deals rapidly with what may be called the 'pre-history' of the problem: that is, the story of the idea of doctrinal development before the nineteenth century. That story has, he considered, little to teach us. For the Fathers, what would now be called 'development of doctrine' was simply a matter of finding better formulations of the 'rule of faith' over against heretics. For the mediaevals, the problem was limited to be a consideration of the relationship between the different Creeds. For the Baroque Scholastics, the issue was that of the theological conclusion – namely, how we may give our assent of faith to truths established by ourselves in theological reasoning. Thus for Schillebeeckx, the topic of development is only a century old; there is no 'traditional thesis' of Catholic theology in this realm.

---

[14]Ibid., pp. 15–16.

[15]'Dogma-ontwikkeling', *Theologisch Woordenboek* I (Roermond 1952), cols. 1087–1106; = *Revelation and Theology*, op. cit., pp. 63–92.

He offered, however, a typology of the 'solutions' to the problem offered in the modern period. Essentially, he identified three basic types of approach: the historical, the logical and the theological. The 'historical' solution involves trying to show through historical research that an unchanging identity holds good as between the various phases in the Church's confession of faith. Schillebeeckx agrees that, often enough, such research can show that there is, at least, no contradiction between those phases, and, that sometimes, moreover, important connexions inter-relate them. Yet history as such will never, he thinks, deliver the goods, since the historical method

can only re-construct explicit thought in all its historical situation, while a great deal of human thought takes place implicitly.[16]

Schillebeeck's 'logical' type of solution is evidently that espoused by Marín-Sola and, more radically, Tuyaerts. On this view, theological reasoning of a logical kind explains both the development of dogma and its unchanging character, Conceptually there is advance – hence development; objectively, however, the theological conclusion is identical with the premisses of faith – hence unchangingness. Schillebeeckx offers two arguments against the idea that logical reasoning is the essential principle of dogmatic development. First, a development of faith can only have a strictly supernatural principle. But consent to the conclusion of a theological argument is by no means wholly dependent on the light of revelation. Evidently, it is also dependent on human reason. Reasoning of a logical kind can be the principle of *theological*, but not of *dogmatic*, development. Secondly, the logical syllogism is itself only a partial formulation of human reasoning when seen as a psychological activity. In Schillebeeckx's words, that syllogism is

only meaningful when it is used as an element of

[16]Ibid., p. 70.

experiential knowledge, since the concept can only grasp reality by an element of experience.[17]

The logical approach, then, must be re-contextualised in a broader picture of how a deepening human understanding – of revelation as of anything else – takes place.

The 'theological' solution stresses, by contrast, religious contact with the reality of revelation itself as the seed-bed of dogmatic development. Here Schillebeeckx draws into the discussion a considerable number of the figures we have looked at in the gallery represented by this book, and especially Newman. Although Schillebeeckx describes this solution sympathetically, he proposes to offer a personal answer to the problem of doctrinal development, using elements from past accounts but highlighting more particularly the mediaeval notion of the 'light of faith'.

Schillebeeckx's theology of doctrinal development is founded on the idea of the inter-relation between nature and grace, as embodied in the work of Thomas. Between the orders of nature and grace there is a real discontinuity, since grace is precisely gratuitious, 'free', with regard to nature. Yet there is also continuity between them, since a single divine Providence embraces them both. If we apply this foundational description of the work of God in humanity to the topic of revelation, we arrive at the conclusion that, whilst all man's natural equipment for understanding truth will play a part in revelation, transcendental dimensions must also be taken into account.

> The natural factors, which also influence the development of dogma, therefore merge again and again into mystery, and are thereby adjusted or defined.[18]

Can we be more precise about how this happens? Schillebeeckx invites his readers to consider the distinction between the content of faith and the act of faith. Faith's

[17]Ibid., p. 74.
[18]Ibid., p. 81.

content issues from public revelation in all its objectivity. Yet its meaning may not be known explicitly from the start, being preceded, perhaps, by a stage consisting of 'implicit impressions' – a term distilled from Newman's vocabulary. The act of faith, on the other hand, is not simply the effect of our encountering the content of revelation – of reading the Bible, or hearing the preaching of the Church's ministers. For here God himself inwardly illuminates our minds, so that we can respond to the content of revelation in a supernatural way. By means of the light of faith, itself an instinct divinely implanted in us, we perceive the content of faith as a mediation of God's own truth. The *lumen fidei* thus enables us to judge whether what confronts is truly something to be believed on the authority of God himself revealing. But the development of doctrine, too, may be understood with the help of these ideas.

The data of faith, the 'given' from out of which we construct the content of revelation, lie embedded in the life of the Church: in the monuments of her Tradition (to use a phrase beloved of Congar) of which the New Testament Scriptures (and the Old in relation to them) are the chief. These data are themselves received by minds subject to growth of both a psychological and a sociological kind: they vary over time in their resources, whether inner – deriving from the psyche, or outer – coming from society. And so, where the perception of the content of revelation is concerned, there will naturally be development. But, on the other hand, the summation of our natural resources and the content of revelation does not specify the full totality of the factors involved. So far left out of the count is the *lumen fidei*, given us in order that we may apprehend the content of revelation as really *revelation* – the result of God revealing. Thus, in the context of human developments in perception, the infused light of faith makes it possible for us to apprehend the connexion between the different phases in which the content of revelation appears to us. For Schillebeeckx, the light of faith is the principle, therefore, not of development but of the continuous, indeed the fundamentally unchanging, character of the reality underlying such development.

Although the light of faith is itself a radiance that can neither distort nor deceive, in some given individual it may be, as Schillebeeckx puts it, 'lost' in consciousness – overwhelmed by other factors in the human situation. Thus we can never know with absolute certainty whether an individual reaction is the result of the working of the light of faith, or no. In a given dogmatic development, the light of faith works at first tentatively, through the consciousness of many individuals, differentiated as that consciousness is in the multifariousness of the human condition in the Church: one person a pious participator in popular devotions, say, another a theologian studying ancient sources. Eventually, however, the various voices echo each other: their testimonies converge. But even then, the mere happening of such a consensual reaction in the community of faith does not suffice to tell us whether an alleged development is genuine, or not. Only the Church's teaching office, with its charism of infallibility, can declare whether such a corporate response has taken place by virtue of the light of faith, and not just on the basis of this-worldly elements. Schillebeeckx thus concludes in a masterly passage:

> The converging activity of the light of faith in the Church's community of faith – together with the Church's infallible teaching office – is the single structural principle of the unchangeable character of the faith throughout all its different phases of development. The laws and factors which cause any human ideology to mature, including implicit thought and reflective reasoning, thus play an active part in the development of dogma. As such, however, they cannot make a datum of faith develop in its properly supernatural element. For this reason, they only play an instrumental part with regard to the activity of the light of faith and the teaching authority of the Church. The light of faith is, however, not revelation, and has, therefore, no creative function which might of its own accord put forward new truths. It is, then, through external stimuli, the rhythm of universally human progress and self-

consciousness, theological investigation and so on that the critical activity of the light of faith and of the Church's teaching office is provided with material. This is why human evolution is so closely interlaced with the development of dogma, why certain dogmas were defined at a late stage, why most are formulated in the language of the period, and so on.[19]

One could well go through this passage, picking up echoes of the various thinkers we have looked at in this study. Thus the stress on implicit thought is Newman's, as is the emphasis on the rôle of the Church's teaching office. The accentuating on the close connexion of human evolution with dogmatic development is reminiscent of Loisy; the insistence that the light of faith cannot in itself put forward new truths picks up an important element in Tyrrell. The acceptance of the contribution of rationality in its reflecting mood echoes Gardeil and Marín-Sola. The transcending of a purely propositional view of revelation follows De Lubac, while being simultaneously a return to Thomas and an anticipation of Rahner.

Schillebeeckx's own theological evolution may have left this essay far behind. As we shall see in the conclusion of this book, his present portrait of the history of Christian reflection is hardly one of doctrinal development at all. It is, rather, a theory of the multiple critical-hermeneutical attempts to recover the 'memory of Jesus' as a spur to human liberation. The attempts found in the dogmatic tradition seem, in this connexion, to have no greater call on our attention, and sometimes less, than many others. Nevertheless, we can be grateful to him for a minor masterpiece which deserves a place in the treasure-house of Catholic thought.

[19]Ibid., p. 91.

II

Yves Congar

Life and Influences

Yves Congar was born on 13 May, 1904 at Sedan in the French Ardennes.[1] His family belonged to the lower bourgeoisie. Unusually for the period, his childhood friends were Jewish and Protestant, spreading seeds of an ecumenical vocation. Despite earlier attraction to medicine, Congar decided in 1921 to enter the Parisian seminary known as 'of the Carmelites', where his spiritual director encouraged him to study Thomism, at the time the most sophisticated theological idom available in the Catholic Church. His mind awakened, he attended the Thomistic courses of the rising philosophical star Jacques Maritain, and frequented retreats given by Maritain's theological mentor, Garrigou-Lagrange. The Neo-Thomist disdain shown by Maritain and Garrigou for the more historically-minded study of Aquinas emerging in the Dominican Order, which they termed 'Palaeo-Thomism', accusing it of antiquarianism, foreshadowed certain conflicts in Congar's later career. Meanwhile, the young ordinand was frequenting the Benedictine abbey of Conques, whence he drew his lifetime love for the Catholic liturgy. He nearly joined the Benedictines, but decided instead for the Dominican noviciate of the Province of France at Amiens, which he entered in 1925.

Congar's serious studies were carried out at the Dominican study-house of Le Saulchoir, then at Kain-la-Tombe in

[1]For Congar's life, see especially J.-P. Jossua, O.P., *Le Père Congar. La théologie au service du peuple de Dieu* (Paris 1967).

248

Belgium, where teachers and pupils had sought refuge from the anti-clerical legislation of the Third French Republic. Thanks to the high standards of its 'regent' or president, Ambroise Gardeil, this institute had reached a level of academic attainment comparable with any university. Historical theology was a particular strength. The young friar read deeply in texts, whether classical, biblical, patristic or medieval. His concern to set Thomas within the context of the thirteenth century led to relations which the historian of medieval philosophy Etienne Gilson, but cooled the ardours of his friendship with the Neo-Thomists.

Congar's master, Marie-Dominique Chenu, had communicated an enthusiasm for the infant Ecumenical Movement, now drawing Protestants and Orthodox together, notably at the Lausanne Faith and Order Conference of 1927. Chenu suggested that a suitable model for a sympathetic Catholic contribution to that movement might be the ecclesiologist of the nineteenth-century German Catholic revival, Johann Adam Möhler. Accordingly, Congar selected as the subject of his 'lectoral' thesis (an internal Dominican degree) in 1928 Möhler's favored theme, the unity of the Church. On the eve of his ordination to the priesthood on 25 July 1930, he prepared himself by meditating on Jesus' high-priestly prayer for the unity of his disciples in John 17, with the help of the commentaries of Thomas and the contemporary biblical scholar Marie-Joseph Lagrange. This he recognised in retrospect as the true launching of his ecumenical vocation.

During two visits to Germany, he discovered the 'High-Church' movement in German Lutheranism, and, on a tour of the places associated with the career of Luther, intuited in the latter 'depths ... which demanded investigation and understanding'. Back in Paris, he was allowed to attend lecture courses by theologians of the Reformed Church of France, who were at the time re-discovering the classical dogmatic Protestantism of Calvin, and thereby preparing the way for the French reception of the anti-liberal neo-orthodoxy of Karl Barth. In time, Congar would be deeply affected by Luther's stress on the primary of grace, and of the

Scriptures, though avoiding Luther's accompanying negations
of the rôle of charity and of tradition. He would also be
influenced by Barth's massive emphasis on the sovereignty of
the revealing, redeeming and reconciling *Word* of God, whilst
regarding Barth's denial that God grants a saving co-causality
to creatures as 'disastrous'.[2] Though, at this early stage,
Protestantism still meant more to him than did Orthodoxy (a
state of things which would later be reversed), he also par-
ticipated in Catholic–Orthodox 'reunions of Franco-Russian
friendship', as these were discreetly called, where he encountered the ideas of Möhler's Orthodox contemporary and counterpart, the lay theologian Alexis Stefanovič Khomiakov.

So far as his own teaching was concerned, he was obliged by
Chenu's absence in Canada – for the founding of the Institute
of Mediaeval Studies at Toronto to take responsibility for a
course of theological propaideutics, 'introduction to theology'.
As part of his preparation, he looked into the work of the
Modernist exegetes and thinkers of the turn of the century.
(Alfred Loisy's monumental autobiography had just appeared.)
The idea came to him that his own generation should rescue
for the Church whatever was of value in the approach of the
Modernists. In his judgment, this meant two things. First, it
meant the application of the historical method to Christian
data – though not a restrictively 'historical-critical' method
where the dimension of faith was epistemologically blotted
out. Secondly, it meant greater attention to the viewpoint of
the experiencing subject, whose needs and concerns shift with
the contours of history itself. In the course of this work, he
discovered the contribution of the highly original Catholic
philosopher Maurice Blondel, whose reflections on the
relation of history and dogma had tried, as we have seen, to
chart a course between the Scylla of Modernism and the
Charybdis of what he dubbed 'Veterism' – essentially, closed-
mindedness to everything that historical study could offer to
the better grasp of a revelation which, though supernatural
and miraculous, was mediated by the texture of history.[2a]

[2]Y. Congar, *Chrétiens en dialogue. Contributions catholiques à l'Oecuménisme* (Paris
1964), pp. ix–lxiv.
[2a]See above, Chapter 5.

Blondel's concept of tradition struck him particularly forcibly.[3]

Congar's lectures on introducing theology, which were the origins of his interest in fundamental theology, were soon supplemented by far more numerous ones on ecclesiology. This was to remain, with ecumenism, the great passion of his life. It gave him the excuse to broaden his contacts, and so extend his sense of the church. This led him to the bi-ritual Byzantine-Latin monastery of Amay, and its ecumenical pioneer founder, Dom Lambert Beauduin, and also to England, where he made Anglican friends and began to acquire a thorough knowledge of the chequered theological history of the Anglican tradition. However, such visits, like his regular excursions to French cities for the preaching of the Christian Unity Octave, were simply punctuations of a domestic round of study and teaching, set within an austere monastic and liturgical framework. This conventual round continued until the outbreak of the Second World War when he found himself first mobilized as a military chaplain, and then immobilized, as a prisoner-of-war at Colditz. There he learned with dismay and stupefaction of the Roman condemnation of Chenu's academic manifesto entitled 'A School of Theology, Le Saulchoir', which had set out the shared theological vision and methods of that house.[4] As late as 1964 he confessed himself unable to comprehend the sense of this action, which he could only regard as based upon informational error. In fact, as later investigation has shown, the charge against Le Saulchoir was 'Semi-Modernism', a slippery concept indeed. In Rome, voices were raised, not least that of the Dominican 'master of the sacred palace', Mariano Cordovani, protesting that the emphasis of the Saulchoir men on historical context would end up by turning theology into cultural anthropology, deprived of any real hold on its divine subject-matter, revelation.

In the creative ferment which characterised the French

[3]Congar's course of theological propaedeutics is substantially present in *La Foi et la théologie* (Tournai 1968).

[4]See on this institution, and its programme, M.-D. Chenu, O.P., *Une Ecole de théologie. Le Saulchoir* (Tournai 1937; Paris 1985).

Catholicism of the immediately post-war years, Congar made a major literary contribution which will be outlined in the next section. However, the hesitations of more conservative Churchmen about his work were increasing. As early as 1947, he was refused permission to publish an article on the position of the Catholic Church vis-à-vis the ecumenical movement which was entering a new phase with the preparation of the first assembly of the World Council of Churches. The Master of the Dominicans warned him against a 'false eirenicism', which might be construed as indifference to specifically Catholic doctrines. Further editions, and any translations, of one of his works were prohibited. Despite these severe vexations, the make of ecumenical links went on, especially among the Orthodox as a result of a lecture tour in the Near East during the winter of 1953–4. In early February of the latter year, he returned to France, to hear the news that, following an article in the defense of the 'priest-worker' movement, to which a number of French Dominicans had lent their support, he was forbidden to teach. He was exiled first to the École Biblique in Jerusalem where, however, he managed to write his only substantial essay on biblical theology, and then, in November 1954, to Blackfriars, Cambridge. Only the kindness of Jean Weber, Bishop of Strasbourg, enabled Congar, at the time of his return to France in December 1955, to resume a pastoral and theological ministry. In retrospect, Congar believed that these difficult years had called forth in him an 'active patience', especially fitted to the work or ecumenism, a 'long process of convergence' as this was, bound up with the inner renewal of each Christian communion.[5]

With the coming of Giuseppe Roncalli to the papal chair as John XXIII in 1959 all was changed. Shortly after the new Pope's announcement of the calling of a General Council, Congar was named as theological consultor to the prepatory commission. At the Second Vatican Council itself, he helped write the 'Message to the World' as its opening, and worked on such major documents as *Dei Verbum* (the 'Dogmatic

[5]Y. Congar, *Chrétiens en dialogue*, op. cit., p. xxi.

Constitution on Divine Revelation'), *Lumen gentium* (the 'Dogmatic Constitution on the Church'), *Gaudium et spes* (the 'Pastoral Constitution on the Church in the Modern World'), *Ad gentes divinitus* (the 'Decree on the Church's Missionary Activity'), *Unitatis redintegratio* (the 'Decree on Ecumenism'), *Presbyterorum ordinis* (the 'Decree on the Life and Ministry of Priests'), and *Dignitatis humanae* (the 'Declaration on Religious Freedom').

Congar on dogma and its development

In *La Foi et la théologie*, his fundamental theology, published in 1968, but substantially a course offered at Le Saulchoir from the late 1930's onwards, Congar situates his account of dogma and its development within an evocation of that great overarching reality, Tradition. As Congar presents the matter, whilst the origin of Tradition lies in the Father's handing-over of the Son to the world, and the Son's subsequent acceptance of betrayal (also, in Latin, *traditio*, a 'handing-over') at the hands of sinful men, this two fold 'productive act', linked to a *masculine* divine symbolism, is received and transmitted in the Church's tradition whose ultimate subject is the Holy Spirit and which Congar conceives in essentially *feminine* terms. The entire Church, lay and clerical together, is the mediate subject of Tradition which she passes on not just as a teaching but as a reality, the reality of Christianity itself. And in terms drawn from Blondel's *'Histoire et dogme'*, Congar insists that Tradition constitutes 'the permanence of a past in a present in whose heart the future is being prepared' – thus transcending the limitations of a fixist conservatism or a falsely radical disregard for continuity.[6] In each age, the Church of Tradition puts forth expressive monuments, ranging from a liturgical text to an artwork, from a theological classic to a saint.

Though all such monuments embody insights into revelation, yet faith cannot for that reason do without dogma proper, presented by Congar as at once a truth and a value: a

[6] Y. Congar, *La Tradition et la vie de l' Eglise* (Paris 1984²), pp. 16–26; 86.

religious truth, filled with helpful significance for the believer's life and destiny. The essential meaning of dogmas is that which the Church's profound intention gives them 'ever the same', independently of the movement of human ideas. Yet of the formulae in which such dogmas are expressed Congar can only say with Galileo Galilei, 'And yet it moves' for they are ever-changing, and the Church's pastors and theologians are duty bound to seek out those that are most effectively 'catholic', universal, in terms *both* of the many different cultures to which her mission takes her, *and* of the ecumenical demands of the re-construction of her integral unity.[7] But it should not be thought that these *desiderata* of Congar's amount to a plea for the deliberate obfuscation of dogma in any sense that the plain Catholic could recognise. He insists that the value of dogma presupposes three things which the history of the centuries since the Protestant Reformation has called into question. And these are: first, the existence of a magisterium in the Church; secondly, the validity of conceptual affirmations concerning what lies beyond the empirical realm; and thirdly, the continuity of that bond which links together in a single chain the historic, revelation-charged facts; the testimony to these facts; the meaning given to these testimonies once the generation of eye-witnesses had passed away; and finally, the formulation of this meaning in the dogmas which the Church proffers to the faithful for their assent.

Congar's discussion of the nature of dogma takes as its most significant background the Modernist crisis of the turn of this century. He describes the origins of Modernism as a 'conjunction between a problem and a philosophic-religious climate'.[8] The *problem* was the tremendous historical and critical achievement of nineteenth century scholars, which necessarily confronted Churchmen with the difference between, on the one hand, the primitive Christian 'given' and, on the other, the dogmatic and institutional expressions of that 'given' which Christianity made its own in later

[7]Y. Congar, *La Foi et la théologie*, op. cit., p. 69.
[8]Ibid., p. 56.

centuries. How should the relationship between these two be conceived? The *climate*, philosophically speaking, was a subtle blend of evolutionism and the doctrines of Kant. Evolutionism, the tendency to construe reality in terms of the biological model offered for the life sciences by Charles Darwin, naturally took development to be 'transformism': a sloughing off of the old, rather than its continued being in a fresh guise. Kantianism criticised all claims to a conceptual knowledge of meta-empirical realities, for which it desired to substitute an ethical affirmation of the values implicit in existence. This same climate, considered religiously, was dominated by a 'desire to rejoin the modern world': in other words, to mediate between the Church's tradition and contemporary culture by some appropriate explanation of the former to the latter.

> In these conditions, the Modernists properly so called proposed a theory not only of dogma and dogmatic formulations, but of revelation itself. To keep religion free of those intellectual categories they deemed to be changing, relative, even outworn, they disengaged religion from intellectuality itself. They unburdened it of the claim, which they judged ruinous, to be a revelation, that is: a divine supply of ideas, of *truths*, conceptual in kind.[9]

Congar finds that the thought of Loisy and Tyrrell corresponds adequately to this summary, though he partially removes from the company of the French exegete and English spiritual theologian his fellow-countryman the philosopher Edouard Le Roy: for while Le Roy believed the positive sense of doctrine to be essentially *practical* – an imperative for conduct, he did not deny that the divine reality must be such as to justify the behaviour thus imposed, and so its later dogmatic representation. However, the Church's magisterium insisted that this is not enough: there is in the dogma concerned a true conceptual articulation, itself the measure

[9]Ibid., p. 57.

and rationale of the religious practice. Yet as this account suggests, this does not prevent dogma from being simultaneously truth *and* value: if pragmatism forgets the first, a 'wholly juridical orthodoxy of the mere letter' forgets the second. Though the Church's doctors and saints have attached the highest importance to certain formulae in which the meaning of the apostolic faith becomes transparent – the *homoousion* of the Arian crisis, the *transubstantiatio* of mediaeval Eucharistic controversy and the Council of Trent, nevertheless, at the end of the day, since faith is a 'power for life and contemplation' it terminates not in its own formulae but in God himself. Or, as Congar puts it, in a characteristic re-casting of Thomas' own statement to this effect, faith finds its end in the convenant relationship which is 'God for us and we ourselves for God'.[10]

After scanning the evidence up to the crisis of interpretation of that idea known as Modernism Congar concludes that the Fathers, notably Gregory Nazianzen, Augustine and Vincent of Lérins, are not without some recognition of doctrinal development, and that, moreover, the Middle Ages 'remained in their line'.

> On the one hand, it was persuaded that all truth lies in Scripture, and all dogma in the articles of the Creed, which comes from the apostles. On the other hand, it admits with equal tranquillity that God does not cease to 'reveal' to the Fathers and the Councils elements of liturgy, discipline and doctrine.[11]

However, what dominated was the idea of faith's unity, and the 'perfect' knowledge of revelation in the apostolic heads of the Church. In the wake of the great Scholastics and their commentators, little interested in history as these were, theologians became absorbed in disengaging what was (merely) logically implicit in revelation. While the First Vatican Council admitted, 'soberly, yet clearly' the existence

[10]Ibid., p. 71.
[11]Ibid., p. 94–5.

of such a thing as doctrinal development, it took the Modernist crisis to shake people out of their ahistorical dogmatic slumbers into reflecting on the conditions of such development. Since then, Congar continues, we have distinguished more successfully between the possibilities of understanding opened up by historical science as such, and those – much richer, from the theological viewpoint – which belong to the 'properly ecclesial and Christian tradition' in the matter of discerning whether and how some truth is included in the apostolic deposit. And Congar proposes as a guiding star the following proposition:

> The fact of a progress in the understanding of the faith finds its foundation in the very nature of revelation as in the proper character of the 'time of the Church', the latter being a community of human beings *en marche*.[12]

Like the Neo-Scholastics of the earlier part of the century, and above all Francisco Marín-Sola, Congar initially describes such doctrinal development as an explicitation of what is still implicit in the normative *donné* or 'given', of the apostolic teaching. As he points out, a reality or a truth can either be perceived in itself, 'in its own contours, or forms', or as enveloped in the gift of another reality or truth. With the Neo-Scholastics, Congar holds that the process of separating out one truth from the original reality may be thoroughly intellectual, and even strictly logical in character: an implicit truth, formally contained in another explicit truth, can be teased out by (deductive) 'explicative' reasoning. If, by contrast, the implicit truth concerned is only *virtually* contained in the truth established earlier, the reasoning process involved will require more *finesse*, what Newman called, in relation to the act of assent, the 'illative sense'. However, Congar, with his more acute feeling for history than the Neo-Thomists, proposes that, in addition, this kind of relationship of implicit to explicit also exists in the *practical* order. The dogmatically implicit can be enveloped in, for

[12]Ibid., p. 99.

example, a liturgical practice. Thus, the doctrine of the sacramentality of the episcopate may be said to have been so 'contained' in the Roman liturgical practice of ordaining the 'archdeacon' – the senior deacon – of the local church to the episcopal order without an intermediate promotion to the presbyterate. Yet Congar is sufficiently Thomist in his fundamental allegiance to add that what is thus implicit in action only becomes consciously explicit through the work of intelligence, of mind in act.

He insists that this business of the implicit element in revelation is not a regrettable necessity owing to human stupidity, but fits in well with revelation's own nature as the 'unveiling of a free and gracious design'. How does he understand this *convenientia*, or 'fittingness' of doctrinal development? He maintains that the Word of the revealing God is not a pure act of God which can function without engaging human co-operation. While classical Protestant theology characteristically fails to recognise the significance of our *agi*, 'acting', conceiving the Church's faith as, rather, a simple mirroring of the Word, and her history as a series of returns to that Word in the face of temptations to syncretism, Catholicism can echo the philosopher Henri Bergson and say, 'God has created creators'. The immanence of God in his creature means that the truth is not simply given to us but also lived out or acted upon – even though everything that is thus lived out is indeed graciously given. Congar finds the enduring value of Newman's essay to lie in its author's abilities to combine the qualities of historian and psychologist, for

> the living-reception of the faithful and the Church follows the conditions proper to the spirit of man.[13]

And here Congar notes, again, in Bergsonian language, that the Church has her own *durée*, her proper mode of temporal existence.

[13]Ibid., p. 104.

This *durée* is characterised at once by a permanence or identity of the work of Christ ... and by the ceaseless visitations of God, appropriated to the Holy Spirit, which theology analyses in its discussion of the 'divine missions'. The Holy Spirit, who is Christ's Spirit, first interiorises the work of Christ, but also, secondly, accomplishes it in never ceasing to 'take from him', our Alpha, to bear him to his plenitude, as our Omega.[14]

These being the fundamental conditions which mark the 'time of the Church', that time may be described as

filled by, in the first place, the free response of men to the word of the prophets, of Christ himself and of the apostles, a word given once for all, a Word itself normative and situating.

This response is conditioned in large part, Congar explains, by the changing circumstances of history. In the *second* place, however, the time of the Church is *also* made up of

divine initiatives or 'missions', given to men to arouse and fulfil a response of faithfulness and holiness.[15]

The development of the original *donné* marries in this way 'purity' with 'plenitude'.

How, in the concrete, does this development work? Congar does not speak of a single, unilateral way, but of ways in the plural. Fundamentally, they may be reduced to two. First, there is the way of 'faithful life', for between faith and the Christian life there is a 'constant coming and going'. Congar is careful to distinguish this position from that of Tyrrell, for whom devotional life enjoyed complete autonomy *vis-à-vis* dogma, and preceded belief. On the contrary, he says, history often shows the Church intervening to prune back a devotion or even to suppress it altogether. Secondly, there is the way

---

[14]Ibid., p. 105–6.
[15]Ibid., p. 106.

of theological precision: here we find faith in its rational mood, thinking out the sense of its own affirmations. Yet, he warns, dogmatisation by reference to this way of 'theological conclusions' alone is rare.

In both 'ways', Congar stresses, development may take place through response to pressures, or currents, in the circumambient secular sphere wherein the Church's life and thought are set.

> Any fact of civilisation can be the starting-point for a movement of thought in the Church. This is only normal, because the Church lives in the world, in time, and she receives assistance so that she may, precisely, offer divine testimony in time, through responding to the questions which history poses.[16]

Finally, Congar must consider how we can make our judgement that some given putative development really is a case of authentic development, one where a relationship of homogeneity unites new expression to the primordial 'fact' or 'given'. To some degree, Congar holds, such a judgement is made by way of teasing out what is logically implicit in an earlier stage of doctrinal truth. However, for Congar this factor plays a much smaller rôle than with earlier Dominican theorists of doctrinal development. What is implicit in revelation is above all the relation of things to the covenant design of the living God; and, in any case, unless some truth is formally attested by the Word of God, it can hardly be proposed to people for their *assent of faith*, though, should it be a logical entailment of truths that are so attested, it may well be presented to them for their *theological agreement*. From this logical or quasi-logical approach, characteristic of Scholasticism both mediaeval and modern. Congar passes on to the more historical manner of proceeding which relies on *documentation* for establishing the homogeneity of development. For Congar, such interrogation of the written witnesses of Tradition is necessary, but only partially effective.

[16]Ibid., p. 111.

Apart from the possible loss or corruption of such evidence in the course of time, an implicit knowledge of later explicit truths is extremely difficult, if not impossible, for a student of the relevant documents to establish. And Congar frankly admits that not all of the early Christian evidence is likely to point towards the later positions of the Church: it is only on the basis of Catholic faith that the historian of doctrine lays aside divergent witnesses as constituting a minority report. This leaves only one other possibility: we must make our judgement by reference to the Church's awareness and to her magisterium. As a Thomist and an historian, Congar is, however, careful to say that in judging on this basis, we must incorporate and use to their full limits the other two 'methods', those of logic and of appeal to documents. His appeal to the faith-awareness of the Church, and the judgement of her magisterium is not, of course, as our investigation of his concept of Tradition should indicate, a counsel of despair. Theologically, the Church is the only subject capable of grasping adequately the internal homogeneity of the revealed 'given' in its self-expression through time. With the assistance of the Holy Spirit, perception of the homogeneity between the apostolic deposit and its later explicitation can be found in the 'sense of the Church', the judges of which are the bearers of the apostolic ministry.

> If the final criterion of the homogeneity of developments is the Church's awareness of the self-identity of her life, and of the conformity of some 'novelty' arising in that life's duration with the form given once for all, then this awareness only receives its definitive character and its value as a criterion in and by the teaching of the episcopal body in communion with the successor of Peter.[17]

Thus the judgement of the hierarchy is the formal element which constitutes Tradition in its dogmatic value.

[17]Ibid., pp. 116–17.

The revelation given once for all, then, is conserved and proposed to all mankind by the Church Christ founded. Though the Church's mediation of revelation issues in objective determinations of its content, namely dogmas, Congar insists that public doctrine must be contextualised within a wider whole. The Church is not only a teacher; she is also 'Mother Church', and her total membership provides, over and above the specific doctrinal contribution of the apostolic ministry with its teaching office, 'the nourishing and educative milieu of faith'.[18]

In these convictions, Congar's theology in the post-conciliar period would register no change. The development of his own theological doctrine was placid, and his view of what theology in the Catholic tradition ought to be knew no interruption. Self-doubt and questioning of a radical kind as to the irreplaceable value and vital importance of the dogmatic tradition, not least in its reflective, theological form, to the Church's preaching, catechesis, worship, devotion and – above all – evangelisation, are not the features of the later Congar's work. To a certain degree, this fact differentiates him from the further evolution of Schillebeeckx, and, in a less marked manner, from that of Rahner. The cause of this parting of the ways may be summed up in a single word: 'hermeneutics'. It is to the unpacking of that bare assertion that, in a 'Retrospect and Prospect' we must, in conclusion, turn.

[18]Ibid., p. 51. I am grateful to Messrs Chapman for their permission to cite in this chapter material from my survey of Congarian theology, *Yves Congar* (London 1989).

12

Conclusion: Retrospect and Prospect

By the decade immediately preceding the opening of the Second Vatican Council in 1962, the idea of doctrinal development appeared to have reached a decent state of theological maturity. Although the topic was, in its modern form, no more than a century old, so much had been written, and of so high a quality, that the ship was safely steaming into harbour. To change the metaphor: what, in the time of Loisy, looked like a wild-eyed, hairy-chested caveman, clutching a tree-stump and threatening to lay waste all around him, had become a civilised elder statesman in dressing-gown and slippers, pulling reflectively on his pipe over a bottle of good port. There are several signs that this was so.

The first was Rahner's pre-conciliar essays which managed to integrate a number of the better thoughts of his predecessors since Newman. They did so with a quite admirable balance and comprehensiveness, leaving no major aspect untouched, and drawing all aspects into a unity. The unified quality of Rahner's presentation derived from two things. First, it came from the detailed inter-connexions Rahner was able to suggest, one thesis complementing and supporting another. Second, it was owed to the light provided by some of Rahner's characteristic theological insights, such as the notion that the *nexus mysteriorum*, the 'criss-crossing of the mysteries', taught by the First Vatican Council, is based ultimately on the fact that all individual doctrines converge on the single mystery of the triune God in his self-communication. If in some future persecution of the Church, or some cultural cataclysm involving the literary production

263

of the race, all the texts to which I have drawn attention in this book perished, Rahner's alone remaining, Catholic theology – as distinct from the history of Catholic theology – would have lost very little. Rahner's work is, therefore, the first reason for saying that, in the decade before the opening of the Second Vatican Council, our subject had come of age.

But secondly, the contributions of both Schillebeeckx and Congar also presuppose that, fundamentally, the problem of doctrinal development has been solved, so that all that remains is to arrange the various authors who helped to bring off this feat in an illuminating order amongst themselves. For Schillebeeckx, whilst the historical, logical and theological approaches to the subject have each their several weaknesses, by a judicious combination of the trio of types we may maximalise the advantages of each and minimise the disadvantages. Like a man sent to fetch water from a well, and provided with a choice of buckets, each of which leaks somewhere, Schillebeeckx does the sensible thing and puts all his buckets inside each other, in the reasonable hope that the sum-total of three leaky buckets will be one more-or-less watertight set of them. In the living stream of the Church's consciousness, the various ways of doctrinal development converge: the way of historical memory, the way of theological logic, and the way of devotion. And this is so even though only the Church's teaching office, with its charism of infallibility, can declare that this convergence has taken place by means of the Holy Spirit, and not from purely human causes.

The same assumption that, basically, the problem of doctrinal development has been solved, and so all we need is to get the elements of the solution into clearer theological and historical perspective also characterises the work of Congar. Congar in effect agreed with Schillebeeckx that what we need to do is to combine three ways of looking at the subject: (in his chosen terms) the way of historical documentation, the dialectical way of scientific reasoning, and that way which consists in consulting the present mind and practice of the Church, and its magisterium. Like the Schillebeeckx of the 1950s, he gave the palm to the third way, whilst insisting, however, on the importance of not neglecting the contributions of the other two,

> Although we must not neglect the two previous ways, indeed we must embrace them and utilise them to the limits of their possibilities, nevertheless, it is the third way alone which is able to take full cognisance of the true nature of the *donné révélé*. For the third way attributes the perception of the homogeneity between a later doctrine and the original revelation to the only subject that adequately corresponds to that *donné révélé*, namely, the Church. The third way takes the Church as she, in fact, thanks to God, actually exists: that is, whole and entire, living from faith, organically structured as a faithful people together with their body of pastors, heirs to the apostles, not in revealing but in guarding and declaring the deposit of faith.[1]

Congar's essay, like Schillebeeckx's, breathes a certain air of satisfaction that the solving of a problem which once seemed so intractable, indeed implacable, can at last be serenely docketed among the assured gains of theological reflection.

And there can be little doubt that such was the impression that these three influential *periti* of the Second Vatican Council gave at that Council itself (technically, Schillebeeckx was simply accredited to the Dutch bishops there). For, if we turn to the Dogmatic Constitution on Divine Revelation, *Dei Verbum*, we shall find only a single brief reference to the theme of doctrinal development, an allusion eloquent in its very conciseness. Manifestly, for the authors of this great text, the subject of doctrinal development seemed altogether unproblematic.

> The Tradition that comes from the apostles makes progress in the Church, with the help of the Holy Spirit. There is a growth in insight into the realities and words that are being passed on. This comes about in various

[1] Y. Congar, *La Foi et la théologie* (Tournai 1962).

ways. It comes through the contemplation and study of believers who ponder these things in their hearts. It comes from the intimate sense of spiritual realities which they experience. And it comes from the preaching of those who have received, along with their right of succession in the episcopate, the sure charism of truth. Thus, as the centuries go by, the Church is always moving towards the plenitude of divine truth, until eventually the words of God are fulfilled in her.[2]

If the serenity and confidence of this passage is not so tangible in Catholic fundamental theology today, the grounds of this shift in attitude may be summed up in three words: pluralism; hermeneutics; reception. By a convenience of the history of modern theology, each term can be associated with, in turn, the last three authors this book has considered: Rahner, Schillebeeckx, Congar – though the effect of the questions those terms represent on their respective theologies was much more dramatic in the cases of Rahner and Schillebeeckx than in that of Congar.

Awareness of the *pluralism* of contemporary intellectual life led Rahner to a less optimistic assessment of the future possibilities of the idea of doctrinal development. In an intellectually pluralistic world, with various ontologies and diverse hermeneutic theories – divergent basic accounts of reality and significance – all jostling for general acceptance and failing to win it, we can no longer, in many areas of reflection, understand each other well enough to have a controversy at all, much less to resolve one. In Rahner's metaphor, a juggler can only 'play with virtuosity' if the number of balls to hand is strictly limited. Today, however, what a learned man knows, compared with what there is to know, seems increasingly microscopic. There are simply, so Rahner fears, too many books, with the result that, not only do the experts know more and more about less and less, but they understand each other less and less as well, and turn into a 'completely dissonant chorus of voices'.[3]

[2]*Dei Verbum* 8.
[3]K. Rahner-H. Fries, *Einigung der Kirchen – reale Möglichkeit* (Freiburg 1983),

Theology mirrors this universal state of affairs. The systematic theologian can no longer cope with all the balls which the historian of doctrine, or the exegete, throws in his direction. In particular, the exegete's science has become so complex that he can expect to master only the merest fragment of his subject matter. And so the ever more technical character of exact scholarship, combined with conflict about the basic presuppositions of theological method, now renders the theologian impotent to judge theology as a whole.

Perhaps, in the Catholic context, it should suffice for the theologian simply to follow the Church's teaching – a rock of strength in an epistemologically uncertain world. But even here 'gnoseological concupiscence', Rahner's term for the desire to know run wild, can find no repose. As soon as we begin to interpret that teaching, and not simply to repeat it, the same problem rears its head. It is reassuring if the bishops and people of the Church like one's interpretation of Church teaching, but suppose that they have not really understood what one was saying? After all, Jansen died in the Church's peace years before there was Jansenism. I can expect no infallible decision about my theology, and so far as the non-infallible interventions of the magisterium are concerned, who would dare say with absolute confidence that it is right in all its deliverances at all points? Rahner concludes his account of theological pluralism by confessing that, while unity of faith brings with it a certain unity in theology, nevertheless, for the rest, theologians must simply live and work, accepting the faith of the Church as their intended norm, and hoping that their partially incommensurable theologies will be shown to be identical eschatologically, at the end of time.[4]

What are the implications of this for the idea of doctrinal development? Such a pluralism is, for Rahner, so radical that one must not only speak of the 'end' of the old type of doctrinal development, but assume that, in the future, the magisterium will be unable to formulate new doctrinal pronouncements.

---

pp. 38–9. For an evaluation of this study, and the debate it aroused, see my '*Einigung der Kirchen*: an Ecumenical Controversy', in *One in Christ* XXI. 2 (1985), pp. 139–66.

[4] Ibid., p. 144.

Today a pluralism exists in regional cultures, philosophies, terminologies, outlooks, theologies, and so on, which can no longer be reduced to any one synthesis, and so vividly has the Church become aware of this that I can no longer imagine that any specific, and at the same time genuinely new proposition can be expressed that can be felt so thoroughly to be an expression of the conscious faith of the whole Church as to be capable of definition.[5]

The 'common theology' which once assisted the magisterium in formulating new teachings is no longer there. Despite the unity of the Creed, the existence of pluralism in theology is a reality that cannot be passed over or ignored. The most that the Church of the future can do is to repeat old doctrines in a fresh way for the sake of guarding them against distortion. And this does not trouble the post-conciliar Rahner, since, as he points out:

In an atheistical age, when the faith is being radically threatened, important decisions of the Church, including definitions – and new ones may be given in the Church of the future – will have to be less a matter of the further material explicitation of revelation and rather aim at safeguarding the basic substance of the Christian faith and seeing that it is presented in new ways in the living preaching of the Church.[6]

Thus, the 'relinquishing' of doctrinal development should not impoverish the Church's life of faith, or ossify her faith-awareness. Instead, or so Rahner hopes, it will lead the Church to concentrate her attention on the central doctrines of Christian revelation, interpreting those doctrines by means of diverse and pluralistic theologies, without attempting to

[5]'The Concept of Infallibility in Catholic Theology', in *Theological Investigations* XIV (Et London 1974), pp. 72–3.

[6]K. Rahner, 'Magisterium', *Sacramentum Mundi* III (London 1969), p. 358. See also idem., 'Pluralism in Theology and the Unity of the Creed', in *Theological Investigations* XI (ET London 1974), pp. 3–23.

recreate a theological uniformity from the multitude of differing hermeneutical schemas.

If, then, *pluralism* led Rahner to distance himself from his own pre-conciliar theology of development, the same rôle in Schillebeeckx's work may be ascribed to the idea of *hermeneutics* thus briefly mentioned. Writing shortly after the Council, Schillebeeckx claimed that theories of doctrinal development were the Catholic answer to the problem of hermeneutics.[7] Even at the time, this claim was not entirely convincing. For, first, the traditional form that hermeneutics has taken in Catholic theology has been twofold: not a theory of doctrinal development only, but also its elder brother, a theory of the senses of Scripture. These two kinds of reflection, concerned as they are with the meaning of apostolic revelation, and notably as found in the texts of the New Testament, seen as a fulfilment of the Old, share patristic roots and a mediaeval flourishing which warrants our calling them 'traditional' in Catholicism. But secondly, and more importantly, if these two enterprises – a theory of doctrinal development and a theory of the senses of Scripture – have been 'hermeneutical', they have been so in a modest, restricted, sense. On the whole, their practitioners have taken meaning for granted and concerned themselves rather with truth. They have assumed that, broadly speaking, when we discuss the Fourth Gospel or the doctrine of justification we know what it is that we are talking about. The very fact that we are able to disagree – that, for example, Catholics and Lutherans might differ about the groundness of the notion of Eucharistic Sacrifice in the passion narratives of the Synoptics, or Dominicans and Franciscans about the consonance of the Immaculate Conception with the universality of Christ's redeeming work – only confirms that this is so. You do not disagree with someone who belongs to another semantic universe; you simply fail to comprehend them. But in three essays of 1967 to 1969, Schillebeeckx put forward a much

---

[7]E. Schillebeeckx, 'Naar een katholiek gebruik van de hermeneutiek: Geloofsidentiteit in het interpreteren van het geloof', in *Geloof bij kenterend getij: Feestbundel W. van de Pol* (Roermond 1967), pp. 78–116; ET in *God the Future of Man* (New York 1968), p. 6.

more radical concept of theological hermeneutics than this.[8] He argued that, thanks to the historicity of man, and more especially, to the overwhelming change of consciousness that humanity was undergoing through the process of secularisation, something more ambitious than this was needful.[9] It would be necessary to go back to scratch, and seek to look at the New Testament using the full set of lenses offered by contemporary philosophical hermeneutics, and notably by structuralist linguistics, logical analysis, phenomenology and the emerging concept of orthopraxy, indebted as this was – in Schillebeeckx's increasing use of it – to the Frankfurt school of critical sociology, itself Marxist, though in a highly revisionist sense.[10]

The increasing estrangement of a substantial portion of the Dutch church from Rome, and Schillebeeckx's decision to become a theological spokesman for its 'critical communities'; the student rebellions of 1968, which first introduced him to the Frankfurt writers; personal tours of both the United States and Latin America where he encountered, respectively, 'Death of God' theology and the beginnings of liberation theology; and encounters with French university chaplains concerned with the vanishing piety of their charges all contributed to Schillebeeckx's distancing from his earlier picture of what, in the Catholic tradition, theology should be. In the face of the fundamental scepticism about the very possibility of revelation which he discerned among his contemporaries, the theologian could no longer, so Schillebeeckx thought, presume the starting-point of belief as expressed in dogma, 'revelation-in-word', and merely search for fresh ways in which to express the deeper underlying reality, 'revelation-in-reality' itself. The theologian must now begin by listening to contemporary secular experience until, from out of its

[8]Ibid., pp. 51–140. These essays are 'Secularisation and Christian Belief'; 'Secular Worship and Church Liturgy'; 'The Church as the Sacrament of Dialogue'.

[9]One must recognise the pastoral concern which underlay this new attitude: 'I felt' (Schillebeeckx wrote) 'an almost feverish sense of urgency', ibid., p. 169.

[10]E. Schillebeeckx, *Geloofsverstaan: interpretatie en kritiek* (Bloemendaal 1972); Et *The Understanding of Faith. Interpretation and Criticism* (London 1974), pp. 20–44; 102–55.

'foreign prophecy', it yields an echo of the Gospel. This Schillebeeckx found, with the help of the 'negative dialectics' of the Frankfurt School, in hope for a better future, conceived – or better, *practised* – as the source of protest and resistance in the name of suffering human beings here and now.[11] He thus arrived at the view that, in the interpretation of the Gospel, oppressed groups occupy a position of hermeneutical privilege: since they experience the negative element in existence more completely than do others, they are the best placed to indicate its positive counterpart – the full dimensions of human hope. In his 1971 study *The Understanding of Faith*, therefore, Schillebeeckx describes theology as not so much interested in the relation between the past – Church Tradition as the mediation of the aboriginal revelation – and the faith-life of the present Church, with its authoritative teaching office, as in the connexion between 'theory' and 'practice'. The liberating power of the Gospel was manifested in the emancipatory *praxis* of Jesus' disciples. Theology's task is to establish the nature of that praxis, to compare and contrast it with its present-day successor, and to ascertain in what way a genuinely evangelical praxis is informed by Christian theory – and yet itself modifies that theory, transforming it as it moves towards the future of man in God.

> Theology must be the critical theory (in a specifically theological manner) of the praxis of faith. Its point of departure is the contemporary praxis of the Church. It analyses the models in which that praxis is presented and the attitudes on which it is based. In correlation with the critical theory of society, it also measures this praxis against its own evangelical claims and thus opens the way for new possibilities, which have, in turn, to be made a living reality in the praxis and faith of the Church community ... The necessary consequence of this situation and the necessary condition for it is that

[11]D. Held, *Introduction to Critical Theory. Horkheimer to Habermas* (London 1980) offers perhaps the best survey in English of the work of the Frankfurt School. Its earlier period is charted in M. Jay, *The Dialectical Imagination* (Boston, Massachusetts 1973).

the believer can only identify himself partially with the empirical Church.[12]

In its scanning of the Jesus tradition, theology will pay especial attention, so Schillebeeckx's massive investigation into the founder of Christianity, *Jesus*, would maintain, to the importance of narratives. Through narrative, celebrated in worship and pronounced tellingly over situations of injustice and oppression, the disturbing memory of the One who stood at the turn of the ages, the 'eschatological prophet', is both fêted in the joy of God and also brought to bear on the inhumanity of man in all its hard facticity. An 'argumentative' Christology – one, namely, which asks after the truth of the Figure at the Church's origin –

> must end up as a story about Jesus, a narrative Christology, and not as an all-embracing, theoretical 'Christological system'.[13]

Schillebeeckx's new theological method carries with it, in addition to the promise of rich insight into the gospels and their spiritual application to the present, seeds of destruction not found in the more classical theological terrain which he has abandoned. Most notably: here revelation and salvation tremble on the brink of absorption into the sea of human consciousness at large. Refusing the luxury of an metaphysic, how can one state the difference between the Church's liturgical remembering of Jesus and, say, Herbert Marcuse's critical remembering of Orpheus?[14] Where our own topic, that of doctrinal development, is concerned, it is difficult to think that the later Schillebeeckx has left sufficient room for the rôle of the Church's public doctrine in his account of Christian believing. While not denying – indeed, affirming – the christological and Trinitarian dogmas, he has ceased to

[12]E. Schillebeeckx, *The Understanding of Faith*, op. cit., pp. 143–4.

[13]Idem., *Jezus, het verhaal van een levende* (Bloemendaal 1974); Et *Jesus. An Experiment in Christology* (London 1979), p. 74.

[14]The criticism, this, of W. L. Portier, 'Schillebeeckx as Critical Theorist: the Impact of Neo-Marxist Social Thought on his Recent Theology', *Thomist* 48. 3 (July 1984).

seek their re-formulation, leaving them, in the main, to one side as conceptual icons that tempt one to pure contemplation rather than the engaged mysticism of political commitment. Such an emancipatory and critical praxis will find greater encouragement in a new christology founded rather on the Synoptic Gospels than on the Gospel of John. Although Schillebeeckx regards the conciliar christology as a faithful reflection, within the Greek patristic framework, of the original New Testament kerygma, proclaiming as it does a Jesus who is at once wholly on God's side and wholly on ours as well, he considers it, nevertheless, a unilateral development, which set restrictive limits to the image of Jesus in the later Church. For the later Christology is too frequently merely *occasioned* by the concrete Jesus of history:

> Jesus of Nazareth, teller of parables, champion of men, one who went about doing good, and was at the same time mystic and exegete of God.[15]

Our own time, in its preoccupation with suffering in a search for meaning and liberation, renders newly pertinent the ante-Nicene christologies which are closer, in Schillebeeckx's view, to the impression left by the Jesus of history in the Synoptic tradition. In thus defining the Christian world of meaning by reference to a triangle – the life of Jesus, contemporary experience, and the theology that mediates between these two, one may, however, miss the crucial help of dogmatic utterances as a raising into intelligibility of the content of the Gospel in ways that are to shape the response to revelation of the Catholic Christian believer for ever afterwards.[15a] The truth of the Gospel falls through our fingers, a quicksilver promise of enlightenment only at the end of time, or becomes a mere fleeting contact, like that of the Haemorrhetic Woman, with the hem of the garments of the Word as he passes by.

[15]Ibid., p. 673.

[15a]The further sections of Schillebeeckx' Christological trilogy: *Gerechtigheid en liefde: Genade en bevrijding* (Baarn 1977; Et *Christ. The Christian Experience in the Modern World*, London, 1980), and *Mensen als Verhaal van God* (Baarn 1989), do not significantly modify this approach. See on the latter, P. Kennedy, O.P., 'Human Beings as the Story of God: Schillebeeckx's Third Christology', *New Blackfriars* 71·836 (1990), pp. 120–131.

The real content of human knowing and believing is the ever present *mystery* of promise – the mystery which is not uttered, which is everywhere reaching towards expression but in itself is never thought. It is this which makes our understanding in faith, which is realised only through a conceptual (or even poetical) interpretation, a ceaseless and fascinating adventure – an experience like that of the believer in the Bible who touched the hem of Jesus' garment.[16]

Despite, however, these concessions to theological agnosticism at the transcendent pole of doctrine, Schillebeeckx's proposals have contributed to theological culture in a variety of projects. These include the enterprises both of 'political theology' and 'narrative theology', as well as the influential school of 'hermeneutical theology', now found in, especially, French-speaking Europe, and of which the philosopher Jean Ladrière and the theologian Claude Geffré are the two great luminaries. For such hermeneutical theologians, the theories of doctrinal development which we have been studying seem not so much wrong as impossibly innocent and naive.

The final key-word in any account of the fate of the idea of doctrinal development must be *reception*, with which term we may link the name of Congar. The notion of the ecclesial reception of doctrine achieved prominence in the 1960s by two quite distinct routes. In part, it arose among historians of the Councils, who noted the way in which successive patristic synods claimed to be 'receiving' the teaching of their predecessors in a fashion that differed from the mere canonical, judicial, confirmation of their *acta*. The idea that a Council or a pope speaking *ex cathedra* may be, not so much the final stamp of approval on a prior process of doctrinal development, working through historical memory, theological logic, and devout contemplation, but, rather, the beginning of a subsequent process of theological reception was a perhaps inevitable follow-up to this discovery by

[16]*God the Future of Man*, op. cit., p. 40.

historians – though, by an unexpected twist of theological history, the Greek Orthodox bishop-theologian John Zizioulas has proposed that the interventions of the Roman popes in disputes over councils, or debated points of doctrine, be understood as, precisely, the final sealing of such an activity of reception.[17]

The second point of entrance of the idea of reception into Catholic theology was the Ecumenical Movement. In the later 1960s, such Catholic ecumenists as Congar discovered the potential of the notion of reception for the movement towards an organically reunited Christendom. A teaching put forward in the Great Church and rejected by a significant body of Christians who then disappeared into schism might more happily be described, not as rejected but as 'not-received'. If someone rejects some tenet, and then is asked to think again, he is being asked to eat his words, if not his hat. But were we simply to say that his spiritual ancestors simply declined to receive an earlier teaching, which teaching we may all sit down and re-receive together, then the ecumenical state of affairs looks much rosier – though the amelioration is achieved at a price. When treated prudently the idea can be a valuable one. By and large, it is so treated by Congar, for whom re-reception is essentially the supplementing – not the supplanting! – of Catholic doctrine by other insights. Thus the Dominican ecclesiologist writes, first, of reception:

> Reception is not constitutive of the juridical quality of a decision. It bears not on the formal aspect of the act but on its content. It does not confer validity. It states, recognises, witnesses that such validity corresponds to the good of the Church, since it concerns a decision (dogma, canons, ethical rules) which must assure the Church's good.[18]

And, again, of re-reception:

[17] J. Zizioulas, 'The Theological Problem of "Reception"', *Centro pro Unione Bulletin* 26 (1984), pp. 3–6.

[18] Y. Congar, O.P., 'La Réception comme réalité ecclésiologique', *Revue des Sciences Philosophiques et Théologiques* 56 (1972), p. 399.

It is to receive a doctrine ... in another context, differently illumined, in synthesis with other values. That changes the equilibrium of the elements, and thus the bearing of things.[19]

But when handled less carefully than here, the ideas of reception and re-reception can be made to throw the entire process of doctrinal development into an indefinitely unattainable future. For who is to say what the result of constant re-reception of magisterial determinations of doctrinal development will be? We shall be cast onto the not so tender mercies of futurologists, and theologians who struggled to bring forward the solutions to the problem of doctrinal development which this book has expounded cannot, after their exhausting efforts, reasonably be expected to turn into prophets as well.

It is, then, desirable for the health of the idea of doctrinal development, as, in general, for the doctrinal consciousness of the Catholic Church, that the operation of these three notions – pluralism, hermeneutics, reception – be kept within determinate bounds. The fundamental strategies by which this may be done are not far to seek. Where *pluralism* is concerned, we must work towards the recreation of a common theological culture, in which each particular theology strives to draw within itself whatever is of value in its rivals, as well as maintaining its own transparency to the public doctrine of the Church. Where *hermeneutics* is concerned, we must insist that the fundamental hermeneutical vantage point to be occupied by the Catholic theologian – whether in his reading of Scripture, or in his evaluation of the human condition – must be that represented by the Church's tradition itself. In that tradition – grasped through its 'monuments', ranging from the Liturgy and sacred art, through the Fathers, the Creeds and the Councils, to the 'sense of the faithful', as these *loci*, 'places', are charted in the classical theologies of the Church – there unfolds, thanks to the Spirit of divine Providence, the authorised interpretation

---

[19]Idem., *Le Concile de Vatican II* (Paris 1984), p. 84.

of both Bible and human living. Finally, where *reception* is concerned, we must treat the idea of re-reception, not as a mortgaging of the achieved fruits of doctrinal development in the name of the future, but as the amplification of the results of that process by the elements of truth found in the teaching of other Christian confessions – elements which are, often enough, simply the forgotten truths of Catholicism itself.[19a]

In the last analysis, what is at stake here is the continuing accessibility of an objective Christian truth. The Scots theologian T. F. Torrance, speaking of the 'conceptual or epistemic consent' which is, for the Greek fathers, at the heart of listening obedience to God's Word, reminds us that, in the religion of which the Nicene Creed is the first great doctrinal confession

> faith was not regarded ... as some form of non-cognitive or non-conceptual relation to God, but was held to involve acts of recognition, apprehension and conception, of a very basic intuitive kind, in the responsible assent of the mind to truth inherent in God's self-revelation to mankind.[20]

And while, in divine revelation, images are of the greatest importance as carriers of meaning, though they are always to be interpreted 'according to the sense given them by the Scriptures' and 'within the whole scope and framework of the biblical narrative and message',[21] there must also be judgement – and hence doctrinal determinations – concerning the significance of what these images connote. It is this objective evangelical truth, expressed in a body of doctrine, which bonds the Church to the 'creative source of its being in the Gospel', and structures its life and mission in accordance

---

[19a]I offer a fuller view of the proper character of distinctively Catholic theology, in conjunction with an overview of its story, in my forthcoming *The Shape of Catholic Theology. An Introduction to its Sources, Principles and History.*

[20]T. F. Torrance, *The Trinitarian Faith. The Evangelical Theology of the Ancient Catholic Church* (Edinburgh 1988), p. 20.

[21]Ibid., p. 120.

with the 'pattern of divine truth' embodied in Christ.[22] This is, of course the very conviction to which Catholicism has given testimony by its continuing fruitfulness in bringing forth doctrine. Dogmatic and ecumenical theology are happily married when the former can, thanks to the latter, borrow from such non-Catholic divines the perspicuous statement of Catholic truth.

[22]Ibid., p. 31.

Appendix: The Idea of Doctrinal Development in Eastern Orthodox Theology

In Eastern Orthodox theology, the idea of dogma possesses specific characteristics of its own – owing to its special relationship with the doctrine of the Spirit, with the Orthodox teaching on Tradition, with the theology of the Councils, and with the notion of the infallibility of the Church as a whole. In this, Orthodox theology has, most notably, preserved one vital feature of the primitive Christian concept of dogma, namely, its inseparable relationship with the liturgical life of the Church.

Negatively, this leads Orthodox spokesmen to draw attention to the apophatic character of dogma. Dogma's negative form (in ruling out certain avenues of thought as culs-de-sac) expresses a self-conscious inadequacy of the human mind before the Christian mystery. Dogma does not exhaust the fullness of revelation, nor that of Christian experience. Put positively: dogma is, in the words of Paul Evdokimov, the 'verbal icon of truth', a symbol of the indescribable mystery.[1] Dogma upholds the mystery; it leads into it; and it expresses it, but apophatically – as in the celebrated case of the dogmatic *horos* of Chalcedon, with its four negative qualifications of the Union. The making of dogma contributes to the keeping of the Church's unity, yet new definition has never been considered as an aim in itself. Rather is it an extraordinary measure directed against disruption of that unity by false teaching.

[1]P. Evdokimov, *L'Orthodoxie* (Neuchâtel 1959).

279

Dogma is seen in contemporary Orthodox thought as, first, doxology, and then, secondly, homology – the profession of the faith. Because of their doxological character, the dogmas are quite naturally affirmed in the course of the baptismal and eucharistic liturgies, as also in iconography. The Orthodox Church celebrates special feasts to commemorate the chief ecumenical councils, which she considers as a continuation of the event of Pentecost, when the Spirit came upon the apostles gathered together in prayer. As the Greek lay theologian Christos Yannaras has written:

> The latent, non-expressed, aim which animates the dogmas and theology of the ancient Church is spiritual. It is theological doxology. There are no dogmatic statements by the Church which could not become doxological hymns in praise of God; there are no Christian hymns which could not be accepted in some measure as a dogmatic comment on the Church's faith. These two aspects – cultus and dogma – are inseparably joined in the Orthodox tradition . . .[2]

For his French counterpart Olivier Clément, a convert to Orthodoxy, dogma is the 'adoration of the human mind', an act of precise thinking, yet not *about* the mystery, but rather *in* it.[3]

The formulation of dogmatic statements is seen by Orthodox writers as a theandric process, in which both God and man are involved. The Holy Spirit co-operates with human actors, as in the words of the 'apostolic council' in Acts 15, 'It has seemed good to the Holy Spirit and to us'. From an historical standpoint, the dogmas of the ecumenical councils were shaped in a human attempt to overcome *aporiai*

---

[2]C. Yannaras, 'Dogma und Verkündigung im orthodoxen Verständnis', *Ostkirchliche Studien* 21 (1972), pp. 132–140; cf. N. A. Nissiotis, 'Remarques sur le renouveau de la Théologie systématique', in *La Pensée orthodoxe* 12 (1966), pp. 125–134.

[3]O. Clément, 'Orthodox Ecclesiology as an Ecclesiology of Communion', in *One in Christ* 6 (1970), p. 102.

and dialectical contradictions.[4] But at the same time, the patristic Church affirmed that she was guided by the Holy Spirit, and, thanks to this guidance, would preserve her identity, and the continuity of her nature and belief, intact. The consensus of bishops, united during a council as bearers of the supreme authority of the Church, is a sign of the presence and operation of the Holy Spirit, while the consensus of the entire People of God, expressed in the reception of the dogmatic definitions by believing Christians as a whole certifies the theandric character of these dogmata.

Orthodox writers sometimes distinguish between the 'biblical character' of dogma, which it owes to its condition as a truth revealed by God, and its 'ecclesiastical character', which follows on from its definition by an ecumenical council and acceptance by the Church as a whole. So far as the vital biblical source is concerned, the need for such a scriptural reference explains the Orthodox hostility not only to the content of the Catholic dogma of Mary's Immaculate Conception (deemed extraneous to, or even contradictory of, the Scriptures) but also to the dogmatic form of belief in the glorious Assumption of the Blessed Virgin in the Catholic Church. Since – according to these theologians – the Bible does not mention Mary's Assumption, and only the liturgical tradition, together with mediaeval Byzantine theology, treats of it, there is no call to dogmatise that event, or to regard it as occupying an integral place in the economy of human salvation. No dogmatic statement can add to the contents of Scripture.[5] Relevant to this is the conviction of an apparent majority of Orthodox theologians that Tradition is not a second source of revelation, parallel to the Bible. Rather is it that reality thanks to which, and owing to the presence of the life-giving Spirit, the Church transmits the sense, and the unity, of Scripture. The Holy Spirit, who, by the inspiration of the biblical authors, embodied revelation in the Bible now assists the Church to remain rooted in the biblical message

[4] S. Bulgakov, 'Na putiach dogmy (posle semi v selenskich soborov)' in *Put'* 9 (1933), pp. 3–35.

[5] J. Meyendorff, 'The Meaning of Tradition', in *Scripture and Ecumenism* (Pittsburgh, Pennsylvania 1965), pp. 43–58.

and to accommodate herself to the exigencies of each epoch by preaching, by the issuing of dogmatic statements, by the teaching of Church fathers, by iconography, and by liturgical worship.[6] Dogma lives in the stream of Tradition, and acts as its witness. It enables believers to accept the truth, as transmitted by living Tradition, and, in case of necessity, separates it from error. Formulated dogma becomes for believers the rule of faith, separating orthodoxy from heresy. The Orthodox Church does not exclude the possibility that she may proclaim fresh dogmatic definitions at some future ecumenical council, should the need to preserve the integrity and purity of faith require it. If, however, the Church extends the rule of faith by new definitions, this does not entail any augmentation or development of Tradition, but rather a deeper knowledge of the truth, within Tradition's stream.[7] The task of dogma, indeed, is not only to protect the truths of faith against error, or to define them in a conceptual manner (as an organic part of the Church's life). That task is also to furnish direction for spiritual and moral living.

Against this backcloth of the general understanding of what dogma is, how do the Orthodox view the idea of doctrinal development as such? The question of doctrinal development does not play in Orthodox thought the major rôle it took on in Catholic reflection since the nineteenth century. Orthodox theologians have tackled the issue chiefly as a reaction to the Catholic dogmatisation of the Immaculate Conception, the primacy and infallibility of the pope, and Mary's Assumption. A majority, it may be, of Orthodox writers register serious reservations about what they take to be the Catholic theory of doctrinal development. Some consider it to involve a 'vitalistic' theory of pre-conscious knowledge which is little different from an admission of blank unawareness, by the ancient Church, of some later points of confessional believing. Again, some regard the movement of Catholic thought on the issue as an attempt to transcend the notion of a closure of revelation with death of the last apostle. Many avoid the term 'evolution of dogmas', but find the phrase 'doctrinal

---

[6]Cf. V. Lossky, *A l'image et à la ressemblance de Dieu* (Paris 1967), p. 166.

[7]Ibid., p. 162; O. Clément, *Transfigurer le temps* (Neuchâtel 1959), p. 194.

development' acceptable at any rate when taken in the sense of a refinement of the language of theological statements, and a deeper understanding of the revealed contents.[8]

For the existence of such a doctrinal development in the Church's history, the formation of dogma at the seven ecumenical Councils constitutes formidable evidence. More widely, Clément has put forward a tripartite scheme, in which Orthodoxy moves through three great periods of doctrinal development: the christological period, consisting of the first eight centuries of the Church's existence; the pneumatological period, running from Photius' council of 879–880 on the *Filioque* to the Constantinopolitan synods of 1341 and 1351 on Palamism; and lastly, the early modern and modern periods which are increasingly dominated by ecclesiological concerns. If in the first period the Christendom of both West and East was absorbed in the truth of the Incarnation and its saving effects, in the second the standpoint of Eastern theologians shifted in a way that went largely unrecognised in Latin Christendom. The new focus of attention on the truth of the Holy Spirit showed doctrinal development proceeding in terms of a different logic from what was happening in the West. Henceforth, Orthodox ecclesiology, the subject matter of the third phase, would be formed under the predominant influence of pneumatology.[9]

In terms of its revealed *content*, however, dogma remains, despite this, immutable: such is the teaching of the Fathers and the common consensus of the Church as a whole.[10] From Chalcedon onwards, the later ecumenical Councils insist that their decrees were no different from the rulings of previous councils, being re-statements by way of protecting

[8]S. Bulgakov, *Pravoslaviye* (Paris 1965), pp. 84–5; idem., 'Dogmat i dogmatica' in *Zyvoie Priedaniie* (Paris 1947), pp. 9–24; V. Lossky, *A l'image et à la ressemblance de Dieu*, op. cit., pp. 158–163; O. Clément, *Trans-figurer le temps*, op. cit., pp. 185–200; Metropolite Seraphim (Lade), *L'Eglise orthodoxe. Les dogmes, la liturgie, la vie spirituelle* (Paris 1952), pp. 18–21; J. Meyendorff, 'The Meaning of Tradition', art. cit., pp. 48–50; D. Staniloae, 'The Orthodox Concept of Tradition and the Development of Doctrine', *Sobornost* 5 (1969), p. 652.

[9]O. Clément, *Transfigurer le temps*, op. cit., pp. 195–200.

[10]P. Evdokimov, *Orthodoxie*, op. cit., p. 000; J. Meyendorff, 'The Meaning of Tradition', art. cit., pp. 50–1.

truth against mis-statements.[11] Many Orthodox theologians are opposed to the idea that earlier dogmatic affirmations can include in tacit or implicit fashion hidden truths of faith that may be teased out by the later Church. They stress that dogma is simply the analysis of what has already (in the apostolic period) been uttered. The fullness of revealed truth is always present, they stress, in the Church, though in dogma that fullness is recapitulated as an expression of the Church's consciousness in a way particularly well-suited to dealing with the problems, and the errors, of some given time. Clément terms this the 'involution' of dogma, not its 'evolution'.[12] The concept of a vital, pre-conceptual state of knowledge is, such writers maintain, effectively indistinguishable from that of a sheer unconsciousness, and this ruptures the common consciousness of the truth of the Church. Consequently, an opinion considered false in one epoch is regarded as true in another – as actually transpired, they allege, in the case of the Immaculate Conception.

Despite Clément's attempt at a periodisation of the history of Orthodox doctrine which will give due weight to each of three successive epochs, far more characteristic of Orthodox theology at large is the immediate confronting of early tradition with modern thought. The Trinitarian and christological determinations of the first seven ecumenical councils are treated as a fundamental system of reference, to be used in developing responses to the questions left undiscussed at those councils – and above all, in the areas of anthropology and ecclesiology. The dogmatisation of the notion of a divine Person provides the warrant for Christian teaching on human personhood, while the doctrine of the Holy Trinity gives us a model to follow in speaking of the unity between local churches.[13] Orthodox theologians reach out immediately to the teaching of the Fathers, without the mediation of mediaeval and early modern theology, whereas,

[11]Ibid. See also: idem, 'Historical Relativism and Authority in Christian Dogma', in *Sobornost* 5 (1969), p. 637; V. Lossky, *A l'image et à la resemblance de Dieu*, op. cit., p. 162.

[12]O. Clément, *Transfigurer le temps*, op. cit., pp. 191–4.

[13]P. Evdókimov, *Orthodoxie*, op. cit.

despite a succession of patristic revivals, Catholic divines must necessarily pay attention also to the high mediaeval doctors and to the fresh direction provided by the Council of Trent.

The pre-Revolutionary Russian academician W. W. Bolotov introduced the distinction, now widespread among the Orthodox, between dogma and dogmatic formulation.[14] Although Orthodoxy is deeply devoted to the dogmas proclaimed by the seven councils, it distinguishes dogma as a living truth in the Church from the historical expression of that truth. The councils never identified their definitions with the fullness of revelation. There is always some kind of antinomy between mystery, as found in revelation, and its rational comprehension in the words of men. Occasionally, an Orthodox writer will go further and rejoice in the predominance of theologoumena over dogmas in Orthodoxy, as did the Russian priest-theologian S. B. Bulgakov. For Bulgakov, freedom is the nerve of theology, and diversity and multiplicity in theological expression constitutes Orthodoxy's beauty and power. Yet this point of view cannot be sundered from its context in Bulgakov's own controversial theological career, in which his personal development of the idea of Sophia, the Wisdom of God, as found in Scripture, the Fathers, and the Byzantine-Slav liturgy and its accompanying iconography, brought down on his head the condemnation of the Moscow Patriarchate as unwarranted innovation, and the sharp criticism of a number of his fellow-theologians as opening the door to a second Gnostic invasion of the Church.[15]

What is of value, to Catholic eyes, in the Orthodox discussion of the idea of doctrinal development is the Eastern stress on the doxological and liturgical dimension of the dogmas. Aware of the spiritual fecundity of the dogmatic formulations, the Orthodox testify in an admirable way to the vitality of the living mystery which underlies the truth now expressed in conceptual form. Although this emphasis on the connexion of the dogmas with the Church's worship

[14]W. W. Bolotov, 'Thesen über das Filioque von einem russischen Theologe', *Revue internationale de théologie* 6 (1898), pp. 671–712.

[15]S. Bulgakov, *Pravoslavije*, op. cit., pp. 196, 224.

and devotion is by no means strange to Catholicism, it is given greater relief in Orthodoxy. At the same time, the Orthodox need the complementary stress of Catholic theological tradition on the peculiar values of the mind, in what may be termed a spirituality of the intelligence at work on its God-given materials.[16]

[16]This appendix is based on a report made for me by Father Wojciech Morawski, O.P., of the Pontifical University of Saint Thomas, Rome. He draws attention to the studies on this subject of a Polish student of Orthodox theology, Wacław Hryniewicz, O.M.I., whose relevant writings are here given as a contribution to the discovery by Western Catholic theology of the, so far, virtually unknown Polish theology of this century, something which the freedoms now enjoyed by the Polish Church, and Polish society, will make possible. They are:

'Apofatyzna teologia', in: *Encyklopedia Katolicka*, I, (Lublin 1973), 745–8.

'Dogmat i jego funkcje w świetle teologii prawosławnej, *Ateneum Kapłanskie* 69.407, pp. 401–419.

'Eklezjologia prawosławna', in W. Granat (ed), *Ku człowiekowi i Bogu w Chrystusie*, II, (Lublin 1974) pp. 376–91.

'Recepcja orzeczeń Magisterium przez wspólnotę Kościoła w świetle teologii prawosławnej', *Zeszyty Naukowe KUL*, 18 (1975), nr 2 (70), pp. 11–27.

Rola Tradycji w interpretacji teologicznej. Analiza współczesnych poglądów dogmatyczno-ekumenicznych (Lublin, 1976).

'Interpretacja dogmatu jako problem ecumeniczny', *Roczniki teologiczno-kanoniczne*, XXIII, (1976), no:.2, pp. 73–85.

Index

Adam, K., 237
Aiello, A. G., 4
Albert of Monaco, 74
Ambrose, 48
Anouilh, J., 57
Anselm, 205
Aristotle, 34, 158
Arnold, M., 134
Athanasius, 18, 48
Augustine, 138, 174, 185, 190, 200, 205, 211, 256
Avis, P., 14–16

Bainvel, J. V., 172, 189
Balfour, A. J., 118
Bagot, bishop, 21
Balsiger, M. U., 9
Balthasar, H. U. von, 16, 195, 197, 204, 208
Barberi, D., 21
Barmann, J., 75
Baronio, C., 36
Barth, K., 201, 249, 250
Bastable, D., 46, 52
Battifol, P., 72, 110, 133
Bauer, W., 11–12, 30
Beauduin, L., 251
Bellarmine, R., 35
Bergson, H., 116, 258
Berruyer, I., 39, 112
Biemer, G., 253
Blanchet, A., 141
Blondel, M., 109, 110, 116, 133, 136–54, 156, 195, 196, 199, 203,

204, 221, 250–1, 253
Bolotov, W. W., 285
Bonnefort, archbishop, 138
Bonniwell, W. R., 178
Bossuet, J. B., 129, 133
Bourgy, P., 236
Bowden, J., 236, 237
Boyer, C., 183, 185–6, 206, 207, 209, 223
Bremond, H., 57, 82, 195
Brent, A., 60–1
Bulgakov, S. B., 281, 283, 285
Bultmann, R., 10–11, 30
Butter, J., 36, 42

Cajetan, cardinal, 179
Calvin, J., 249
Cenci, P., 80
Chadwick, H., 119
Chadwick, O., 38, 39, 53, 69, 129
Chantraine, G., 195
Chenu, M. d., 160, 194, 237–8, 249, 250, 251
Clément, O., 280, 283, 284
Congar, Y., 13, 14, 235, 245, 248–62, 264–5, 266, 275–6
Cordovani, M., 251
Corot, J. B. C., 88
Crehan, J., 14
Crews, C. F., 116
Cupitt, D., 120
Cyril of Alexandria, 208

D'Achaval, H. N., 53

Daniélou, J., 185
Dante, 195
Darwin, C., 46, 255
Davis, C., 14
De Boyer de Sainte Suzanne, R., 78
De Grandmaison, L., 172, 187–9, 198
D'Hulst, M., 73
De la Brosse, O., 238
Dell'Isola, M., 78
De Lubac, H., 139, 142, 151, 154, 183, 185, 186, 194, 195–213, 221, 222
De Petter, D., 236, 237
Descartes, R., 138
Deschamps, cardinal, 137
Dessain, C. S., 17, 25, 53, 64
Dhanis, E., 190–3
Diem, H., 176
Dodds, E. R., 84
Dubarle, D., 141
Duchesne, L., 72, 73, 108

Eadmer, 192
Ephraim, 37
Evdokimov, P., 279, 283, 284

Fabro, C., 215
Feyerabend, P., 173
Flanagan, J. S., 64
Franzelin, J. B., 5, 36
Frederick William IV, 21
Fries, H., 235, 269
Froude, H., 19
Froude, J. A., 57
Fuller, R., 3

Gadamer, H. G., 16
Gagnebet, M. R., 166, 207
Galilei, G., 89, 254
Gardeil, A., 134, 155, 176, 177, 178, 186, 206, 225, 247, 249
Gardeil, H. D., 155, 157
Garrigou-Lagrange, R., 165–166, 248
Gauthier, P., 139, 140, 142, 153
Geffré, C., 135, 274

Geiselmann, J. R., 5
Gladstone, W. E., 24, 65–7, 129
Gornall, T., 66
Gregory the Great, 37
Gregory Nazianzen, 256
Guardini, R., 216
Guitton, J., 83–85, 112–13
Günther, A., 169

Hammans, A., 4, 206
Hanson, R. P. C., 2–3
Harnack, A. von, 7–9; 30, 74, 87, 96–100, 149
Hegel, G. F. W., 200
Heidegger, M., 214–15, 237
Heiler, F., 2, 3, 75
Held, M., 271
Herford, V., 121
Hilkert, M. C., 240
Hitler, A., 155, 227
Honecker, M., 214
Houtin, A., 78, 80–82,
Hryniewicz, W., 286
Huby, J., 211
Hügel, F. von, 57, 58, 72, 74, 79, 85, 115, 143
Husserl, E., 237

Icard, M., 73
Irenaeus, 143

James, W., 118
Jay, M., 271
Jansen, C., 267
John Damascene, 174
John of Saint Thomas, 179
John XXIII, 212, 252

Kant, I., 155, 156, 161, 224,
Kasper, W., 5, 28
Keble, J., 19, 22
Kelly, W. J., 215
Kennedy, P., 236, 273
Kenyon, J., 57
Ker, I. T., 17, 19, 22, 41, 52, 56
Khomiakov, A. S., 250
Kingsley, C., 23

Kuhn, T., 173
Küng, H., 14
Kurtz, L. R., 74

Laberthonnière, L., 80, 138
Lade, S., 283
Ladrière, J., 274
Lagrange, M. J., 75, 93, 105, 249
Lash, N., 46, 48, 55, 56, 57, 58, 70
Lebreton, J., 196
Lefèvre, F., 138
Leibniz, G., 136
Leo I, 20, 116
Leo XIII, 25, 73, 92, 114, 122, 179
Leonard, E., 121
Le Roy, E., 133, 137, 255
Lévesque, P., 93
Linus, pope, 72
Lipner, J., 16
Lobato, A., 165
Locke, J., 44
Loisy, A., 57, 71–113, 116, 120, 133,
    139–40, 144, 146, 148, 149, 157,
    247, 255
Lonergan, B., 14
Lösch, A., 234
Lossky, V., 282, 283, 284
Lotz, J. B., 214
Lugo, J. de, 38–9
Luther, M., 89, 249, 250
Lynch, J., 59

Maier, E., 205
Maine de Biran, 136, 204
Malebranche, N., 138
Malherbe, J., 135
Manning, H. E., 24, 67, 70
Marcel, G., 239
Marause, H., 272
Marín-Sola, F., 178–183, 186, 209–
    210, 225, 226, 243, 247, 256
Maritain, J., 248
Maritain, R., 144
Marlé, R., 78, 142
Marty, E., 196
Marx, K., 237
Mercier, D., 121, 122

Merleau-Ponty, M., 237, 239
Meyendorff, J., 281, 283, 284
Meynell, H., 173
Mignot, E. I., 74
Mill, J. S., 130
Minon, A., 234–235
Misner, P., 24, 49, 63, 65, 70
Möhler, J. A., 5, 234, 249, 250
Moran, V., 83
Morawski, W., 286
Müller, N., 214
Murray, J. C., 4
McCool, G., 215
McDermott, J. M., 197
MacNeice, L., 84

Nédoncelle, M., 197
Neri, P., 22
Neufeld, K. H., 206
Newman, J. H., 1, 2, 5, 13, 17–70,
    74, 95, 107, 112, 116, 122, 123,
    139, 171, 187, 188, 197, 203, 205,
    221, 233, 244, 245, 247, 256, 258,
    263
Newton, I., 18
Nienaltowski, H. R., 5, 234
Nissiotis, N. A., 280

Orbán, L., 169
Origen, 57

Pascal, B., 138, 196
Patfoort, A., 238
Perrone, G., 59–62
Pelikan, J., 4
Petre, M. D., 78, 114, 116
Photius, 283
Pius IX, 23, 24, 45, 58–9, 62
Pius X, 75, 79, 104, 121, 138
Pius XI, 212
Pius XII, 206
Plotinus, 84
Popper, K., 173
Portier, W. L., 272
Poulat, E., 72, 73, 75, 77, 78, 80, 81,
    85, 92, 107, 112
Poussin, N., 188

Pryzwara, E., 214
Pusey, E. B., 19

Rahner, H., 214
Rahner, K., 13, 14, 59, 212–13, 214–235, 262, 263–4, 266–9
Reding, M., 237
Renan, E., 71
Richard, cardinal, 92
Rizzo, A., 185
Royer, R., 137
Rousselot, P., 142, 151, 154, 159, 193, 195–213, 222, 247

Sabatier, A., 125–8
Sabatier, P., 87
Sagovsky, N., 114, 134
Sales, M., 206
Sanday, W., 75
Sauras, E., 179
Schelstrate, E. de, 38
Schillebeeckx, E., 13, 14, 235, 236–47, 262, 264, 265, 266, 269–74
Schindler, D. L., 175
Schlier, H., 176
Schneemelcher, P., 11
Schoenl, W., 120
Schrodt, P., 7, 176
Schultenover, D. J., 115, 116
Schweitzer, A., 122
Siewerth, G., 214
Simonin, H. D., 193–4
Socrates, 139
Sophocles, 56
Staniloae, D., 283
Stephenson, A. A., 54
Stresemann, G., 227
Suárez, F., 114, 179, 180–2

Taylor, A. J. P., 227
Teilhard de Chardon, P., 195, 196

Thomas Aquinas, 94, 95, 110, 115, 130, 156, 164, 174, 179, 180, 182, 185, 193, 196, 197, 200, 202, 205, 207, 238, 239, 240, 244, 247, 249
Thomas de Vio, 179
Tilliette, X. de, 141
Trevor, M., 17
Toinet, P., 111
Torrance, T. F., 277
Turner, H. R. W., 8
Tuyaerts, M. M., 183, 184, 243
Tyrrell, G., 57, 58, 114–35, 155, 157, 159, 160, 163, 165, 195, 220, 223, 247

Valensin, A., 195, 196
Vidler, A., 78, 81, 83, 89,
Voncent of Lérins, 35, 99, 256
Virgoulay, R., 152
Vorgrimler, H., 195, 196, 214, 215
Voss, G., 235

Ward, B., 120
Ward, W., 17, 25, 91, 116
Weaver, M. J., 24, 70
Weber, J., 252
Wehrlé, J., 139, 140, 141, 142, 148
Welte, B., 214
Wenzel, P., 169
Werner, M., 9–10, 12, 30
Williams, R., 12
Wiseman, N., 22, 116, 119
Wittgenstein L., 241
Wong, J. H. P., 215

Yannaras, C., 280
Yeats, W. B., 84

Zahn-Harncak, A. von, 7
Zizioulas, J., 275